CASEBOOK SERIES

PUBLISHED

Jane Austen: *Emma* DAVID LODGE
Jane Austen: *'Northanger Abbey' & 'Persuasion'* B.C. SOUTHAM
Jane Austen: *'Sense and Sensibility', 'Pride and Prejudice' & 'Mansfield Park'*
 B.C. SOUTHAM
Beckett: *Waiting for Godot* RUBY COHN
William Blake: *Songs of Innocence and Experience* MARGARET BOTTRALL
Charlotte Brontë: *'Jane Eyre' & 'Villette'* MIRIAM ALLOTT
Emily Brontë: *Wuthering Heights* MIRIAN ALLOTT
Browning: *'Men and Women' & Other Poems* J.R. WATSON
Bunyan: *The Pilgrim's Progress* ROGER SHARROCK
Chaucer: *Canterbury Tales* J.J. ANDERSON
Coleridge: *'The Ancient Mariner' & Other Poems* ALUN R. JONES & WILLIAM ...
Congreve: *Comedies* PATRICK LYONS
Conrad: *'Heart of Darkness', 'Nostromo' & 'Under Western Eyes'* C.B. COX
Conrad: *The Secret Agent* IAN WATT
Dickens: *Bleak House* A.E. DYSON
Dickens: *'Hard Times', 'Great Expectations' & 'Our Mutual Friend'* NORMAN PAGE
Dickens: *'Dombey and Son' & 'Little Dorrit'* ALAN SHELSTON
Donne: *Sons and Sonets* JULIAN LOVELOCK
George Eliot: *Middlemarch* PATRICK SWINDEN
George Eliot: *'The Mill on the Floss' & 'Silas Marner'* R.P. DRAPER
T.S. Eliot: *Four Quartets* BERNARD BERGONZI
T.S. Eliot: *'Prufrock', 'Gerontion', 'Ash Wednesday' & Other Shorter Poems*
 B.C. SOUTHAM
T.S. Eliot: *The Waste Land* C.B. COX & ARNOLD P. HINCHLIFFE
T.S. Eliot: *Plays* ARNOLD P. HINCHLIFFE
Henry Fielding: *Tom Jones* NEIL COMPTON
E.M. Forster: *A Passage to India* MALCOLM BRADBURY
William Golding: *Novels 1954-64* NORMAN PAGE
Hardy: *The Tragic Novels* R.P. DRAPER
Hardy: *Poems* JAMES GIBSON & TREVOR JOHNSON
Hardy: *Three Pastoral Novels* R.P. DRAPER
Gerard Manley Hopkins: MARGARET BOTTRALL
Henry James: *'Washington Square' & 'The Portrait of a Lady'* ALAN SHELSTON
Jonson: *Volpone* JONAS A. BARISH
Jonson: *'Every Man in his Humour' & 'The Alchemist'* R.V. HOLDSWORTH
James Joyce: *'Dubliners' & 'A Portrait of the Artist as a Young Man'* MORRIS BEJA
Keats: *Odes* G.S. FRASER
Keats: *Narrative Poems* JOHN SPENCER HILL
D.H. Lawrence: *Sons and Lovers* GAMINI SALGADO
D.H. Lawrence: *'The Rainbow' & 'Women in Love'* COLIN CLARKE
Lowry: *Under the Volcano* GORDON BOWKER
Marlowe: *Doctor Faustus* JOHN JUMP
Marlowe: *'Tamburlaine the Great', 'Edward the Second' & 'The...'*
 JOHN RUSSELL BROWN
Marvell: *Poems* ARTHUR POLLARD
Milton: *Paradise Lost* A.E. DYSON & JULIAN LOVELOCK
O'Casey: *'Juno and the Paycock' & ... Gunman'* RONALD AYLING
John Osborne: *Look Back...*

OTHER CASEBOOKS ARE IN PREPARATION

William Blake

Songs of Innocence and Experience

A CASEBOOK

EDITED BY

MARGARET BOTTRALL

M

MACMILLAN

First published 1970
6th reprint 1989

Published by
MACMILLAN EDUCATION LTD
Houndmills, Basingstoke, Hampshire RG21 2XS
and London
Companies and representatives
throughout the world

Printed in Hong Kong

ISBN 0-333-09392-5

CONTENTS

ACKNOWLEDGEMENTS

W. B. Yeats, 'William Blake and the Imagination', from *Essays and Introductions* (Mr M. B. Yeats and The Macmillan Company; © Mrs W. B. Yeats 1961); T. S. Eliot, 'William Blake', from *The Sacred Wood* (Methuen & Co. Ltd); J. Wicksteed, 'An Expository Essay addressed to Max Plowman', prefacing *Blake's Innocence and Experience* (J. M. Dent & Sons Ltd); J. Harvey Darton, *Children's Books in England* (Cambridge University Press and Mr Morley Kennerly); S. F. Bolt, 'The Songs of Innocence', from *Politics and Letters* (1947); Wolf Mankowitz, 'The Songs of Experience', from *Politics and Letters* (1947); C. M. Bowra, '*Songs of Innocence and Experience*', from *The Romantic Imagination* (Oxford University Press and Harvard University Press); 'Blake after Two Centuries', from *University of Toronto Quarterly*, XXVII (1957) (Professor Northrop Frye and The University of Toronto Press); F. W. Bateson, introduction to *Selection of Blake's Poems* (Heinemann Educational Books Ltd and Barnes & Noble Inc.); R. F. Gleckner, 'Point of View and Context in Blake's Songs', from *Bulletin of the New York Public Library*, LXI (Nov. 1957) (The New York Public Library); M. Nurmi, 'Blake's Revisions of "The Tyger" ', from *Publications of the Modern Language Association of America*, LXXI (1956) (The Modern Language Association of America); 'The Nether-world of Alchemy', from *Sewanee Review*, LXXI (Summer 1963) iii (Routledge & Kegan Paul Ltd and Princeton University Press; © The University of the South, assigned to the Bollingen Foundation and the National Gallery of Art 1963), an abridgement of chapter 16, ' "The Tyger" ', of *Blake and Tradition* by Kathleen Raine – the A. W. Mellon Lectures in the Fine Arts, Bollingen Series, XXXV 11 (Princeton University Press, 1968; © the Trustees of the National Gallery of Art, Washington, D.C., 1968).

GENERAL EDITOR'S PREFACE

The Casebook series, launched in 1968, has become a well-regarded library of critical studies. The central concern of the series remains the 'single-author' volume, but suggestions from the academic community have led to an extension of the original plan, to include occasional volumes on such general themes as literary 'schools' and genres.

Each volume in the central category deals either with one well-known and influential work by an individual author, or with closely related works by one writer. The main section consists of critical readings, mostly modern, collected from books and journals. A selection of reviews and comments by the author's contemporaries is also included, and sometimes comment from the author himself. The Editor's introduction charts the reputation of the work or works from the first appearance to the present time.

Volumes in the 'general themes' category are variable in structure but follow the basic purpose of the series in presenting an integrated selection of readings, with an Introduction which explores the theme and discusses the literary and critical issues involved.

A single volume can represent no more than a small selection of critical opinions. Some critics are excluded for reasons of space, and it is hoped that readers will pursue the suggestions for further reading in the Select Bibliography. Other contributions are severed from their original context, to which some readers may wish to turn. Indeed, if they take a hint from the critics represented here, they certainly will.

A. E. DYSON

INTRODUCTION

THERE are several good reasons why the Songs of Innocence and Experience form the best introduction to the poetry of William Blake. Though they represent only a small fraction of his output, and by themselves do not give an adequate impression of his powerful originality and creative energy, they are the most immediately intelligible and attractive of all his writings. The power of the Songs to arrest and delight at first encounter is undeniable. Children feel it, poets acknowledge it. Their apparent simplicity of diction and pattern has been their chief passport to popularity. Today, critical exegesis has laid bare, even in these seemingly direct little poems, complexities of meaning undreamed of by Blake's earlier admirers, and maybe unsuspected by Blake himself; but the Songs have always held their own because of their poetic purity. They are utterly free from literary affectations and from moral attitudinising. They act on us with the immediacy of a scent or a melody. They do, indeed, stand up to and repay pondering, investigation, analysis; but the best of them have the spell-binding power peculiar to pure lyrics, and this is probably the most important thing about them.

In their original form they exemplified that combination of word and design which makes Blake's work so unlike any other poet's. They belong to a period of poetic vigour; and Blake himself continued to think about them, altering the sequence of poems over the years, in a way that suggests that he recognised their lasting significance. When he combined *Songs of Experience* with the Innocence series, issued five years earlier, and described them on the title-page as 'Shewing the Two Contrary States of the Human Soul', he indicated their relevance to the rest of his written work. In *The Marriage of Heaven and Hell*, contemporaneous with *Songs of Experience*, he declared, 'Without Contraries is no progression.' This conception is fundamental to Blake's interpretation of the nature of man and society; and the Songs are central and indispensable to our understanding of Blake because they do present, in concentrated, crystallised form, many of the themes developed and elaborated in the so-called Prophetic Books.

But it is not necessary to be familiar with the complicated mythology and symbolism of the later writings in order to read the Songs satisfactorily – that is to say, sensitively and with an apprehension of their depth of meaning. Indeed it seems inept to bring to bear on them an interpretative apparatus which derives from the study of the whole corpus of Blake's works. Not only does this practice, indulged in by some very able Blake scholars, tend to obfuscate rather than enlighten; it rests on the supposition that the poet was a systematic and consistent thinker, whose fundamental interpretation of reality never radically altered. Surely the sequence of his works and the tenor of his life suggest strongly that his mind was capacious and the very opposite of rigid. That he finally reconciled the gospel of liberty with the gospel of forgiveness is in itself a proof of the long distance that he travelled. To read the Songs in the light of the later Prophetic Books therefore seems a misguided enterprise.

There are, however, many links that connect the Songs with other writings of Blake's prime. It is an advantage to the reader of *Songs of Innocence* to know the pastoral songs in *Poetical Sketches* (1783), and to consider how in *The Book of Thel* (1789) Blake treats some of the more hazardous implications of innocence, at the very same time as he was producing the lyrics. It is an advantage to have read *The Island in the Moon*, that unpublished, rumbustious, farcical satire, in which, improbably enough, three of the Songs of Innocence appear in their earliest guise. Nobody who had done so would be likely to mistake Blake himself for an innocent, in the sense of a simple, artless singer piping his native woodnotes wild. Similarly, Songs of Experience are better understood if they are taken alongside *The Marriage of Heaven and*

Hell, and *Visions of the Daughters of Albion*, which also belong to the early 1790s. The one reinforces the irony, the other the passionate indignation, of the poet who in the Songs denounced hypocrisy, tyranny, jealousy and repression. And indispensable to an understanding of *Songs of Experience* is a knowledge of the poems in the notebook which Blake used for drafting.

But what matters most is the interaction of the two series of Songs. We certainly cannot see the point of *Songs of Experience* unless we read it together with, and as a commentary on, the earlier series. Nor can the full import of *Songs of Innocence* be gauged without knowledge of its sequel. The extent to which the two groups throw light upon one another is so great that they are sometimes regarded as inseparable. This view does violence to the known facts. *Songs of Innocence* appeared in 1789. *Songs of Experience* was advertised in a prospectus in 1793 as a separate, companion volume; but it has not survived except in combination with the earlier collection.[1] At first Blake merely bound them together. In the second edition he gave the *Songs* their joint title-page, and most of the surviving copies comprise both series. Blake did, however, continue to issue separate copies of *Songs of Innocence*, which suggests that he reckoned it could stand on its own feet as a children's book. *Songs of Experience* undoubtedly stemmed from *Songs of Innocence*; but we have no evidence that the two series were conceived as an entity or were composed concurrently.

That Blake's reputation as a poet during his lifetime was very limited is not surprising in view of the manner in which his compositions were produced and distributed. The only one of his works to be conventionally printed was the early *Poetical Sketches*, and even that was not put on the market. The exquisite little volumes of the Songs were hand-written, illustrated, etched, coloured and sold by Blake himself, with the assistance of his wife. They were purchased by a few well-wishers and connoisseurs, who did, in fact, make some of the poems known to a

[1] J. T. Smith, in the Biographical Sketch of Blake included in vol. II of *Nollekens and his Times* (1828), prints a descriptive list of the illustrations to a single copy of *Songs of Experience*, 'now extremely rare'.

rather wider circle. They were even introduced to the German reading-public by Henry Crabb Robinson, who, in an article contributed in 1811 to a periodical published in Hamburg, *Vaterlandisches Museum*,[1] included 'The Tyger' and four other songs. These were quoted in English, and were also translated into German in their original metres by the Dr Julius who was responsible for translating the article itself. This dealt with the pictures as well as the poetry, and was written long before Crabb Robinson had actually met Blake. Though he remained to the end deeply puzzled by Blake's imaginative utterances, he did more than anyone else to make this strange genius known to the foremost literary men of the day. It was through Crabb Robinson that Southey called on Blake and that Hazlitt read him, and he was responsible for fostering Wordsworth's interest in him. In so far as Blake enjoyed any poetic reputation while he lived, it was on account of his lyrics. His other works were usually dismissed as unintelligible, if not downright mad.

When he died in 1827, obituary notices appeared in the *Literary Gazette*, *Gentleman's Magazine* and *Annual Register*, but these commemorate the designer and illustrator, not the poet. They pay tribute to Blake's beauty of character and lament his penury, but ignore his writings. In the following year J. T. Smith, who was Keeper of Prints and Drawings in the British Museum, included a biographical sketch of Blake in the second volume of *Nollekens and his Times*.[2] Here, too, it is the artist who mainly engages the writer's attention, though Smith does mention the early Songs and the tunes which Blake composed for them, as well as 'his later poetry, if it may be so called, attached to his plates'. This, 'though it was certainly in some parts enigmatically curious as to its application, yet it was not wholly uninteresting'. Smith adds that though Blake was no church-goer, he was neither a free-

[1] Vol. II, pp. 107–31. It was entitled 'William Blake, Künstler, Dichter und religiöser Schwärmer'. Crabb Robinson's original essay has not survived, but an English translation of the German is to be found in 'An early appreciation of William Blake', by K. A. Esdaile, in *Library*, V 229–56.

[2] Published by Henry Colburn, 1828. Smith's biographical sketch was reprinted in Arthur Symons, *William Blake* (1907).

thinker nor irreligious. 'Through life, his Bible was everything with him.'[1]

It was again Blake's reputation as a pictorial artist that secured his inclusion in Allan Cunningham's *Lives of the most eminent British Painters, Sculptors and Architects*, published in 1830. This book had a wide circulation, and gave currency to many anecdotes about Blake and his wife. In the second edition more attention was given to the poetry, and there was less emphasis on the wildness and madness of Blake's imagination. An article, provoked by Cunningham's *Life* in its unrevised form, was published in 1830 in the *London University Magazine*. It has been reproduced in full in this collection, as a remarkably independent and penetrating appreciation of Blake's genius.

In 1839 J. J. Garth Wilkinson published anonymously an edition of *Songs of Innocence and Experience*. In the preface Wilkinson censures Allan Cunningham for judging Blake by superficial criteria, but himself speaks disparagingly of the later works, with the exception of the illustrations to the Book of Job. But for putting the *Songs* on the market for the first time, he deserves to be remembered.

The first full-length study, combining biography with criticism, was Alexander Gilchrist's *Life of William Blake*, which appeared in 1863. This delightful book brought to the notice of a wide public the man whom Gilchrist called 'Pictor Ignotus'. He collected data from people who had known Blake in his latter years, and treated his theme with enthusiastic sympathy. Gilchrist died before the book was completed, but it was finished by his wife and the two Rossetti brothers. D. G. Rossetti added a selection of poems from the Notebook as well as from published sources, and the second edition (1880) included a list of all Blake's known engravings, drawings, paintings, etc., and an essay by James Smetham.

Blake's importance as a creative artist was established by Gilchrist's *Life*. It evoked several long reviews, including those by James Smetham and James Thomson, extracts from which appear in this volume, and gave rise to Swinburne's book-length

[1] Symons's edition, p. 361.

study, published in 1868. This is not a balanced critical assessment, but rather an impassioned tribute to Blake's originality and power. Swinburne could not himself make much of the later writings, but he enunciated a principle that was destined to be extremely fruitful – namely, that Blake's work must not be judged piecemeal, but that the critic is in duty bound to consider the worth of what at first may appear hopelessly esoteric and unrewarding. He also brought to the reading of the lyrical poems a concentrated attention that points the way forward to Blake scholarship. In spite of rhapsodising, he looks at the variant drafts and traces connections between one poem and another. The chapter on the lyrics has worn better than the rest of the book.

The proclamation of Blake's genius by Gilchrist's associates struck some readers as absurdly extravagant. H. G. Hewlett contributed a shrewd article on Blake's 'Imperfect Genius' to the *Contemporary Review* (XXXVI (1876) 756–84). He stressed the derivative elements in Blake's Songs and Ossianic writings, and remarked that those who professed to interpret his poems seldom agreed as to their meaning – a fair comment, even today. Hewlett expected Blake's reputation to decline, as a result of his having been wildly over-praised, but this did not happen. The image of Blake as arch-Romantic rebel continued to exercise a powerful fascination.

W. B. Yeats's collection of essays *Ideas of Good and Evil* (1903) included two lyrical pieces on Blake. He had earlier made a far more weighty contribution to Blake studies, in the three-volume edition of *The Works of William Blake, Poetic, Symbolic and Critical* (1893), which he undertook in collaboration with Edwin J. Ellis. This provided facsimiles of the Prophetic Books and an elaborate exposition of their symbolism. These interpretations carry little conviction nowadays, and the text is unreliable. But this edition generated much interest in Blake's mythology; and, though his editorial work has been quite superseded, Yeats shines out among those who have been students of Blake. Throughout his own poetic life he drew inspiration from the earlier visionary, with whom he felt a strong, compelling affinity.[1]

[1] Among critical studies comparing Blake and Yeats may be men-

After Yeats came Arthur Symons, who appended to his appreciative essay a most useful collection of primary sources for Blake's biography. Also in 1907 appeared an important French study, Pierre Berger's *William Blake: mysticisme et poésie*, a more systematic study of the corpus of the writings than any previously attempted.[1] Behind the work of both these critics stands the first scholarly edition of the lyrical poems, John Sampson's, published in 1905 by the Oxford University Press. Not until the 1920s, however, did the critical study of Blake receive another strong impetus.

In 1921 Sir Geoffrey Keynes, the scholar who has done more than any other single man to help Blake students, produced his *Bibliography of William Blake*; in 1925 his annotated three-volume edition of the *Writings* appeared; and in 1927 came the invaluable one-volume edition of *The Poetry and Prose of William Blake*.[2] In 1924 appeared S. Foster Damon's very important interpretative book, *William Blake: his Philosophy and Symbols*, still indispensable to the serious student of Blake; and in 1927 came Max Plowman's useful little guide, *Introduction to the Study of William Blake*.[3] To this centenary year also belongs the first edition of Mona Wilson's well-known biography, *The Life of William Blake*.

In 1928 the first book entirely devoted to the Songs was published. This was Joseph Wicksteed's commentary, with reproductions of all the engravings and manuscript drafts. This is an important publication, especially for anyone who wants to read the poems as Blake wished them to be read, that is, in

---

tioned M. E. Rudd, *Divided Image* (1953) and Hazard Adams, *Blake and Yeats: the contrary vision* (1955).

[1] English edition *William Blake, Poet and Mystic*, authorised translation by Daniel H. Conner (1914). This contains a useful bibliography.

[2] The standard edition since 1957 has been *The Complete Writings of William Blake, with All Variant Readings*, edited by Keynes and published by the Nonesuch Press. The Oxford Standard Authors edition (1966) is a photographic reprint of this, plus additions, corrections, a new preface and some supplementary material.

[3] A new edition, with notes by R. H. Ward, was published in 1967.

conjunction with the designs.[1] Wicksteed had already explored
Blake's iconography in his monograph on the illustrations to the
Book of Job (1910). His poem-by-poem analysis of the Songs
was a pioneer effort; and though his interpretation of their symbolism is open to challenge, and his tone of voice may occasionally irritate, his readings are always careful and imaginative.

During the thirties there was a comparative lull in Blake
studies, but an immense amount of scholarly investigation and
interpretative criticism has been produced during the last
twenty-five years. Some Blake devotees have sought to elucidate
his poetry and pictures by reference to literary and religious
sources; others have concentrated on the social content of Blake's
work and tried to 'place' him in his contemporary context.

J. Bronowski's *William Blake: A Man without a Mask* (1944)
was the first detailed exposition of Blake's poetic involvement
with the political and social problems of his own day. Because
it is easily available (Penguin Books, 1954) no extract is given here
from the passages on the Songs; but Bronowski's treatment is
thought-provoking, especially as regards *Songs of Experience*.
Ten years later, David V. Erdman's *Blake: Prophet against
Empire* (1954) expounded the view of Blake as a poet of social
vision and humane protest. Its sub-title is 'A poet's interpretation
of the history of his own time'. It is an excellent corrective to the
notion that Blake was an isolated dreamer. Erdman finds the kind
of evidence he requires in many of the Songs of Experience,
superlatively in 'London'; but his arguments should be read in the
framework of the whole volume. The persuasiveness of the part
depends on the cumulative effect of the total argument.[2]

[1] In 1955 the Trianon Press in Paris published for the William
Blake Trust an exquisite hand-coloured facsimile of the Songs in a
strictly limited and very costly edition. In 1967 a coloured reproduction of *Songs of Innocence and Experience*, with an introduction and
commentary by Sir Geoffrey Keynes, was published by Rupert Hart-
Davis in association with the Trianon Press. A coloured microfilm of
the Fitzwilliam Museum copy of *Songs of Innocence and Experience*
should be obtainable from Micro Methods Ltd, East Ardsley, Wake-
field, Yorks.
[2] Two books in similar vein, Bernard Blackstone's *English Blake*

The value of this kind of criticism has been well expressed by M. H. Abrams:

No amount of historical explanation can make Blake out to be other than a phoenix among poets; but if we put his work into its historical and intellectual context, and alongside that of his poetic contemporaries of the 1790s, we find at least that he is not a freak without historical causes, but that he responded to the common circumstances in ways markedly similar. . . .[1]

The socio-political approach, however, has its obvious limitations, for Blake's interior life is of the first importance. He was essentially a religious poet, more concerned with eternity than with the productions of time; he constantly said so, and he expected to be believed. Those scholars who have devoted their energies to examining the sources that fed Blake's imagination and influenced his poetic thinking are abundantly justified.

Among the critics primarily concerned with Blake as a poet whose creativity was nourished by extensive reading, as well as by direct visionary experience, Northrop Frye has been the most influential. His *Fearful Symmetry* (1947) demonstrates Blake's continuous indebtedness to the Bible, and the extent to which Milton haunted him. Though a difficult book, it suggested new and fruitful ways of reading the poetry, both lyric and 'epic', and linked together in a more or less coherent system Blake's symbolically expressed ideas. To reproduce in isolation what Frye has to say about the Songs would be futile; he relates them to Orc and Urizen, youth and age; the pastoralism of Innocence is an aspect of Beulah, and so forth. Very valuably, however, Frye insists on the vigour and lack of sentimentality in *Songs of Innocence*, and in praise of *Songs of Experience* exclaims, 'Contempt and horror have never spoken more clearly in English poetry.' He makes the important point that among the things satirised by *Songs of Experience* is the state of Innocence itself,

(1949) and Mark Schorer's *William Blake: the Politics of Vision* (1946), are briefly described in the Select Bibliography.

[1] *Romanticism Reconsidered* (Selected Papers from the English Institute, University of Columbia, 1963) p. 42.

and that, conversely, *Songs of Innocence* make the hypocrisies of Experience the more shameful by providing a contrast, thus contributing a satirical element of their own. In *Fearful Symmetry* there are no such detailed exegeses of individual lyrics as were to be undertaken in the 1950s and 1960s by followers of Frye; but it proved to be an enormously stimulating book.

The Neoplatonic elements in Blake's thinking have been studied by two critics in particular, George M. Harper (*The Neoplatonism of William Blake*, 1961) and Kathleen Raine; the latter has used some of the Songs to illustrate his indebtedness to hermetic, alchemical and other occult writings, in the course of tracing his debts to Antiquity throughout his creative life.

During the last ten or fifteen years there has been a shift in Blake studies away from the huge tangles of the Prophetic Books towards the elucidation of the lyrical poems. The first readers of *Songs of Innocence and Experience* were far more struck by Blake's unaffected, moving simplicity of diction and imagery than by the symbolic method he employed. When the Rossettis printed the lyrics that existed in draft in the Notebook and the Pickering manuscript they acknowledged that the import of some of these was extremely hard to grasp; 'The mental Traveller', for instance, or 'The Crystal Cabinet' are more obviously cryptic than any of the songs published in Blake's lifetime. Learned periodicals in the United States and Canada have printed scores of articles on individual lyrics over the past few years; and it would have been possible, by reproducing interpretations by critics whose fundamental assumptions are widely diverse, if not actually opposed, seriously to undermine an unsophisticated reader's faith in the validity of literary criticism.[1] Rival readings of 'The Voice of the Ancient Bard' and 'Earth's Answer', even of such apparently artless poems as 'The Blossom' or 'Infant Joy', could occupy many pages; and the upshot might be confusion and incredulity. What you find in Blake depends largely on what you

[1] In the definitive edition of *The Poetry and Prose of William Blake* by H. Bloom and D. V. Erdman (1965) Harold Bloom excludes from his commentary any consideration of the Songs, 'for which a wealth of criticism is available elsewhere'.

expect to find. He is like Shakespeare in that. It also depends on where you start from. The two studies of 'The Tyger' included in this volume, each admirable in its way and according to its own terms of reference, reinforce this point. It has therefore seemed more useful to reprint, in the main, essays and excerpts which treat the Songs collectively.

During the last decade, four important studies specifically concerned with the lyrical poems have appeared. In 1959 Robert F. Gleckner produced *The Piper and the Bard*. This critic regards the Songs as 'integral parts of the growth of Blake's poetic ability, his philosophical-religious-aesthetic concepts and his own very special techniques for conveying these concepts'. Through close reading of most of the Songs, plus *Tiriel*, *Thel*, *The Marriage of Heaven and Hell* and *Visions of the Daughters of Albion*, Gleckner discovers the 'key-elements of an organic and ever-developing system, that began with the seeds of innocence and resulted finally in the Prophetic Books'. This exhaustive ransacking of symbols he regards as a far more fruitful method of approach than the kind of commentary that seeks to elucidate Blake's poetry 'in terms of mysticism, antinomianism, occultism, neoplatonism, psychology, sociology and anthropology'. At his best Gleckner interprets individual poems in an illuminating way; but sometimes the 'system' blinds him to simple probabilities, and his explications become over-elaborate and implausible.

Hazard Adams's *William Blake: a Reading of the Lyrical Poems* was published in 1963. It is an important book, with a very useful bibliography, but the critical method is rather odd. Adams assumes a constant, traditional, archetypal symbolism in Blake's lyrical poems, and works backwards from the 1803 poems in the Pickering manuscript to interpret the Songs of Innocence and Experience. He is less committed to the notion of a self-sufficient system than Gleckner, but notes that 'the best essays on Blake's lyrics seem constantly in danger of expanding into book-length statements. The true Blakean feels that to explain a single line of Blake he must somehow explain all of him. . . . He finds it necessary to move from a rhetorical or narrowly contextual interest to an archetypal one.' In Hazard Adams's view, 'The shorter poems, like the prophetic books in this respect, evoke a vast world of particulars, shading and shifting into one another and modifying one another's meaning, not reflecting the world as we "know" it, but attempting to organise the world of poetic symbolism – using language to burst through the forms of our knowledge.'

In 1964 appeared *Innocence and Experience*, by E. D. Hirsch Jr, in which the Songs are used as searchlights to illuminate the whole period of Blake's poetic maturity. Mr Hirsch opposes those who try to interpret the whole of Blake's work as though it were structured by a permanent set of ideas. He maintains, with common sense as well as scholarship, that Blake was a man who strove to incorporate in his work whatever appeared to be true at the time of writing. But in claiming that Blake underwent a radical change of heart and mind between writing the first and second series of Songs, so that the two books represent 'mutually exclusive states', this critic ignores a good deal of evidence and indulges in some special pleading. His commentaries on the individual Songs, however, are often delicately perceptive and quite free from pretentiousness.

D. G. Gillham's *Blake's Contrary States* was published by the Cambridge University Press in 1966, sub-titled 'The Songs of Innocence and Experience as Dramatic Poems'. Instead of trying to interpret the lyrics along biographical-psychological lines, Mr Gillham emphasises the characteristically dialectical mode of Blake's thinking. He maintains that the Songs of Innocence and Experience were conceived as a unified entity, and that they constitute an exploration of 'possible states of being and feeling in which spiritual energy expresses itself'. One of the great merits of this book is that it presents the Songs as enjoyable and enlightening, and makes them intelligible without calling on any esoteric knowledge for their elucidation. It seems rather irresponsible, in the mid-sixties, to be quite so unaffected by other men's scholarship as Mr Gillham appears to be; but there is a danger that the Songs, having been subjected to a vast amount of erudite scrutiny, may take on a daunting aspect. They used to be considered trifling. That verdict was certainly mistaken; but was Blake really quite so portentous as some of his recent critics make out?

What this collection of critical comments finally reflects is the survival-power of truly original genius. Blake's importance is ever more widely acknowledged; his vision makes itself manifest as the desire to understand it increases. Only a handful of people, mostly young painters, recognised during Blake's lifetime that he was a man in a million. He was rescued from oblivion a hundred years ago, and the work of interpretation began; arbitrarily at first, but with increasing scrupulousness and regard for factual evidence. Nobody would pretend that even now the bulk of Blake's poetry is easily accessible, or that it is ever likely to become so. Much of his later work is marred by the eccentricities of a seer driven in upon himself and writing cryptically. But surely of all the Romantic poets Blake is the one who now speaks most tellingly to our condition; and in *Songs of Innocence and Experience* he speaks with an economy, a directness and a poetic penetration that compel response.

MARGARET BOTTRALL

PART ONE

Blake: Aphorisms and Extracts from Letters

APHORISMS

Without Contraries is no progression. Attraction and Repulsion, Reason and Energy, Love and Hate, are necessary to Human existence.

From these contraries spring what the religious call Good & Evil. Good is the passive that obeys Reason. Evil is the active springing from Energy.

Good is Heaven. Evil is Hell.

(from *The Marriage of Heaven and Hell*, 1790–3)

A Spirit and a Vision are not, as the modern philosophy supposes, a cloudy vapour, or a nothing: they are organized and minutely articulated beyond all that the mortal and perishing nature can produce. He who does not imagine in stronger and better lineaments, and in stronger and better light than his perishing and mortal eye can see, does not imagine at all. . . .

(from *A Descriptive Catalogue*, 1809)

Man Passes on, but States remain for Ever; he passes thro' them like a traveller who may as well suppose that the places he has passed thro' exist no more, as a Man may suppose that the States he has pass'd thro' Exist no more. Every thing is Eternal.

(from the Notebook: *Additions to Blake's Catalogue of Pictures, etc.*, 1810)

LETTERS

WILLIAM BLAKE TO DR TRUSLER (16 August 1799)

Revd Sir,

I find more & more that my Style of Designing is a Species by itself, & in this which I send you have been compell'd by my Genius or Angel to follow where he led; if I were to act otherwise it would not fulfill the purpose for which alone I live, which is, in conjunction with such men as my friend Cumberland, to renew the lost Art of the Greeks.

I attempted every morning for a fortnight together to follow your Dictate, but when I found my attempts were in vain, resolv'd to shew an independence which I know will please an Author better than slavishly following the track of another, however admirable that track may be. At any rate, my Excuse must be: I could not do otherwise; it was out of my power!

I know I begged of you to give me your Ideas, & promised to build on them; here I counted without my host. I now find my mistake. . . . But I hope that none of my Designs will be destitute of Infinite Particulars which will present themselves to the Contemplator. And tho' I call them Mine, I know that they are not Mine, being of the same opinion with Milton when he says* That the Muse visits his Slumbers & awakes & governs his Song when Morn purples the East, & being also in the predicament of that prophet who says: I cannot go beyond the command of the Lord, to speak good or bad. . . .†

WILLIAM BLAKE TO DR TRUSLER (23 August 1799)

Revd Sir,

I really am sorry that you are fall'n out with the Spiritual World, Especially if I should have to answer for it. I feel very sorry that your Ideas & Mine on Moral Painting differ so

---

* [*Editor's note:*] *Paradise Lost*, VII 29–30.
† [*Editor's note:*] Numbers XXIV 13.

much as to have made you angry with my method of Study. If I am wrong, I am wrong in good company. I had hoped your plan comprehended All Species of this Art, & Especially that you would not regret that Species which gives Existence to Every other, namely, Visions of Eternity. You say that I want somebody to Elucidate my Ideas. But you ought to know that What is Grand is necessarily obscure to Weak men. That which can be made explicit to the Idiot is not worth my care. The wisest of the Ancients consider'd what is not too Explicit as the fittest for Instruction, because it rouzes the faculties to act. I name Moses, Solomon, Esop, Homer, Plato.

. . . I perceive that your Eye is perverted by Caricature Prints, which ought not to abound so much as they do. Fun I love, but too much Fun is of all things the most loathsom. Mirth is better than Fun, & Happiness is better than Mirth. I feel that a Man may be happy in This World. And I know that This World is a World of Imagination & Vision. I see Every thing I paint In This World, but Every body does not see alike. To the Eyes of a Miser a Guinea is more beautiful than the Sun, & a bag worn with the use of Money has more beautiful proportions than a Vine filled with Grapes. The tree which moves some to tears of joy is in the Eyes of others only a Green thing that stands in the way. Some See Nature all Ridicule and Deformity, & by these I shall not regulate my proportions; & Some Scarce see Nature at all. But to the Eyes of the Man of Imagination, Nature is Imagination itself. As a man is, So he sees. As the Eye is formed, such are its Powers. You certainly Mistake, when you say that the Visions of Fancy are not to be found in This World. To Me This World is all One continued Vision of Fancy or Imagination, & I feel Flatter'd when I am told so. What is it sets Homer, Virgil & Milton in so high a rank of Art? Why is the Bible more Entertaining & Instructive than any other book? Is it not because they are addressed to the Imagination, which is Spiritual Sensation, & but mediately to the Understanding or Reason? Such is True Painting, and such was alone valued by the Greeks & the best modern Artists. . . .

But I am happy to find a Great Majority of Fellow Mortals

who can Elucidate My Visions, & Particularly they have been Elucidated by Children, who have taken a greater delight in contemplating my Pictures than I even hoped. Neither Youth nor Childhood is Folly or Incapacity. Some Children are Fools & so are some Old Men. But There is a vast Majority on the side of Imagination or Spiritual Sensation. . . .

PART TWO

Contemporary Impressions

BENJAMIN HEATH MALKIN

MR BLAKE has long been known to the order of men among whom he ranks; and is highly esteemed by those, who can distinguish excellence under the disguise of singularity. Enthusiastic and high-flown notions on the subject of religion have hitherto, as they usually do, prevented his general reception, as a son of taste and of the muses. The sceptic and the rational believer, uniting their forces against the visionary, pursue and scare a warm and brilliant imagination, with the hue and cry of madness. Not contented with bringing down the reasonings of the mystical philosopher, as they well may, to this degraded level, they apply the test of cold calculation and mathematical proof to departments of the mind which are privileged to appeal from so narrow and rigorous a tribunal. They criticise the representations of corporeal beauty, and the allegoric emblems of mental perfections; the image of the visible world, which appeals to the senses for a testimony to its truth, or the type of futurity and the immortal soul, which identifies itself with our hopes and with our hearts, as if they were syllogisms or theorems, demonstrable propositions or consecutive corollaries. By them have the higher powers of this artist been kept from public notice, and his genius tied down, as far as possible, to the mechanical department of his profession. By them, in short, has he been stigmatised as an engraver, who might do tolerably well, if he was not mad. But men, whose names will bear them out, in what they affirm, have now taken up his cause. . . .

Neither is the capacity of this untutored proficient limited to his professional occupation. He has made several irregular and unfinished attempts at poetry. He has dared to venture on the

ancient simplicity; and feeling it in his own character and manners, has succeeded better than those, who have only seen it
through a glass. His genius in this line assimilates more with the
bold and careless freedom, peculiar to our writers at the latter end
of the sixteenth, and former parts of the seventeenth century,
than with the polished phraseology, and just, but subdued
thought of the eighteenth. As the public have hitherto had no
opportunity of passing sentence on his poetical powers, I shall
trespass on your patience, while I introduce a few specimens from
a collection, circulated only among the author's friends, and
richly embellished by his pencil.

[Malkin proceeds to quote 'Laughing Song', 'Holy Thursday',
'The Divine Image', 'How sweet I roam'd,' 'I love the jocund
dance', 'The Tyger'. He makes comparisons with songs by Ben
Jonson.]

(from *A Father's Memoirs of his Child*, 1806)

HENRY CRABB ROBINSON

I SHOWED Hazlitt Blake's *Young*.* He saw no merit in them as
designs. I read him some of the poems. He was much struck with
them, and expressed himself with his usual strength and singularity. 'They are beautiful,' he said, 'and only too deep for the
vulgar. He has no sense of the ludicrous, and, as to a God, a worm
crawling in a privy is as worthy an object as any other, all being
to him indifferent. So to Blake the Chimney Sweeper, etc. He is
ruined by vain struggles to get rid of what presses on his brain –
he attempts impossibles.' I added, 'He is like a man who lifts a
burden too heavy for him; he bears it an instant, it then falls on
and crushes him.' W. Hazlitt preferred the 'Chimney Sweeper'.

(from Robinson's Diary, 10 March 1811)

I will put down as they occur to me without method all I can
recollect of the conversation of this remarkable man. Shall I call

* [*Editor's note:*] Illustrations to Edward Young's *Night Thoughts*.

him Artist or Genius – or Mystic – or Madman? Probably he is all. He has a most interesting appearance. He is now old – pale with a Socratic countenance, and an expression of great sweetness, but bordering on weakness – except when his features are animated by expression, and then he has an air of inspiration about him. The conversation was on art, and on poetry, and on religion; but it was my object, and I was successful, in drawing him out, and so getting from him an avowal of his *peculiar* sentiments. I was aware before of the nature of his impressions, or I should at times have been at a loss to understand him. . . . He at another time spoke of his paintings as being what he had seen in his visions. And when he said *my visions* it was in the ordinary unemphatic tone in which we speak of trivial matters that everyone understands and cares nothing about. In the same tone he said repeatedly, the 'Spirit told me.' I took occasion to say – You use the same word as Socrates used. What resemblance do you suppose there is between your spirit and the spirit of Socrates? 'The same as between our countenance.' He paused and added – 'I was Socrates.' And then, as if correcting himself, 'A sort of brother. I must have had conversations with him. So I had with Jesus Christ. I have an obscure recollection of having been with both of them.' . . .

On my asking in what light he viewed the great question concerning the Divinity of Jesus Christ, he said – '*He is the only God.*' But then he added – 'And so am I and so are you.' Now he had just before (and this occasioned my question) been speaking of the errors of Jesus Christ – He was wrong in suffering Himself to be crucified. He should not have attacked the Government. He had no business with such matters. On my inquiring how he reconciled this with the sanctity and divine qualities of Jesus, he said He was not then become the Father. Connecting as well as one can these fragmentary sentiments, it would be hard to give Blake's station between Christianity, Platonism, and Spinosism. Yet he professes to be very hostile to Plato, and reproaches Wordsworth with being not a Christian but a Platonist.

It is one of the subtle remarks of Hume on certain religious speculations that the tendency of them is to make men indifferent

to whatever takes place by destroying all ideas of good and evil.
I took occasion to apply this remark to something Blake said. If
so, I said, there is no use in discipline or education, no difference
between good and evil. He hastily broke in on me – 'There is no
use in education. I hold it wrong. It is the great sin. It is eating
of the tree of the knowledge of good and evil. That was the fault
of Plato – he knew of nothing but of the virtues and vices and
good and evil. There is nothing in all that. Everything is good in
God's eyes.' On my putting the obvious question – Is there
nothing absolutely evil in what men do? 'I am no judge of that.
Perhaps not in God's eyes.' . . .

It is easier to repeat the personal remarks of Blake than these
metaphysical speculations so nearly allied to the most opposite
systems. He spoke with seeming complacency of himself – said
he acted by command. The spirit said to him, 'Blake, be an artist
and nothing else.' In this there is felicity. His eye glistened while
he spoke of the joy of devoting himself solely to divine art. 'Art
is inspiration. When Michael Angelo or Raphael or Mr Flaxman
does any of his fine things, he does them in the spirit.' Blake said,
'I should be sorry if I had any earthly fame, for whatever natural
glory a man has is so much detracted from his spiritual glory. I
wish to do nothing for profit. I wish to live for art. I want
nothing whatever. I am quite happy.'

(from Robinson's Diary, 10 December 1825)

IT was at the latter end of the year 1825 that I put in writing my
recollections of this most remarkable man. . . . He died in the
year 1827. I have therefore now revised what I wrote . . . without
any attempt to reduce to order, or make consistent the wild and
strange rhapsodies uttered by this insane man of genius, thinking
it better to put down what I find as it occurs, though I am aware
of the objection that may justly be made to the recording the
ravings of insanity in which it may be said there can be found no
principle, as there is no ascertainable law of mental association
which is obeyed; and from which therefore nothing can be
learned.

This would be perfectly true of *mere* madness – but does not apply to that form of insanity ordinarily called monomania, and may be disregarded in a case like the present in which the subject of the remark was unquestionably what a German would call a *Verunglückter Genie*, whose theosophic dreams bear a close resemblance to those of *Swedenborg* – whose genius as an artist was praised by no less men than *Flaxman* and *Fuseli* – and whose poems were thought worthy republication by the biographer of *Swedenborg* (*Wilkinson*), and of which Wordsworth said after reading a number – they were the 'Songs of Innocence and Experience showing the two opposite sides of the human soul' – 'There is no doubt this poor man was mad, but there is something in the madness of this man which interests me more than the sanity of Lord Byron and Walter Scott!' The German painter *Götzenberger** (a man indeed who ought not to be named *after the others* as an authority for my writing about Blake) said, on his returning to Germany about the time at which I am now arrived, 'I saw in England many men of talents, but only three men of genius, Coleridge, Flaxman and Blake, and of these Blake was the greatest.'

(from *Reminiscences*, 1869)

S. T. COLERIDGE

P.S. I have this morning been reading a strange publication – viz. Poems with very wild and interesting pictures, as the swathing – etched (I suppose) but it is said – printed and painted by the Author, W. Blake. He is a man of Genius – and I apprehend, a Swedenborgian – certainly, a mystic *emphatically*. You perhaps smile at *my* calling another Poet, a *Mystic*; but verily I am in the

* [*Editor's note:*] Crabb Robinson's Diary, 2 February 1827, records that he took Götzenberger to visit Blake, and that 'the young painter from Germany ... seemed highly gratified by the designs' which Blake had made for Dante's *Divina Commedia*. 'Mrs Aders says G. considers B. as the first & Flaxman as the second man he has seen in England. ...'

very mire of common-place common-sense compared with
Mr Blake, apo- or rather ana-calyptic Poet, and Painter!
    (Postscript of letter to H. F. Cary, dated 6 February 1818)

I return you Blake's poesies, metrical and graphic, with thanks.
With this and the Book I have sent a rude scrawl as to the order
in which I was pleased by the several poems. . . .
    I begin with my Dyspathies that I may forget them: and have
uninterrupted space for Loves and Sympathies. Title page and the
following emblem contain all the faults of the Drawings with as
few beauties as could be in the compositions of a man who was
capable of such faults + such beauties. – The faults – despotism in
symbols, amounting in the Title page to the μισητόν, and occasionally, irregular unmodified Lines of the Inanimate, sometimes
as the effect of rigidity and sometimes of exossation – like a wet
tendon. So likewise the ambiguity of the Drapery. Is it a garment
– or the body incised and scored out? The *Limpness* (= the
effect of Vinegar on an egg) in the upper one of the two prostrate
figures in the Title page, and the *eye*-likeness of the twig pos-
teriorly on the second – and the strait line down the waist-coat of
pinky gold-beater's skin in the next drawing, with the I don't
know whatness of the countenance, as if the mouth had been
formed by the habit of placing the tongue, not contemptuously,
but stupidly, between the lower gums and the lower jaw – these
are the only *repulsive* faults I have noticed. The figure, however,
of the second leaf (abstracted from the *expression* of the countenance given it by something about the mouth and the inter-
space from the lower lip to the chin) is such as only a Master
learned in his art could produce.
    N.B. **I** signifies, It gave me pleasure. **H**, still greater – **H̄**, and
greater still. **Θ**, in the highest degree, **o**, in the lowest.*
    Shepherd **I**. Spring **I** (last Stanza **H**). Holy Thursday **H̄**.
Laughing Song **H**. Nurse's Song **I**. The Divine Image **Θ**. The
Lamb **H**. The little Black Boy **Θ**: yea **Θ + Θ**! Infant Joy **H̄**. (N.b.
for the 3 last lines I should wish – When wilt thou smile, or – O

        * **o** means that I am perplexed and have no opinion.

smile, O smile! I'll sing the while – For a Babe two days old does not, cannot *smile* – and innocence and the very truth of Nature must go together. Infancy is too holy a thing to be ornamented.) – Echoing Green **I** (the figures **H**, and of the second leaf **H̄**). The Cradle Song **I**. The School boy **H̄**. Night Θ. On another's Sorrow **I**. A Dream? – The little Boy lost **I** (the drawing **H**). The little boy found **I**. The Blossom **o**. The Chimney Sweeper **o**. The Voice of the ancient Bard **o**.

Introduction **H**. Earth's Answer **H**. Infant Sorrow **I**. The Clod and the Pebble **I**. The Garden of Love **H**. The Fly **I**. The Tyger **H**. A little Boy lost **H**. Holy Thursday **I**. P. 13, **o**. Nurse's Song **o**. The little girl lost and found (the ornaments most exquisite, the poem **I**). Chimney Sweeper in the Snow **o**. To Tirzah – and The Poison Tree **I** and yet **o**. A little girl lost **o** (I would have had it omitted – not for the want of innocence in the poem, but from the too probable want of it in many readers). London **I**. The sick Rose **I**. *The little Vagabond* – Tho' I cannot approve altogether of this last poem and have been inclined to think that the error which is most *likely* to beset the scholars of Emanuel Swedenborg is that of utterly demerging the tremendous incompatibilities with an evil will that arise out of the essential Holiness of the abysmal Aseity in the Love of the eternal *Person* – and thus giving temptation to weak minds to sink this Love itself into *good nature*, & yet still I disapprove the mood of mind in this wild poem so much less than I do the servile, blind worm, wrap-rascal scurf-coat of FEAR of the *modern Saints* (whose whole being is a Lie, to themselves as well as to their Brethren), that I should laugh with good conscience in watching a Saint of the new stamp, one of the Fixt Stars of our eleemosynary Advertisements, groaning in wind-pipe! and with the whites of his Eyes upraised at the *audacity* of this poem! – anything rather than *this* degredation† of Humanity, and therein of the Incarnate Divinity!

(from a letter to C. A. Tulk, 12 February 1818)

† with which how can we alter 'Our Father'?

CHARLES LAMB

BLAKE is a real name, I assure you, and a most extraordinary man, if he be still living. He is the Robert [William] Blake, whose wild designs accompany a splendid folio edition of the *Night Thoughts*, which you may have seen, in one of which he pictures the parting of soul and body by a solid mass of human form floating off, God knows how, from a lumpish mass (fac Simile to itself) left behind on the dying bed. He paints in water colours marvellous strange pictures, visions of his brain, which he asserts that he has seen. They have great merit. He has *seen* the old Welsh bards on Snowdon – he has seen the Beautifullest, the strongest, and the Ugliest Man, left alone from the Massacre of the Britons by the Romans, and has painted them from memory (I have seen his paintings) and asserts them to be as good as the figures of Raphael and Angelo, but not better, as they had precisely the same retro-visions and prophetic visions with themself [himself]. The painters in oil (which he will have it that neither of them practised) he affirms to have been the ruin of art, and affirms that all the while he was engaged in his Water paintings, Titian was disturbing him, Titian the Ill Genius of Oil Painting. His Pictures – one in particular, the Canterbury Pilgrims (far above Stothard's)– have great merit, but hard, dry, yet with grace. His poems have been sold hitherto only in Manuscript. I never read them: but a friend at my desire procured the 'Sweep Song' ['The Chimney Sweeper']. There is one to a tiger, which I have heard recited, beginning:

> Tiger, Tiger, burning bright,
> Thro' the desarts of the night,

which is glorious, but alas! I have not the book; for the man is flown, whither I know not – to Hades or a Mad House. But I must look on him as one of the most extraordinary persons of the age. . . .

(from a letter to Bernard Barton, 15 May 1824)

[E. V. Lucas annotates this letter: William Blake was at this time sixty-six years of age. He was living in poverty and neglect at 3 Fountain Court, Strand. Blake made 537 illustrations to Young's *Night Thoughts*, of which only forty-seven were published. Lamb is, however, thinking of his edition of Blair's *Grave*. The exhibition of his works was held in 1809, and it was for this that Blake wrote the descriptive catalogue. Lamb had sent 'The Chimney Sweeper', in the *Songs of Innocence*, to James Montgomery for his *Chimney-Sweepers' Friend and Climbing Boys' Album*, 1824, a little book designed to ameliorate the lot of those children, in whose interest a society existed. Barton also contributed something. It was Blake's poem which had excited Barton's curiosity. Probably he thought that Lamb wrote it. Lamb's mistake concerning Blake's name is curious in so far that it was Blake's brother Robert who in a vision revealed to the poet the method by which the *Songs of Innocence* were to be reproduced. He died in 1787. It might be added that Lamb's enthusiasm for Blake seems to have converted Barton, who, in 1830, was corresponding with John Linnell, the painter, about him.]

JOHN LINNELL

THERE is one thing I must mention: I never in all my conversations with him [Blake] could for a moment feel that there was the least justice in calling him insane; he could always explain his paradoxes satisfactorily when he pleased, but to many he spoke so that 'hearing they might *not* hear'. He was more like the ancient patterns of virtue than I ever expected to see in this world; he feared nothing so much as being rich, lest he should lose his spiritual riches. He was at the same time the most sublime in his expressions, with the simplicity and gentleness of a child, though never wanting in energy when called for.

(from a letter to Bernard Barton, 3 April 1830)

ALLAN CUNNINGHAM

HE removed to 28 Poland Street. Here he commenced that series of works which give him a right to be numbered among the men of genius of his country. In sketching designs, engraving plates, writing songs, and composing music, he employed his time, with his wife sitting at his side, encouraging him in all his undertakings. As he drew the figure he meditated the song which was to accompany it, and the music to which the verse was to be sung, was the offspring too of the same moment. Of his music there are no specimens – he wanted the art of noting it down – if it equalled many of his drawings, and some of his songs, we have lost melodies of real value.

The first fruits were the *Songs of Innocence and Experience*, a work original and natural, and of high merit, both in poetry and in painting. It consists of some sixty-five or seventy scenes, presenting images of youth and manhood – of domestic sadness, and fireside joy – of the gaiety and innocence, and happiness of childhood. Every scene has its poetical accompaniment, curiously interwoven with the group or the landscape, and forming, from the beauty of the colour and the prettiness of the pencilling, a very fair picture of itself. Those designs are in general highly poetical; more allied, however, to heaven than to earth – a kind of spiritual abstractions, and indicating a better world and fuller happiness than mortals enjoy. . . .

But then he imagined himself under spiritual influences; he saw the forms and listened to the voices of the worthies of other days; the past and future were before him, and he heard, in imagination, even that awful voice which called on Adam amongst the trees of the garden. In this kind of dreaming abstraction, he lived much of his life; all his works are stamped with it; and though they owe much of their mysticism and obscurity to the circumstance, there can be no doubt that they also owe to it much of their singular loveliness and beauty. It was wonderful that he could thus, month after month, and year after year, lay down his graver after it had won him his daily wages, and retire from the battle for bread, to disport his fancy amid scenes of more than earthly splendour, and creatures pure as unfallen dew.

In this lay the weakness and the strength of Blake, and those who desire to feel the character of his compositions, must be familiar with his history and the peculiarities of his mind. He was by nature a poet, a dreamer, and an enthusiast. The eminence which it had been the first ambition of his youth to climb, was visible before him, and he saw on its ascent or on its summit those who had started earlier in the race of fame. He felt conscious of his own merit, but was not aware of the thousand obstacles which were ready to interpose. He thought that he had but to sing songs and draw designs, and become great and famous. The crosses which genius is heir to had been wholly unforeseen – and they befell him early; he wanted the skill of hand, and fine tact of fancy and taste, to impress upon the offspring of his thoughts that popular shape, which gives such productions immediate circulation. His works were looked coldly on by the world, and were only esteemed by men of poetic minds, or those who were fond of things out of the common way. He earned a little fame, but no money by these speculations, and had to depend for bread on the labours of his graver.

All this neither crushed his spirit, nor induced him to work more in the way of the world; but it had a visible influence upon his mind. He became more seriously thoughtful, avoided the company of men, and lived in the manner of a hermit, in that vast wilderness, London. Necessity made him frugal, and honesty and independence prescribed plain clothes, homely fare, and a cheap habitation. He was thus compelled more than ever to retire to worlds of his own creating, and seek solace in visions of paradise for the joys which the earth denied him. By frequent indulgence in these imaginings, he gradually began to believe in the reality of what dreaming fancy painted – the pictured forms which swarmed before his eyes assumed, in his apprehension, the stability of positive revelations, and he mistook the vivid figures, which his professional imagination shaped, for the poets, and heroes, and princes of old. Amongst his friends, he at length ventured to intimate that the designs on which he was engaged were not from his own mind, but copied from grand works revealed to him in visions; and those who believed that, would readily lend an ear to the assurance that he was commanded to execute his performances by a celestial tongue!

> (from 'Life of Blake', in *Lives of the most eminent British Painters, Sculptors and Architects*, vol. II 1830))

CAROLINE BOWLES AND ROBERT SOUTHEY

I AM longing to see some of Blake's engravings from his own extraordinary designs, of which I first heard from yourself. Do you know whether they are scarce, or dear? They are certainly not generally known. Cunningham's life of him in the *Family Library* has strengthened the interest for Blake and his works with which your account first inspired me. Mad though he might be, he was gifted and good, and a most happy being. I should have delighted in him, and would fain know how it fares with the faithful, affectionate partner of his honourable life. . . .

> (from C.B. to R.S., 27 April 1830)

I HAVE nothing of Blake's but his designs for Blair's *Grave*, which were published with the poem. His still stranger designs for his own compositions in verse were not ready for sale when I saw him, nor did I ever hear that they were so. Much as he is to be admired, he was at that time so evidently insane, that the predominant feeling in conversing with him, or even looking at him, could only be sorrow and compassion. . . . I came away from the visit with so sad a feeling that I never repeated it. . . .*
You could not have delighted in him – his madness was too evi-

---

* [*Editor's note:*] Henry Crabb Robinson recorded in his diary, 24 July 1811: 'Late to C. Lamb's. Found a very large party there. Southey had been with Blake, and had admired both his designs and his poetic talents, at the same time that he held him for a decided madman. Blake, he says, spoke of his visions with the diffidence that is usual with such people, and did not seem to expect that he should be believed. He showed Southey a perfectly mad poem called *Jerusalem*, Oxford Street is in Jerusalem. . . .'

dent, too fearful. It gave his eyes an expression such as you would expect to see in one who was possessed. . . .

(from R.S. to C.B., 8 May 1830)

ANON. (? C. A. TULK)

SCARCELY had we finished the perusal of that highly interesting and splendid article of Campbell's upon Flaxman's genius and works, when we had the productions of a kindred spirit brought afresh before the public by Allan Cunningham, in a work celebrating the triumph of English art.

Every one must have smiled at this would-be imitation of Vasari; but in this instance we have not to laugh, but rather to complain, first, of the insertion of stories which are falsely coloured; then of the stealing, borrowing or copying a considerable portion of the life from *Nolleken's Own Times* [sic]; and, last of all, of a smile of contempt when speaking of Blake's private sentiments and feelings, which certainly is not becoming or respectful in a fellow artist. In our opinion, it was rather foolish of Mr Cunningham to attempt the life of so extraordinary a man as Blake, the peculiar character of whose mind he could no more comprehend, than he could produce rival works in either poetry or painting. Thus far with Mr Allan [Cunningham]; we will now proceed to a subject far more agreeable than a mere review of the Lives of the Painters.

The public have had only a slight glimpse of the noble *Songs of Innocence and Experience*, by William Blake, but even that has laid open great beauties to its view. It is a curious circumstance, and well worthy the attention of all persons, that in this age of reason, Englishmen should have allowed two such men as Flaxman and Blake, to pass from this life without evincing the smallest regard for them. Perhaps 'reason stumbles all night over bones of the dead', as Blake elegantly expressed it, and pays but small attention to real genius; or it may be partly accounted for through the want of a good philosophy, which, Mad. De Stael says, has not as yet been taught in England. These, perhaps, are a few of the many reasons why Blake and Flaxman have been buried in obscurity; but we have a confident hope that Coleridge, Blake and Flaxman are the forerunners of a more elevated and purer system, which has even now begun to take root in the breast of the English nation; they have laid the foundation for future minds – Coleridge, for the development of a more internal philosophy – Blake and Flaxman, for a purer and more ennobling sentiment in works of art.

After having preluded in this manner, let us direct our eyes to the beauties of Blake's poems. [The 'Introduction' to *Songs of Experience*.] Around these lines the stars are rolling their resplendent orbs, and in the cloud on which the song floats, a human form is lying, anxiously surveying their courses: these are a few wild notes struck forth by the hand of a master. But let us continue to look over his notes, bright both with poetry and forms divine, which demonstrate an intimate knowledge of the passions and feelings of the human breast. ['A Poison Tree'].

If Blake had lived in Germany, by this time he would have had commentators of the highest order upon every one of his effusions; but here, so little attention is paid to works of the mind, and so much to natural knowledge, that England, in the eyes of the thinking world, seems fast sinking into a lethargy, appearing as if the 'Poison Tree' had poured its soporific distillation over its body, which now lies under it almost dead and lifeless. But in that country where freedom of thought is allowed to the utmost extent, there the lethargic influence is most quickly dispelled; the elasticity of the mind occasions a partial depression, but it soon recovers its natural tone, and springs forth with freshness of life, gladdening the world; England being the lungs by which Europe breathes freely, which without her would become putrid, or else break forth into eruptions, like the French Revolution. All this, then, results from that perfect freedom of thought which reigns in England, and this it is which inspires with delight all good men, when they behold this country free from the chains of both mind or [*sic*] body; and through this very freedom the poets and artists of England have rivalled, nay, even surpassed, the works of the ancients; for, together with all the beauty which the ancients possessed, the *English alone*, of all nations in Europe, have practially, and not theoretically, developed in their works of art a higher principle and sentiment, which conducts from the merely sensual delight of form to a contemplation of the beauties of the soul. The powers, then, of both mind and body having been freely exercised, the result is a genius, who stands forth as a representative of his race; and thus we may say, Blake in his single person united all the grand combination of art and mind, poetry, music and painting; we may carry the simile still further, and say, that as England is the least fettered by the minds of other nations, so Blake poured forth his effusions in his own grand style, copying no one, (*nolumus leges Angliae mutari,*) but breathing spirit and life into his works; and though shaping forms from the world of his creative and sportive imagination, yet he still remembered he was a moral as well as intellectual citizen of England, bound both to love and instruct her. These ought to be the ruling principles of all artists and poets. Flaxman and Blake thought it a still higher honour to be celebrated for their innocence and beauty of sentiment, than for a mere sensual representation of forms. Their internal aesthetic produced a similar external, not by any means inferior to the mere form-painter, and in this respect superior, that there was a Promethean fire which glowed in their productions, purifying the soul from the gross imperfections of the natural mind.

Let it not, then, be passed over as trifling, how and after what fashion artists work, for as the closer a composer combines music with the feelings in the same proportion does he attain to excellence, and so far does he travel from that excellence when the feelings are cut off from the music; in the same manner, artists who exert an immense influence over the passions and feelings of men, having pure souls, exalt rather than degrade the minds of those who contemplate their works. Exerting this moral influence on the state of society, respect ought to be paid to them, on other grounds than that of their being the mere producers of beautiful forms.

The Greeks in their institutions took especial care of the artist and the poet, as men who presented to their eyes the deeds and

actions of their gods and heroes; and we are well aware that they
inspired the Greek states with an intense desire of rivalling their
ancestors in glory. Now this consideration alone ought to be of
great weight with us, and yet there is a still higher principle to be
drawn from the fine arts, for they instruct the moden nations
rather in the beauty of peace, than in war.

This grand combination of art succeeds in every particular,
painting being the flesh, poetry the bones, and music the nerves
of Blake's work.

The figures surrounding and enclosing the poems, produce
fresh delight. They are equally tinged by a poetical idea, and
though sometimes it is difficult to understand his wandering
flights, yet the extraordinary power developed in the handling of
both arts astonish [sic] as well as delight. Here and there figures
are introduced, which, like the spirits in Macbeth, pass quickly
from the sight; yet they every one of them have been well
digested in a brain of genius; and we should endeavour rather to
unlock the prison-door in which we are placed, and gain an
insight into his powerful mind, than rail and scoff at him as a
dreamer and madman.

For instance, Albion, with which the world is very little
acquainted, seems the embodying of Blake's ideas on the present
state of England; he viewed it, not with the eyes of ordinary men,
but contemplated it rather as a province of one grand man, in
which diseases and crimes are continually engendered, and on
this account he poured forth his poetical effusions somewhat in
the style of Novalis, mourning over the crimes and errors of his
dear country: and it is more extraordinary still that, like Novalis,
he contemplated the natural world as the mere outbirth of the
thought, and lived and existed in that world for which we are
created. Horrid forms and visions pervade this Albion, for they
were the only representatives, in his opinion, of the present state
of mankind. No great genius wrote without having a plan, and
so in this, a light is frequently thrown across the pictures, which
partly discover the interior designs of the Poet. We are perfectly
aware of the present state of public opinion on this kind of man,
but we know at the same time, that every genius has a certain

end to perform, and always runs before his contemporaries, and for that reason is not generally understood. This is our candid opinion with respect to Blake, but we hope that hereafter his merits will be more generally acknowledged.

We now proceed to the other poems. ['A Cradle Song', 'The Divine Image', 'The Garden of Love'.] This ['The Garden of Love'] is a curious and mystical poem, which as yet can be but partially understood – but at the same time it is highly poetical. Now approaching a new subject, the elegant dream of Thel, which seems born in the perfume of the lily, so charming, so fairy-like, are all its illustrations, there is only one work that we remember like it in excellence, the *Sakontola*, for it wears all the freshness of Indian simplicity and innocence.

The titlepage of this mazy dream contains a specimen of his utmost elegance in design: two beautiful figures are chasing one another in gentle sport, and the Peri Thel is looking on the fairy land. A few specimens of this poem will suffice to show its interest:

> A Speech* addressed to Thel by a Cloud.

This little work is the fanciful product of a rich imagination, drawing, colouring, poetry, have united to form a beautiful whole; all the figures teem with elegance, and convey sentiments which are noble, though veiled under a fairy tale. With this last extract we conclude for the present, earnestly recommending the works of our author to the attention of the English nation, whereby their taste may be improved in the fine arts, as well as gratification derived from the perusal of his poetry.† [Quotes from *Thel*, 'Why cannot the ear . . . vale of Har'.]

> ('The Inventions of William Blake, Painter and Poet', an
> unsigned article in *London University Magazine*, II (1830))‡

* [*Editor's note:*] In fact, the dialogue is quoted: 'Virgin, know'st thou not . . . to find his partner in the vale.'

† Blake and Coleridge, when in company, seemed like congenial beings of another sphere, breathing for a while on our earth; which may easily be perceived from the similarity of thought pervading their works.

‡ [*Editor's note:*] Keynes conjectures that the author of this article

FREDERICK TATHAM

In youth he surprised everyone with his vigour and activity. In age he impressed all with his unfading ardour and unabated energy. His beautiful grey locks hung upon his shoulders; and dressing as he always did in latter years in black, he looked, even in person, although without any effort towards eccentricity, to be of no ordinary character. In youth, he was nimble; in old age, venerable. His disposition was cheerful and lively, and was never depressed by any cares but those springing out of his art. He was the attached friend of all who knew him, and a favourite with everyone but those who oppressed him, and against such his noble and impetuous spirit boiled, and fell upon the aggressor like a water-spout from the troubled deep. Yet, like Moses, he was one of the meekest of men. His patience was almost incredible: he could be the lamb; he could plod as a camel; he could roar as a lion. He was everything but subtle; the serpent had no share in his nature; secrecy was unknown to him. He would relate those things of himself that others make it their utmost endeavour to conceal. He was possessed of a peculiar obstinacy, that always bristled up when he was either unnecessarily opposed or invited out to show like a lion or a bear. Many anecdotes could be related in which there is sufficient evidence to prove that many of his eccentric speeches were thrown forth more as a piece of sarcasm upon the inquirer than from his real opinion. If he thought a question were put merely for a desire to learn, no man could give advice more reasonably and more kindly; but if that same question were put for idle curiosity, he retaliated by such an eccentric answer as left the inquirer more afield than ever. He then made an enigma of a plain question: hence arose many vague reports of his oddities. He was particularly so upon religion. His writings

---

may have been C. A. Tulk, the eminent Swedenborgian who was a friend of Coleridge (see p. 39). Tulk was a supporter of the newly-established University of London. He possessed a copy of *Poetical Sketches* presented to him, and inscribed, by Blake. See G. Keynes, *Blake Studies* (1949) p. 98.

abounded with these sallies of independent opinion. He detested priestcraft and religious cant. . . . Irritated by hypocrisy and the unequivocal yielding of weak and interested men, he said and wrote unwarrantable arguments; but unalloyed and unencumbered by opposition, he was in all essential points orthodox in belief. . . .

Fuseli and Flaxman both said that Blake was the greatest man in the country, and that there would come a time when his works would be invaluable. Before Fuseli knew Blake, he used to fill his pictures with all sorts of fashionable ornaments and tawdry embellishments. Blake's simplicity imbued the minds of all who knew him; his life was a pattern, and has been spoken of as such from the pulpit. His abstraction from the world, his power of self-denial, his detestation of hypocrisy and gain, his hatred of gold and the things that perish, rendered him indeed well able to have exclaimed: 'In innocency I have washed my hands.'

(from 'Life of William Blake', *c.* 1832)

J. J. GARTH WILKINSON

THE present volume contains nearly all that is excellent in Blake's poetry; and great, rare, and manifest is the excellence that is here. The faults are equally conspicuous, and he who runs may read them. They amount to an utter want of elaboration, and even, in many cases, to an inattention to the ordinary rules of grammar. Yet the Songs of Innocence, at least, are quite free from the dark becloudment which rolled and billowed over Blake in his later days. He here transcended Self, and escaped from the isolation which Self involves; and, as it then ever is, his expanding affections embraced universal man, and, without violating, beautified and hallowed even his individual peculiarities. Accordingly, many of these delicious lays belong to the Era as well as to the Author. They are remarkable for the transparent depth of thought which constitutes true simplicity – they give us glimpses

of all that is holiest in the childhood of the world and the individual – they abound with the sweetest touches of that pastoral life,
by which the Golden Age may be still visibly represented to the
Iron one – they delineate full-orbed age, ripe with the seeds of a
second infancy, which is 'the Kingdom of Heaven'. The latter
half of the volume, comprising the Songs of Experience, consists,
it is true, of darker themes; but they, too, are well and wonderfully
sung, and ought to be preserved, because, in contrastive connection with the Songs of Innocence, they do convey a powerful
impression of THE TWO CONTRARY STATES OF THE HUMAN SOUL.

(from preface to *Songs of Innocence and Experience*, 1839)

EDWARD QUILLINAN

AMONG some new books that I have been looking at ... I
observed C. Lamb's Letters, & *Blake's* Poems – and as I was
glancing over them for an hour or two, it seemed to me that both
publications had the fault of *too much*. In Lamb's *too much* (for
some may be well enough) of childish fun, or rather that strain
at fun which is the trivial imitation of child's fun; – and *some* of
Blake's verses, illustrated in the book you possess, want in this
publication* the poetry of the painting to support them. They
seemed to sound very like nonsense-verses as we read them
aloud. Some of them, I say; for others have a real charm in their
wildness & oddness. Do not suppose I undervalue the man. I
have on the contrary a sort of tenderness for him that makes me
perhaps to over-estimate the value of many of his verses. He &
that good old wife of his, as described by Allan Cunningham, are
two very interesting persons in my mind....

[After receiving Robinson's reply, Quillinan wrote from
Longrigg House.] ... How can you say I wrote slightingly of

* [*Editor's note:*] I have been unable to trace any 'new' edition of
Blake around this date. It appears that the reference must be to Garth
Wilkinson's plain text of *Songs of Innocence and Experience*, published
by Pickering in 1839. Quillinan is contrasting it with an 'illuminated'
copy of the Songs which Crabb Robinson had purchased from Blake.

Blake? He is one of my pet spoilt children of genius – Your book made him so, & Allan Cunningham's life of him. He is more than ever safe in my goodwill *now* – I understand him & his wife better now than ever. I only objected to some trivial verses; well in your illustrated book, but somewhat weak for unadorned publication. . . .

(from letters to H. Crabb Robinson,
27 July and 12 August 1848)

SAMUEL PALMER

BLAKE, once known, can never be forgotten. His knowledge was various and extensive, and his conversation so nervous and brilliant that, if recorded at the time, it would have thrown much light upon his character, and in no way lessened him in the estimation of those who knew him only by his works. . . .

In him you saw at once the Maker, the Inventor; one of the few in any age: a fitting companion for Dante. He was energy itself, and shed around him a kindling influence; an atmosphere of life, full of the ideal. To walk with him in the country, was to perceive a soul of beauty through the forms of matter; and the high gloomy buildings between which, from his study window,* a glimpse was caught of the Thames and the Surrey shore, assumed a kind of grandeur from the man dwelling near them. Those may laugh at this, who never knew such a one as Blake, but of him it is the simple truth. . . .

He was a man without a mask; his aim simple, his path straight forwards, and his wants few: so he was free, noble and happy. . . .

His voice and manner were quiet, yet all awake with intellect. Above the tricks of littleness, or the least taint of affectation, with a natural dignity which few would have dared to affront, he was gentle and affectionate, loving to be with little children and to talk about them. . . .

Declining, like Socrates, whom in many respects he resembled, the common objects of ambition, and pitying the scuffle to obtain

* [*Editor's note:*] In Fountain Court, the Strand.

them, he thought that no one could be truly great who had not
humbled himself 'even as a little child'. This was a subject he
loved to dwell upon and to illustrate.

(from a letter to Alexander Gilchrist, 1855)

PART THREE

Comments and Critiques
1863–1907

ALEXANDER GILCHRIST

HE taught Mrs Blake to take off the impressions with care and delicacy, which such plates signally needed; and also to help in tinting them from his drawings with right artistic feeling; in all which tasks she, to her honour, much delighted. The size of the plates was small, for the sake of economising copper; something under five inches by three. The number of engraved pages in the *Songs of Innocence* alone was twenty-seven. They were done up in boards by Mrs Blake's hand, forming a small octavo; so that the poet and his wife did everything in making the book, – writing, designing, printing, engraving, – everything except manufacturing the paper: the very ink, or colour rather, they did make. Never before surely was a man so literally the author of his own book. '*Songs of Innocence, the author and printer W. Blake,* 1789' is the title. Copies still occur occasionally; though the two series bound together in one volume, each with its own title-page, and a general one added, is the more usual state.

First of the Poems let me speak, harsh as seems their divorce from the Design which blends with them, forming warp and woof in one texture. It is like pulling up a daisy by the roots from the greensward out of which it springs. To me many years ago, first reading these weird Songs in their appropriate environment of equally spiritual form and hue, the effect was as that of an angelic voice singing to oaten pipe, such as Arcadians tell of; or, as if a spiritual magician were summoning before human eyes, and through a human medium, images and scenes of divine loveliness; and in the pauses of the strain we seem to catch the rustling of angelic wings. The Golden Age independent of Space or Time, object of vague sighs and dreams from many generations of struggling humanity – an Eden such as childhood sees, is brought nearer than ever poet brought it before. For this poet was in assured possession of the Golden Age within the chambers of his own mind. As we read, fugitive glimpses open, clear as brief, of our buried childhood, of an unseen world present, past, to come; we are endowed with new spiritual sight, with unwonted intuitions, bright visitants from finer realms of thought, which ever elude us, ever hover near. We encounter familiar objects, in unfamiliar, transfigured aspects, simple expression and deep meanings, type and antitype. True, there are palpable irregularities, metrical licence, lapse of grammar, and even of orthography; but often the sweetest melody, most daring eloquence of rhythm, and what is more, appropriate rhythm. They are *unfinished* poems: yet would finish have bettered their bold and careless freedom? Would it not have brushed away the delicate bloom? that visible spontaneity, so rare and great a charm, the eloquent attribute of our old English ballads and of the early Songs of all nations. The most deceptively perfect wax-model is no substitute for the living flower. The form is, in these Songs, a transparent medium of the spiritual thought, not an opaque body. 'He has dared to venture', writes Malkin, not irrelevantly, 'on the ancient simplicity, and feeling it in his own character and manners, has succeeded' better than those who have only seen it through a glass.

There is the same divine *afflatus* as in the *Poetical Sketches*, but fuller: a maturity of expression, despite surviving negligences, and of thought and motive. The 'Child Angel', as we ventured to call the Poet in earlier years, no longer merely sportive and innocently wanton, wears a brow of thought; a glance of insight has passed into

> A sense sublime
> Of something far more deeply interfused

in Nature, a feeling of 'the burthen of the mystery of things'; though still possessed by widest sympathies with all that is simple and innocent, with echoing laughter, little lamb, a flower's blossom, with 'emmet wildered and forlorn'.

These poems have a unity and mutual relationship, the influence of which is much impaired if they be read otherwise than as a whole. They are given entire in the Second Volume, to which I refer my reader, if not of decisively unpoetic turn.

Who but Blake, with his pure heart, his simple exalted character, could have transfigured a commonplace meeting of Charity Children at St Paul's, as he has done in the 'Holy Thursday'? A picture at once tender and grand. The bold images, by a wise instinct resorted to at the close of the first and second stanzas and opening of the third, are in the highest degree imaginative; they are true as only Poetry can be.

How vocal is the poem 'Spring', despite imperfect rhymes. From addressing the child, the poet, by a transition not infrequent with him, passes out of himself into the child's person, showing a chameleon sympathy with childlike feelings. Can we not see the little three-year-old prattler stroking the white lamb, her feelings made articulate for her? Even more remarkable is the poem entitled 'The Lamb', sweet hymn of tender infantine sentiment appropriate to that perennial image of meekness; to which the fierce eloquence of 'The Tyger', in the *Songs of Experience*, is an antitype. In 'The Lamb' the poet again changes person to that of a child. Of lyrical beauty, take as a sample 'The Laughing Song', with its happy *ring* of merry innocent voices. This and 'The Nurse's Song' are more in the style of his early poems, but, as we said, of far maturer execution. I scarcely need call attention to the delicate simplicity of the little pastoral, entitled 'The Shepherd': to the picturesqueness in a warmer hue, the delightful domesticity, the expressive melody of 'The Ecchoing Green': or to the lovely sympathy and piety which irradiate the touching 'Cradle Song'. More enchanting still is the stir of fancy and sympathy which animates 'The Dream', that

> Did weave a shade o'er my angel-guarded bed;

of an emmet that had

> Lost her way,
> Where on grass methought I lay.

Few are the readers, I should think, who can fail to appreciate the symbolic grandeur of 'The Little Boy Lost' and 'The Little Boy Found', or the enigmatic tenderness of the 'Blossom' and the

'Divine Image'; and the verses 'On Another's Sorrow', express some of Blake's favourite religious ideas, his abiding notions on the subject of the Godhead, which surely suggest the kernel of Christian feeling. A similar tinge of the divine colours the lines called 'Night', with its revelation of angelic guardians, believed in with unquestioning piety by Blake, who makes us in our turn conscious, as we read, of angelic noiseless footsteps. For a nobler depth of religious beauty, with accordant grandeur of sentiment and language, I know no parallel nor hint elsewhere of such a poem as 'The Little Black Boy' –

My mother bore me in the southern wild.

We may read these poems again and again, and they continue fresh as at first. There is something unsating in them, a perfume as of a growing violet, which renews itself as fast as it is inhaled.

One poem, 'The Chimney Sweeper', still calls for special notice. This and 'Holy Thursday' are remarkable as an anticipation of the daring choice of homely subject, of the yet more daringly familiar manner, nay, of the very metre and trick of style adopted by Wordsworth in a portion of those memorable 'experiments in poetry' – the *Lyrical Ballads* – in 'The Reverie of Poor Susan', for instance (not written till 1797), the 'Star Gazers', and 'The Power of Music' (both 1806). The little Sweep's dream has the spiritual touch peculiar to Blake's hand. This poem, I may add, was extracted thirty-five years later in a curious little volume (1824) of James Montgomery's editing, as friend of the then unprotected Climbing Boys. It was entitled, *The Chimney Sweeper's Friend and Climbing Boy's Album;* a miscellany of verse and prose, original and borrowed, with illustrations by Robert Cruikshank. Charles Lamb, one of the living authors applied to by the kind-hearted Sheffield poet, while declining the task of rhyming on such a subject, sent a copy of this poem from the *Songs of Innocence*, communicating it as 'from a very rare and curious little work'. At line five, 'little Tom Dacre' is transformed, by a sly blunder of Lamb's, into 'little Tom Toddy'. The poem on the same subject in the *Songs of Experience*, inferior poetically, but in an accordant key of gloom, would have been the more apposite to Montgomery's volume.

The tender loveliness of these poems will hardly reappear in Blake's subsequent writing. Darker phases of feeling, more sombre colours, profounder meanings, ruder eloquence, characterise the *Songs of Experience* of five years later.

In 1789, the year in which Blake's hand engraved the *Songs of Innocence*, Wordsworth was finishing his versified 'Evening Walk' on the Goldsmith model; Crabbe ('Pope in worsted stockings', as Hazlitt christened him), famous six years before by his *Village*, was publishing one of his minor quartos, *The Newspaper;* and Mrs Charlotte Smith, not undeservedly popular, was accorded a fifth edition within five years, of her *Elegiac Sonnets*, one or two of which still merit the praise of being good sonnets, among the best in a bad time. In these years, Hayley, Mason, Hannah More, Jago, Downman, Helen Maria Williams, were among the active producers of poetry; Cumberland, Holcroft, Inchbald, Burgoyne, of the acting drama of the day; Peter Pindar, and *Pasquin* Williams, of the satire.

The designs, simultaneous offspring with the poems, which in the most literal sense illuminate the Songs of Innocence, consist of poetized domestic scenes. The drawing and draperies are grand in style as graceful, though covering few inches' space; the colour pure, delicate, yet in effect rich and full. The mere tinting of the text and of the free ornamental border often makes a refined picture. The costumes of the period are idealized, the landscape given in pastoral and symbolic hints. Sometimes these drawings almost suffer from being looked at as a book and held close, instead of at due distance as pictures, where they become more effective. In composition, colour, pervading feeling, they are lyrical to the eye, as the Songs to the ear.

On the whole, the designs to the Songs of Innocence are finer as well as more pertinent to the poems; more closely interwoven with them, than those which accompany the Songs of Experience.

(from *Life of William Blake*, 1863)

JAMES THOMSON

I AM merely writing a few remarks on the poet, not sketching the life and character of the man; but I may be allowed to call the attention of readers to this wonderful life and character. Blake was always poor in world's wealth, always rich in spiritual wealth, happy and contented and assured, living with God. As to his soul's salvation, I do not believe that he ever gave it a thought, any more than a child thinks of the question whether its loving parents will continue to feed and clothe and cherish it. He had none of the feverish raptures and hypochondriac remorses which even in the best of those who are commonly called saints excite a certain contemptuous pity in the midst of love and admiration: he was a thoroughly healthy and happy religious soul, whose happiness was thoroughly unselfish and noble. As to the 'Christian Evidences', as they are termed, of which the mass of good people are so enamoured, in trying to argue themselves and others into a sort of belief in a sort (and such a sort!) of deity, he would have no more dreamed of appealing to them than he would have tried elaborately to argue himself into a belief in the existence of the sun. 'I feel the warmth, I see the light and see by the light: what do you want to argue about? You may call it sun, moon, comet, star, or Will-o'-the-Wisp, if it so pleases you; all I know and care for is this, that day by day it warms and lights me.' Such would have been the sum of his reply to any questioner; for he was emphatically a seer, and had the disdain of all seers for the pretensions of gropers and guessers who are blind. Like Swedenborg, he always relates things heard and seen; more purely a mystic than Swedenborg, he does not condescend to dialectics and scholastic divinity. Those who fancy that a dozen stony syllogisms seal up the perennial fountain of our deepest questions, will affirm that Blake's belief was an illusion. But an illusion constant and self-consistent and harmonious with the world throughout the whole of a man's life, wherein does this differ from a reality? Metaphysically we are absolutely unable to prove any existence; we believe that those things really exist which we find pretty constant and consistent in their relations to us – a very sound practical but very unsound philosophical belief. Blake and Swedenborg and other true mystics (Jesus among them) undoubtedly had senses other than ours. It is as futile for us to argue against the reality of their perceptions as it would be false in us to pretend that our perceptions are the same. As, however, Blake was supremely a mystic, it is but fair to add that he (and the same may be affirmed of Jesus) was unlike common Christians as thoroughly as he was unlike common atheists; he lived in a sphere far removed from both. In the clash of the creeds, it is always a comfort to remember that sects with their sectaries, orthodox and heterodox, could not intersect at all, if they were not in the same plane. Blake's esteem for argumentation may be read in one couplet:

> If the sun and moon should doubt
> They'd immediately go out.

The wisdom and the celestial simplicity of this little piece* prepared me to love the author and all that he had done; yet the selections from his poems and other writings were a revelation far richer than my hopes.

His object [in 'Auguries of Innocence'] was not to expand a small fact into a universal truth, but to concentrate the full essence of a universal truth into a small fact. . . . The sharply cut symbol leaves a distinct and enduring impression, where the abstract dogma would have perhaps made no impression at all. . . .

[The imagery of the Prophetic Books.] Every man living in seclusion and developing an intense interior life, gradually comes to give a quite peculiar significance to certain words and phrases and emblems. Metaphors which to the common bookwrights and journalists are mere handy counters, symbols almost as abstract and unrelated in thought to the things they represent as are the x and y and z used in solving an algebraic problem, are for *him* burdened with rich and various freights of spiritual experience;

* [*Editor's note:*] 'The Divine Image', the first of Blake's poems that he had read.

they are ships in which he has sailed over uncharted seas to un-
mapped shores, with which he has struggled through wild tem-
pests and been tranced in divine calms, in which he has returned
with treasures from all the zones; and he loves them as a sailor
loves his ship. His writings must thus appear, to any one reading
them for the first time, very obscure, and often very ludicrous;
the strange reader sees a battered old hull, where the writer sees
a marvellous circumnavigation. But we ought not to be kept from
studying these writings by any apparent obscurity and ludicrous-
ness, if we have found in the easily comprehended vernacular
writings of the same man (as in Blake we certainly *have* found)
sincerity and wisdom and beauty. . . .

> (from a review of Gilchrist's *Life* originally published
> in the *National Reformer*, 1866, signed B. V.)

A. C. SWINBURNE

To attest by word or work the identity of things which never
can become identical, was no part of Blake's object in life. What
work it fell to his lot to do, that, having faith in the fates, he
believed the best work possible, and performed to admiration.
It is in consequence of this belief that, apart from all conjectural
or problematic theory, the work he did is absolutely good.
Intolerant he was by nature to a degree noticeable even among
free-thinkers and prophets; but the strange forms assumed by
this intolerance are best explicable by the singular facts of his
training – his perfect ignorance of well-known ordinary things
and imperfect quaint knowledge of much that lay well out of the
usual way. He retained always an excellent arrogance and a wholly
laudable self-reliance; being incapable of weak-eyed doubts or
any shuffling modesty. His great tenderness had a lining of contempt – his fiery self-assertion a kernel of loyalty. No one, it is
evident, had ever a more intense and noble enjoyment of good
or great works in other men – took sharper or deeper delight in
the sense of a loyal admiration: being of his nature noble, fearless,
and fond of all things good; a man made for believing. This royal
temper of mind goes properly with a keen relish of what excel-

lence or greatness a man may have in himself. Those must be readiest to feel and to express unalloyed and lofty pleasure in the great powers and deeds of a neighbour, who, while standing clear alike of reptile modesty and pretentious presumption, perceive and know in themselves such qualities as give them a right to admire and a right to applaud. If a man thinks meanly of himself, he can hardly in reason think much of his judgment; if he depreciates the value of his own work, he depreciates also the value of his praise....

The present critic has not (happily) to preach the gospel as delivered by Blake; he has merely, if possible, to make the text of that gospel a little more readable. And this must be worth doing, if it be worth while to touch on Blake's work at all. What is true of all poets and artists worth judging is especially true of him; that critics who attempt to judge him piecemeal do not in effect judge him at all, but someone quite different from him, and some one (to any serious student) probably more inexplicable than the real man. For what are we to make of a man whose work deserves crowning one day and hooting the next? If the *Songs* be so good, are not those that praise them bound to examine and try what merit may be latent in the 'Prophecies'? – bound at least to explain as best they may how the one comes to be worth so much and the other worth nothing? ... We are not bound to accept Blake's mysticism; we are bound to take some account of it. A disciple must take his master's word for proof of the thing preached. This it would be folly to expect of a biographer; even Boswell falls short of this, having courage on some points to branch off from the strait pathway of his teacher and strike into a small speculative track of his own. But a biographer must be capable of expounding the evangel (or, if such a word could be, the 'dysangel') of his hero, however far he may be from thinking it worth acceptance. And this, one must admit, the writers on Blake have on the whole failed of doing.... To pluck the heart out of Blake's mystery is a task which every man must be left to attempt for himself; for this prophet is certainly not 'easier to be played on than a pipe'....

First then for the Songs of Innocence and Experience. These at a first naming recall only that incomparable charm of form in which they first came out clothed, and hence vex the souls of men with regretful comparison. For here by hard necessity we miss the lovely and luminous setting of designs, which makes the Songs precious and pleasurable to those who know or care for little else of the master's doing; the infinite delight of those drawings, sweeter to see than music to hear, where herb and stem break into grace of shape and blossom of form, and the branch-work is full of little flames and flowers, catching as it were from the verse enclosed the fragrant heat and delicate sound they seem to give back; where colour lapses into light and light assumes feature in colour. If elsewhere the artist's strange strength of thought and hand is more visible, nowhere is there such pure sweetness and singleness of design in his work. All the tremulous and tender splendour of spring is mixed into the written word and coloured draught; every page has the smell of April. Over all things given, the sleep of flocks and the growth of leaves, the laughter in dividing lips of flowers and the music at the moulded mouth of the flute-player, there is cast a pure fine veil of light, softer than sleep and keener than sunshine. The sweetness of sky and leaf, of grass and water – the bright light life of bird and child and beast – is so to speak kept fresh by some graver sense of faithful and mysterious love, explained and vivified by a con-science and purpose in the artist's hand and mind. Such a fiery outbreak of spring, such an insurrection of fierce floral life and radiant riot of childish power and pleasure, no poet or painter ever gave before: such lustre of green leaves and flushed limbs, kindled cloud and fervent fleece, was never wrought into speech or shape. Nevertheless this decorative work is after all the mere husk and shell of the Songs. These also, we may notice, have to some extent shared the comparative popularity of the designs which serve as framework to them. They have absolutely achieved the dignity of a reprint; have had a chance before now of swim-ming for life; whereas most of Blake's offspring have been thrown into Lethe bound hand and foot, without hope of ever striking out in one fair effort. Perhaps on some accounts this preference has been not unreasonable. What was written for children can hardly offend men; and the obscurities and audacities of the prophet would here have been clearly out of place. It is indeed some relief to a neophyte serving in the outer courts of such an intricate and cloudy temple, to come upon this little side-chapel set about with the simplest wreaths and smelling of the fields rather than incense, where all the singing is done by clear children's voices to the briefest and least complex tunes. Not at first without a sense of release does the human mind get quit for a little of the clouds of Urizen, the fires of Orc, and all the Titanic apparatus of prophecy. And these poems are really unequalled in their kind. Such verse was never written for children since verse-writing began. Only in a few of those faultless fragments of childish rhyme which float without name or form upon the memories of men shall we find such a pure clear cadence of verse, such rapid ring and flow of lyric laughter, such sweet and direct choice of the just word and figure, such an impeccable simplicity; nowhere but here such a tender wisdom of holiness, such a light and perfume of innocence. Nothing like this was ever written on that text of the lion and the lamb; no such heaven of sinless animal life was ever conceived so intensely and sweetly.

> And there the lion's ruddy eyes
>   Shall flow with tears of gold,
> And pitying the tender cries,
>   And walking round the fold,
> Saying *Wrath by His meekness*
> *And by His health sickness*
> *Is driven away*
> *From our immortal day.*
> *And now beside thee, bleating lamb,*
>   *I can lie down and sleep,*
> *Or think on Him who bore thy name,*
>   *Graze after thee, and weep.**

The leap and fall of the verse is so perfect as to make it a fit

---

* [*Editor's note:*] All Swinburne's quotations are taken from Alexander Gilchrist's *Life of William Blake, with Selections from his Poems and other Writings*, 2 vols. (1863).

garment and covering for the profound tenderness of faith and
soft strength of innocent impulse embodied in it. But the whole
of this hymn of 'Night' is wholly beautiful; being perhaps one of
the two poems of loftiest loveliness among all the Songs of
Innocence. The other is that called 'The Little Black Boy'; a
poem especially exquisite for its noble forbearance from vulgar
pathos and achievement of the highest and most poignant sweetness of speech and sense; in which the poet's mysticism is baptized
with pure water and taught to speak as from faultless lips of
children, to such effect as this.

> And we are put on earth a little space
> *That we may learn to bear the beams of love;*
> And these black bodies and this sunburnt face
> Are like a cloud and like a shady grove.

Other poems of a very perfect beauty are those of 'The Piper',
'The Lamb', 'The Chimney Sweeper', and 'The two-days-old
Baby';* all, for the music in them, more like the notes of birds
caught up and given back than the modulated measure of
human verse. One cannot say, being so slight and seemingly
wrong in metrical form, how they come to be so absolutely right;
but right even in point of verses and words they assuredly are.
Add fuller formal completion of rhyme and rhythm to that song
of 'Infant Joy', and you have broken up the soft birdlike perfection of clear light sound which gives it beauty; the little bodily
melody of soulless and painless laughter.

Against all articulate authority we do however class several of
the Songs of Experience higher for the great qualities of verse
than anything in the earlier division of these poems. If the Songs
of Innocence have the shape and smell of leaves or buds, these
have in them the light and sound of fire or the sea. Entering
among them, a fresher savour and a larger breath strikes one upon
the lips and forehead. In the first part we are shown who they
are who have or who deserve the gift of spiritual sight: in the
second, what things there are for them to see when that gift has
been given. Innocence, the quality of beasts and children, has the
keenest eyes; and such eyes alone can discern and interpret the

* [*Editor's note:*] 'Infant Joy'.

actual mysteries of experience. It is natural that this second part, dealing as it does with such things as underlie the outer forms of the first part, should rise higher and dive deeper in point of mere words. These give the distilled perfume and extracted blood of the veins in the rose-leaf, the sharp, liquid, intense spirit crushed out of the broken kernel in the fruit. The last of the Songs of Innocence is a prelude to these poems; in it the poet summons to judgment the young and single-spirited, that by right of the natural impulse of delight in them they may give sentence against the preachers of convention and assumption; and in the first poem of the second series he, by the same 'voice of the bard', calls upon earth herself, the mother of all these, to arise and become free: since upon her limbs also are bound the fetters, and upon her forehead also has fallen the shadow, of a jealous law: from which nevertheless, by faithful following of instinct and divine liberal impulse, earth and man shall obtain deliverance.

> Hear the voice of the bard!
> Who present, past, and future sees:
> Whose ears have heard
> The ancient Word
> That walked among the silent trees:
> Calling the lapsèd soul
> And weeping in the evening dew;
> That might control
> The starry pole
> And fallen fallen light renew!

If they will hear the Word, earth and the dwellers upon earth shall be made again as little children; shall regain the strong simplicity of eye and hand proper to the pure and single of heart; and for them inspiration shall do the work of innocence; let them but once abjure the doctrine by which comes sin and the law by which comes prohibition. Therefore must the appeal be made; that the blind may see and the deaf hear, and the unity of body and spirit be made manifest in perfect freedom: and that to the innocent even the liberty of 'sin' may be conceded. For if the soul suffer by the body's doing, are not both degraded? and if the body be oppressed for the soul's sake, are not both the losers?

> O Earth, O Earth, return!
>   Arise from out the dewy grass!
> Night is worn,
> And the morn
>   Rises from the slumberous mass.
> Turn away no more;
>   Why wilt thou turn away?
> The starry shore,
> The watery floor,
>   Are given thee till the break of day.

For so long, during the night of law and oppression of material form, the divine evidences hidden under sky and sea are left her; even 'till the break of day'. Will she not get quit of this spiritual bondage to the heavy body of things, to the encumbrance of deaf clay and blind vegetation, before the light comes that shall redeem and reveal? But the earth, being yet in subjection to the creator of men, the jealous God who divided nature against herself – father of woman and man, legislator of sex and race – makes blind and bitter answer as in sleep, 'her locks covered with grey despair'.

> Prisoned on this watery shore,
>   Starry Jealousy does keep my den:
> Cold and hoar,
> Weeping o'er,
>   I hear the father of the ancient men.

Thus, in the poet's mind, Nature and Religion are the two fetters of life, one on the right wrist, the other on the left; an obscure material force on this hand, and on that a mournful imperious law: the law of divine jealousy, the government of a God who weeps over his creature and subject with unprofitable tears, and rules by forbidding and dividing: the *Urizen* of the Prophetic Books, clothed with the coldness and the grief of remote sky and jealous cloud. Here as always, the cry is as much for light as for licence, the appeal not more against prohibition than against obscurity.

> Can the sower sow by night,
> Or the ploughman in darkness plough?

In the Songs of Innocence there is no such glory of metre or sonorous beauty of lyrical work as here. No possible effect of verse can be finer in a great brief way than that given in the second and last stanzas of the first part of this poem. It recalls within one's ear the long relapse of recoiling water and wash of the refluent wave; in the third and fourth lines sinking suppressed as with equal pulses and soft sobbing noise of ebb, to climb again in the fifth line with a rapid clamour of ripples and strong ensuing strain of weightier sound, lifted with the lift of the running and ringing sea.

Here also is that most famous of Blake's lyrics, 'The Tyger'; a poem beyond praise for its fervent beauty and vigour of music. It appears by the manuscript that this was written with some pains; the cancels and various readings bear marks of frequent rehandling. One of the latter is worth transcription for its own excellence and also in proof of the artist's real care for details, which his rapid instinctive way of work has induced some to disbelieve in.

> Burnt in distant deeps or skies
> The cruel fire of thine eyes?
> Could heart descend or wings aspire?*
> What the hand dare seize the fire?

* Could God bring down his heart to the making of a thing so deadly and strong? or could any lesser demonic force of nature take to itself wings and fly high enough to assume power equal to such a creation? Could spiritual force so far descend or material force so far aspire? Or, when the very stars, and all the armed children of heaven, the 'helmed cherubim' that guide and the 'sworded seraphim' that guard their several plants, wept for pity and fear at sight of this new force of monstrous matter seen in the deepest night as a fire of menace to man –

> Did he smile his work to see?
> Did he who made the lamb make thee?

We may add another cancelled reading to show how delicately the poem has been perfected; although by an oversight of the writer's most copies hitherto have retained some trace of the rough first draught, neglecting in one line a change necessary to save the sense as well as to complete the sentence.

> And when thy heart began to beat,
> What dread hand and what dread feet

Nor has Blake left us anything of more profound and perfect value than 'The Human Abstract'; a little mythical vision of the growth of error; through soft sophistries of pity and faith, subtle humility of abstinence and fear, under which the pure simple nature lies corrupted and strangled; through selfish loves which prepare a way for cruelty, and cruelty that works by spiritual abasement and awe.

> Soon spreads the dismal shade
> Of Mystery over his head;
> And the caterpillar and fly
> Feed on the Mystery.

> And it bears the fruit of Deceit,
> Ruddy and sweet to eat;
> And the raven his nest has made
> In the thickest shade.

Under the shadow of this tree of mystery,* rooted in artificial

---

> Could fetch it from the furnace deep
> And in thy horrid ribs dare steep?
> In what clay and in what mould
> Were thine eyes of fury rolled?

Having cancelled this stanza or sketched ghost of a stanza, Blake in his hurry of rejection did not at once remember to alter the last line of the preceding one; leaving thus a stone of some size and slipperiness for editorial feet to trip upon, until the recovery of that nobler reading –

> What dread hand *framed thy* dread feet?

Nor was this little 'rock of offence' cleared from the channel of the poem even by the editor of 1827, who was yet not afraid of laying hand upon the text. So grave a flaw in so short and so great a lyric was well worth the pains of removing and is yet worth the pains of accounting for; on which ground this note must be of value to all who take in verse with eye and ear instead of touching it merely with eyelash and finger-tip in the manner of sand-blind students.

* Compare the passage in 'Ahania' where the growth of it is defined; rooted in the rock of separation, watered with the tears of a jealous God, shot up from sparks and fallen germs of material good; being after all a growth of mere error, and vegetable (not spiritual) life; the belief, all the meaner kind of devouring things take shelter and eat of the fruit of its branches; the sweet poison of false faith, painted on its outer husk with the likeness of all things noble and desirable; and in the deepest implication of barren branch and deadly leaf, the bird of death, with priests for worshippers ('the priests of the raven of dawn', loud of lip and hoarse of throat until the light of day have risen), finds house and resting-place. Only in the 'miscreative brain' of fallen men can such a thing strike its tortuous root and bring forth its fatal flower; nowhere else in all nature can the tyrants of divided matter and moral law, 'Gods of the earth and sea', find soil that will bear such fruit.

Nowhere has Blake set forth his spiritual creed more clearly and earnestly than in the last of the Songs of Experience. Tirzah, in his mythology, represents the mere separate and human nature, mother of the perishing body and daughter of the 'religion' which occupies itself with laying down laws for the flesh; which, while pretending (and that in all good faith) to despise the body and bring it into subjection as with control of bit and bridle, does implicitly overrate its power upon the soul for evil or good, and thus falls foul of fact on all sides by assuming that spirit and flesh are twain, and that things pleasant and good for the one can properly be loathsome or poisonous to the other. This 'religion' or 'moral law', the inexplicable prophet has chosen to baptize under the singular type of Rahab – the 'harlot virgin-mother', impure by dint of chastity and forbearance from such things as are pure to the pure of heart: for in this creed the one thing unclean is the belief in uncleanness, the one thing forbidden is to believe in the existence of forbidden things. Of this mystical mother and her daughter we shall have to take some further account when once fairly afloat on those windy waters of prophecy through which all who would know Blake to any purpose must be content to steer with such pilotage as they can get. For the present it will be enough to note how eager and how direct is the appeal here made against any rule or reasoning based on

---

topmost stem of it made into a cross whereon to nail the dead redeemer and friend of men.

reference to the mere sexual and external nature of man – the nature made for ephemeral life and speedy death, kept alive 'to work and weep' only through that mercy which 'changed death into sleep'; how intense the reliance on redemption from such a law by the grace of imaginative insight and spiritual freedom, typified in 'the death of Jesus'.* Nor are any of these poems finer in structure or nobler in metrical form.

This present edition of the *Songs of Experience*† is richer by one of Blake's most admirable poems of childhood – a division of his work always of especial value for its fresh and sweet strength of feeling and of words. In this newly recovered 'Cradle Song' are perhaps the two loveliest lines of his writing:

> Sleep, sleep: in thy sleep
> Little sorrows sit and weep.‡

* Compare again in the *Vision of the Last Judgment* (II 163), that definition of the 'Divine body of the Saviour, the true Vine of Eternity', as 'the Human Imagination, who appeared to me as coming to judgment among his saints, and throwing off the Temporal that the Eternal might be established'. The whole of that subtle and eloquent rhapsody is about the best commentary attainable on Blake's mystical writings and designs. It is impossible to overstate the debt of gratitude due from all students of Blake to the transcriber and editor of the *Vision*, whose indefatigable sense and patient taste have made it legible for all. To have extracted it piecemeal from the chaos of notes jotted down by Blake in the most inconceivable way, would have been a praiseworthy labour enough; but without addition or omission to have constructed these abortive fragments into a whole so available and so admirable, is a labour beyond praise.

† [*Editor's note:*] i.e. Rossetti's in Gilchrist's *Life of Blake*.

‡ This exquisite verse did not fall into its place by chance; the poem has been more than once revised. Its opening stanza stood originally thus:

> Sleep, sleep; in thy sleep
> Thou wilt every secret keep;
> Sleep, sleep, beauty bright,
> Thou shalt taste the joys of night.

Before recasting the whole, Blake altered the second line into –

> Canst thou any secret keep?

The gist of the song is this; the speaker, watching a girl newly born, compares her innocuous infancy with the power that through beauty

Before parting from this chief lyrical work of the poet's, we may notice (rather for its convenience as an explanation than its merit as a piece of verse) this projected 'Motto to the Songs of Innocence and of Experience', which editors have left hitherto in manuscript:

> The good are attracted by men's perceptions,
>   And think not for themselves
> Till Experience teaches them how to catch
>   And to cage the Fairies and Elves.
>
> And then the Knave begins to snarl,
>   And the Hypocrite to howl;
> And all his* good friends show their private ends,
>   And the Eagle is known from the Owl.

---

will one day be hers, her blameless wiles and undeveloped desires with the strong and subtle qualities now dormant which the years will assuredly awaken within her; seeing as it were the whole woman asleep in the child, he smells future fruit in the unblown bud. On retouching his work, Blake thus wound up the moral and tune of this song in a stanza forming by its rhymes an exact antiphonal complement to the end of the first 'Cradle Song'.

> When thy little heart does wake,
> Then the dreadful lightnings break
> From thy cheek and from thine eye,
> O'er the youthful harvests nigh;
> Infant wiles and infant smiles
> Heaven and earth of peace beguiles.

The epithet 'infant' has supplanted that of 'female', which was perhaps better: as to the grammatical licence, Blake followed in that the Elizabethan fashion which made the rule of sound predominate over all others. The song, if it loses simplicity, seems to gain significance by this expansion of the dim original idea; and beauty by expression of the peril latent in a life whose smiles as yet breed no strife between friends, kindle no fire among the unripe shocks of growing corn; but whose words shall hereafter be as very swords, and her eyes as lightning; *teterrima belli causa.*

* 'His', the good man's: this lax piece of grammar (shifting from singular to plural and back again without much tangible provocation) is not infrequent with Blake, and would hardly be worth righting if that were feasible. A remarkable instance is but too patent in the final

Experience must do the work of innocence as soon as conscience begins to take the place of instinct, reflection of perception; but the moment experience begins upon this work, men raise against her the conventional clamour of envy and stupidity. She teaches how to entrap and retain such fugitive delights as children and animals enjoy without seeking to catch or cage them; but this teaching the world calls sin, and the law of material religion condemns: the face of Tirzah is set against it, in the 'shame and pride' of sex.

> Thou, mother of my mortal part,
> With cruelty didst mould my heart,
> And with false self-deceiving fears
> Didst bind my nostrils, eyes, and ears.

And thus those who live in subjection to the senses would in their turn bring the senses into subjection; unable to see beyond the body, they find it worth while to refuse the body its right to freedom.

In these hurried notes on the Songs an effort has been made to get that done which is most absolutely necessary – not that which might have been most facile or most delightful. Analytic remark has been bestowed on those poems only which really cannot dispense with it in the eyes of most men. Many others need no herald or interpreter, demand no usher or outrider: some of these are among Blake's best, some again almost among his worst.*

'chorus' of the *Marriage of Heaven and Hell*. Such rough licence is given or taken by old poets; and Blake's English is always beautiful enough to be pardonable where it slips or halts: especially as its errors are always those of a rapid lyrical style, never of a tortuous or verbose ingenuity: it stammers and slips occasionally, but never goes into convulsions like that of some later versifiers.

* Such we must consider, for instance, the second 'Little Boy Lost', which looks at first more of a riddle and less worth solution than the haziest section of the Prophetic Books. A cancelled reading taken from the rough copy in the 'Ideas' will at all events make one stanza more amenable to reason:

> I love myself; so does the bird
> That picks up crumbs around the door.

Poems in which a doctrine or subject once before nobly stated and illustrated is re-asserted in a shallower way and exemplified in a feebler form,* require at our hands no written or spoken

---

Blake was rather given to erase a comparatively reasonable reading and substitute something which cannot be confidently deciphered by the most daring self-reliance of audacious ingenuity, until the reader has found some means of pitching his fancy for a moment in the ordinary key of the prophet's. This uncomfortable little poem is in effect merely an allegoric or fabulous appeal against the oppression of formulas (or family 'textualism' of the blind and unctuous sort) which refuse to single and simple insight, to the outspoken innocence of a child's laughing or confused analysis, a right to exist on any terms: just as the companion poem is an appeal, so vague as to fall decidedly flat, against the externals of moral fashion. Both, but especially the 'Girl', have some executive merit: not overmuch. To the surprising final query, 'Are such things done on Albion's shore?' one is provoked to respond, 'On the whole, not, as far as we can see'; but the Albion of Blake's verse is never this weaving and spinning country of our working days; it is rather some inscrutable remote land of Titanic visions, moated with silent white mist instead of solid and sonorous surf, and peopled with vague pre-Adamite giants symbolic of more than we can safely define or conceive. An inkling of the meaning may, if anything can, be extracted from some parts of the *Jerusalem*; but probably no one will try.

* With more time and room to work in, we might have noticed in these less dramatic and seemingly less original poems of the second series which take up from the opposite point of view matters already handled to such splendid effect in the Songs of Innocence, a depth and warmth of moral quality worth remark; infinite tenderness of heart and fiery pity for all that suffer wrong; something of Hugo's or Shelley's passionate compassion for those who lie open to 'all the oppression that is done under the sun'; something of the anguish and labour, the fever-heat of sleepless mercy and love incurable which is common to those two great poets. The second 'Holy Thursday' is doubtless far enough below the high level of the first; but the second 'Chimney Sweeper' as certainly has a full share of this passionate grace of pain and pity. Blake's love of children never wrung out into his work a more pungent pathos or keener taste of tears than in the last verse of this poem. It stood thus in the first draught:

> And because I am happy and dance and sing
> They think they have done me no injury,
> And are gone to praise God and his priest and king,
> Who wrap themselves up in our misery.

signs of either assent or dissent. Such poems, as the editor has well indicated, have places here among their betters: none of them, it may be added, without some shell of outward beauty or seed of inward value. The simpler poems claim only praise; and of this they cannot fail from any reader whose good word is in the least worth having. Those of a subtler kind (often, as must now be clear enough, the best worth study) claim more than this if they are to have fair play. It is pleasant enough to commend and to enjoy the palpable excellence of Blake's work; but another thing is simply and thoroughly requisite – to understand what the workman was after. First get well hold of the mystic, and you will then at once get a better view and comprehension of the painter and poet. And if through fear of tedium or offence a student refuses to be at such pains, he will find himself, while following Blake's trace as poet or painter, brought up sharply within a very short tether. 'It is easy', says Blake himself in the *Jerusalem*, 'to acknowledge a man to be great and good while we derogate from him in the trifles and small articles of that goodness; whose alone are his friends who admire his minute powers.'

(from *William Blake: a critical essay*, 1868)

JAMES SMETHAM

IF we wished by a single question to sound the depths of a man's mind and capacity for the judgment of works of pure imagination, we know of none we should be so content to put as this one, 'What think you of William Blake?' He is one of those crucial tests which, at once, manifest the whole man of art and criticism. He is a stumbling-block to all pretenders, to all conventional

---

The quiet tremulous anger of that, its childish sorrow and contempt, are no less true than subtle in effect. It recalls another floating fragment of verse on social wrongs which shall be rescued from the chaos of the 'Ideas':

> There souls of men are bought and sold,
> And milk-fed infancy, for gold;
> And youths to slaughter-houses led,
> And maidens, for a bit of bread.

learnedness, to all merely technical excellence. . . . In him there is an utter freedom from pretence.

Of Blake's conditions and limitations as a general thinker we shall have hereafter to speak. Thought with him leaned largely to the side of imagery rather than to the side of organised philosophy; and we shall have to be on our guard, while reading the record of his views and opinions, against the dogmatism which was more frequently based on exalted fancies than on the rock of abiding reason and truth. He never dreamed of questioning the correctness of his impressions. To him all thought came with the clearness and veracity of vision. The conceptive faculty, working with a perception of outward facts singularly narrow and imperfect, projected every idea boldly into the sphere of the actual. What he *thought*, he *saw*, to all intents and purposes, and it was this sudden and sharp crystallisation of inward notions into outward and visible signs which produced that impression on many beholders, that reason was unseated – a surmise which his biography* regards so seriously as to devote a chapter to the consideration of the question, 'Mad or not mad?' If we say on this point at once that, without attempting definitions or distinctions, and while holding his substantial genius in the highest esteem, having long studied both his character and his works, we cannot but, on the whole, lean to the opinion that, somewhere in the wonderful compound of flesh and spirit – somewhere in those recesses where the one runs into the other – he was 'slightly touched', we shall save ourselves the necessity of attempting to defend certain phases of his work, while maintaining an unqualified admiration for the mass and manner of his thoughts.

When he was a little over thirty years of age Blake collected and published one of his sweetest and most original works, the *Songs of Innocence*, engraving the poem [*sic*] in a singular way with delightful designs on copper. These plates, a remnant of which we have had the good fortune to see, are somewhat like rude, deep-cut casts in copper, from engraved wood blocks. They were

* [*Editor's note:*] Gilchrist.

drawn on the copper with some thick liquid, impervious to acid; the plate was then immersed in aquafortis, and 'bitten' away, so that the design remained in relief. These he printed with his own hand, in various tones of brown, blue and grey, tinting them afterwards by hand into a sort of rainbow-coloured, innocent page, in which the thrilling music of the verse, and the gentle bedazzlement of the lines and colours so intermingle, that the mind hangs in a pleasant uncertainty as to whether it is a picture that is singing or a song which has newly budded and blossomed into colour and form. All is what the title imports; and though they have been, of late years, frequently quoted, and lose half their sweetness away from the embowering leaves and tendrils which clasp them, running gaily in and out among the lines, we cannot but gratify ourselves and our readers with one light peal of the fairy bells: [Smetham then quotes in full 'Sweet dreams form a shade O'er my lovely infant's head'.] This is the tone of them; there are many such strains as these that deserve to be much better known than they are, notwithstanding the bad grammar that mingles with their innocent music. . . .

He stands, and must always stand, eminently alone. The fountain of thought and knowledge to others, he could never be the head of a school. What is best in him is wholly inimitable. 'The fire of God was in him.' And as, all through his works, this subtle element plays and penetrates, so in all he did and said, the ethereal force flamed outward, warming all who knew how to use it aright, scorching or scathing all who come impertinently near it. He can never be popular in the ordinary sense of the word, write we never so many songs in his praise, simply because the region in which he lived was remote from the common concerns of life, and still more by reason of the truth of the 'mystic sentence' uttered by his own lips. . . .

> Nor is it possible to thought
> A greater than itself to know.

(from 'Essay on William Blake', 1869)

W. M. ROSSETTI

THE character of Blake's poetry bears, it need hardly be said, a considerable affinity to that of his work in the art of design; he himself, it is said, thought the former the finer of the two. There is, however, no little difference between them, when their main elements are considered proportionally. In both, Blake almost totally ignores actual life and its evolution, and the passions and interactions of men as elicited by the wear and tear of real society. True, individual instances might be cited where he has in view some topic of the day, or some incident of life, simple or harrowing, such as social or dramatic writers might take cognizance of. But these also he treats with a primitiveness of singularity which, if it does not remove the objects from our sympathy – and a few cases of very highly sympathetic treatment are to be found – does at least leave them within the region of the ideal, or sometimes of the intangible. As a rule, Blake does not deal at all with the complicated practical interests of life, or the influence of these upon character; but he possesses the large range of primordial emotion, from the utter innocence and happy unconscious instinct of infancy, up to the fervours of the prophet, inspired to announce, to judge, and to reprobate.

This range of feeling and of faculty is, as we have just said, expressed equally in the designs and in the poetry of Blake, but not in the same proportions. In the designs, the energetic, the splendid, the majestic, the grand, the portentous, the terrific, play the larger part, and constitute the finer portion of the work; while the softer emotions, and the perception of what is gentle in its loveliness, are both less prominent in quantity, and realized with less mastery and sureness. In the poems these conditions are reversed. We find Blake expressing frequently and with the most limpid and final perfection – in some of its essential aspects, unsurpassed, or indeed unequalled – the innocent and simple impulses of human nature; the laughter and prattle of a baby, the vivid transforming freshness of youthful love, the depth and self-devotion of parental affection, the trust in the Father whom the

eye hath not seen. Very noble utterance is also given from time
to time to some subject of discipline or of awe to the human soul,
or even of terror: but generally it is not with these topics that
Blake deals in his lyrical poems. He reserves them for his Prophetic Books, written in a style which, though poetical and rhapsodic,
does not bring the works within the pale of verse, and barely
allows them to obtain access to the human understanding. It is in
these scriptures, rather than in the poems properly so called, that
we have to seek for the written counterpart of that supernatural
stress and that sense of the appalling – now profound in its
quietude, now almost bacchant in its orgies – which tell upon us
so potently in his designs; and certainly the written form of all
this is by no means equal to the plastic one. Leaving these
Prophetic Books for the present, we may say of the other rhyth-
mic poems that the spiritual intuition of which we have already
spoken as Blake's most central faculty, and a lyric outflow the
purest and most spontaneous, fashioning the composition in its
general mould, and directing aright each word and cadence, are
the most observable and precious qualities. This statement as to
the wording and cadences must of course be understood with
limitation; for Blake, exquisitely true to the mark as he can come
in such matters, is often also palpably faulty – transgressing even
the obvious laws of grammar and of metre. Power of thought is
likewise largely present in several cases; not of analytic or reasoning thought, for which Blake had as little turn in his poems as
liking in his *dicta*, but broad and strong intellectual perception,
telling in aid of that still higher and primary faculty of intuition. . . .

The comparative merit of the Songs of Innocence and the later-
written Songs of Experience has been debated by competent
critics, with diverse conclusions. To me it seems that the finest
compositions in the *Experience* are fully as admirable as the finest
in the *Innocence*; the unsuccessful items, however, being more
numerous, and the faulty elements throughout producing a more
damaging effect. The tone of thought, necessarily more varied,

is also, in a sense, more elevated, but not so constantly well sustained or at unity with itself.

(from prefatory memoir to *The Poetical Works of William Blake*, 1874)

D. G. ROSSETTI

HAVING spoken so far of Blake's influence as a painter, I should be glad if I could point out that the simplicity and purity of his style as a lyrical poet had also exercised some sway. But, indeed, he is so far removed from all ordinary apprehensions in most of his poems, or more or less in all, and they have been so little spread abroad, that it will be impossible to attribute to them any decided place among the impulses which have directed the extraordinary mass of poetry, displaying power of one or another kind, which has been brought before us, from his day to our own. . . .

Little need be added to what has already been said in the *Life** respecting the Songs of Innocence and Experience. The first series is incomparably the more beautiful of the two, being indeed almost flawless in essential respects; while in the second series, the five years intervening between the two had proved sufficient for obscurity and the darker mental phases of Blake's writing to set in and greatly mar its poetic value. This contrast is more especially evident in those pieces whose subjects tally in one and the other series. For instance, there can be no comparison between the first 'Chimney Sweeper', which touches with such perfect simplicity the true pathetic chord of its subject, and the second, tinged somewhat with the commonplaces, if also with the truth, of social discontent. However, very perfect and noble examples of Blake's metaphysical poetry occur among the Songs

* [*Editor's note:*] By Alexander Gilchrist (1863). D. G. Rossetti edited a selection of Blake's poems for the second edition (1880).

of Experience, such as 'Christian Forbearance'* and 'The Human Abstract'.

(from *Works*, ed. W. M. Rossetti, 1886)

W. B. YEATS

THERE have been men who loved the future like a mistress, and the future mixed her breath into their breath and shook her hair about them, and hid them from the understanding of their times. William Blake was one of these men, and if he spoke confusedly and obscurely it was because he spoke of things for whose speaking he could find no models in the world he knew. He announced the religion of art, of which no man dreamed in the world he knew; and he understood it more perfectly than the thousands of subtle spirits who have received its baptism in the world we know, because, in the beginning of important things – in the beginning of love, in the beginning of the day, in the beginning of any work – there is a moment when we understand more perfectly than we understand again until all is finished. In his time educated people believed that they amused themselves with books of imagination, but that they 'made their souls' by listening to sermons and by doing or by not doing certain things. When they had to explain why serious people like themselves honoured the great poets greatly they were hard put to it for lack of good reasons. In our time we are agreed that we 'make our souls' out of some one of the great poets of ancient times, or out of Shelley or Wordsworth, or Goethe or Balzac, or Flaubert, or Count Tolstoy, in the books he wrote before he became a prophet and fell into a lesser order, or out of Mr Whistler's pictures, while we amuse ourselves, or, at best, make a poorer sort of soul, by listening to sermons or by doing or by not doing certain things. We write of great writers, even of writers whose beauty would once have seemed an unholy beauty, with rapt sentences like those our

* [*Editor's Note:*] Title given in Notebook to first draft of 'A Poison Tree'.

fathers kept for the beatitudes and mysteries of the Church; and no matter what we believe with our lips, we believe with our hearts that beautiful things, as Browning said in his one prose essay that was not in verse, have 'lain burningly on the Divine hand', and that when time has begun to wither, the Divine hand will fall heavily on bad taste and vulgarity. When no man believed these things William Blake believed them, and began that preaching against the Philistines, which is as the preaching of the Middle Ages against the Saracen.

He had learned from Jacob Boehme and from old alchemist writers that imagination was the first emanation of divinity, 'the body of God', 'the Divine members', and he drew the deduction, which they did not draw, that the imaginative arts were therefore the greatest of Divine revelations, and that the sympathy with all living things, sinful and righteous alike, which the imaginative arts awaken, is that forgiveness of sins commanded by Christ. The reason, and by the reason he meant deductions from the observations of the senses, binds us to mortality because it binds us to the senses, and divides us from each other by showing us our clashing interests; but imagination divides us from mortality by the immortality of beauty, and binds us to each other by opening the secret doors of all hearts. He cried again and again that every thing that lives is holy, and that nothing is unholy except things that do not live – lethargies, and cruelties, and timidities, and that denial of imagination which is the root they grew from in old times. Passions, because most living, are most holy – and this was a scandalous paradox in his time – and man shall enter eternity borne upon their wings.

And he understood this so literally that certain drawings to *Vala*, had he carried them beyond the first faint pencillings, the first faint washes of colour, would have been a pretty scandal to his time and to our time. The sensations of this 'foolish body', this 'phantom of the earth and water', were in themselves but half-living things, 'vegetative' things, but passion that 'eternal glory' made them a part of the body of God.

This philosophy kept him more simply a poet than any poet of his time, for it made him content to express every beautiful

feeling that came into his head without troubling about its utility
or chaining it to any utility. Sometimes one feels, even when one
is reading poets of a better time – Tennyson or Wordsworth, let
us say – that they have troubled the energy and simplicity of their
imaginative passions by asking whether they were for the helping
or for the hindrance of the world, instead of believing that all
beautiful things have 'lain burningly on the Divine hand'. But
when one reads Blake, it is as though the spray of an inexhaustible
fountain of beauty was blown into our faces, and not merely
when one reads the Songs of Innocence, or the lyrics he wished to
call 'The Ideas of Good and Evil', but when one reads those
Prophetic Works in which he spoke confusedly and obscurely
because he spoke of things for whose speaking he could find no
models in the world about him. He was a symbolist who had to
invent his symbols; and his counties of England, with their
correspondence to tribes of Israel, and his mountains and rivers,
with their correspondence to parts of a man's body, are arbitrary
as some of the symbolism in the *Axël* of the symbolist Villiers De
L'Isle-Adam is arbitrary, while they mix incongruous things as
Axël does not. He was a man crying out for a mythology, and
trying to make one because he could not find one to his hand.
Had he been a Catholic of Dante's time he would have been well
content with Mary and the angels; or had he been a scholar of our
time he would have taken his symbols where Wagner took his,
from Norse mythology; or have followed, with the help of Professor Rhys, that pathway into Welsh mythology which he found
in *Jerusalem*; or have gone to Ireland and chosen for his symbols
the sacred mountains, along whose sides the peasant still sees
enchanted fires, and the divinities which have not faded from the
belief, if they have faded from the prayers of simple hearts; and
have spoken without mixing incongruous things because he spoke
of things that had been long steeped in emotion; and have been
less obscure because a traditional mythology stood on the thres-
hold of his meaning and on the margin of his sacred darkness. If
'Enitharmon' had been named Freia, or Gwydeon, or Danu, and
made live in Ancient Norway, or Ancient Wales, or Ancient
Ireland, we would have forgotten that her maker was a mystic;

and the hymn of her harping, that is in *Vala*, would but have reminded us of many ancient hymns.

'The joy of woman is the death of her most best beloved
'Who dies for love of her
'In torments of fierce jealousy & pangs of adoration.
'The lover's night bears on my song
'And the nine spheres rejoice beneath my powerful control.

'They sing unceasing to the notes of my immortal hand.
'The solemn, silent moon
'Reverberates the living harmony upon my limbs.
'The birds & beasts rejoice & play,
'And every one seeks for his mate to prove his inmost joy.

'Furious & terrible they sport & red the nether deeps;
'The deep lifts up his rugged head,
'And lost in infinite humming wings vanishes with a cry.
'The fading cry is ever dying,
'The living voice is ever living in its inmost joy.'

(first published in *Academy*, 19 June 1897, and
reprinted in *Essays*, 1924)

ARTHUR SYMONS

IT was in 1794 that Blake engraved the *Songs of Experience*. Four of the Prophetic Books had preceded it, but here Blake returns to the clear and simple form of the *Songs of Innocence*, deepening it with meaning and heightening it with ardour. Along with this fierier art the symbolic contents of what, in the Songs of Innocence, had been hardly more than child's strayings in earthly or divine Edens, becomes angelic, and speaks with more deliberately hid or doubled meanings. Even 'The Tyger', by which Lamb was to know that here was 'one of the most extraordinary persons of the age', is not only a sublime song about a flame-like beast, but contains some hint that 'the tigers of wrath are wiser than the horses of instruction'. In this book, and in the poems which shortly followed it, in that manuscript book whose contents have sometimes been labelled, after a rejected title of Blake's, 'Ideas of Good and Evil', we see Blake more wholly and more evenly himself than anywhere else in his work. From these central poems we can distinguish the complete type of Blake as a poet.

Blake is the only poet who sees all temporal things under the form of eternity. To him reality is merely a symbol, and he catches at its terms, hastily and faultily, as he catches at the lines of the drawing-master, to represent, as in a faint image, the clear and shining outlines of what he sees with the imagination; through the eye, not with it, as he says. Where other poets use reality as a spring-board into space, he uses it as a foothold on his return from flight. Even Wordsworth seemed to him a kind of atheist, who mistook the changing signs of 'vegetable nature' for the unchanging realities of the imagination. 'Natural objects', he wrote in a copy of Wordsworth, 'always did and now do weaken, deaden, and obliterate imagination in me. Wordsworth must know that what he writes valuable is not to be found in nature.' And so his poetry is the most abstract of all poetry, although in a sense the most concrete. It is everywhere an affirmation, the register of vision; never observation. To him observation was one of the daughters of memory, and he had no use for her among his Muses, which were all eternal, and the children of the imagination. 'Imagination', he said, 'has nothing to do with memory.' For the most part he is just conscious that what he sees as 'an old man grey' is no more than a 'frowning thistle':

> For double the vision my eyes do see,
> And a double vision is always with me.
> With my inward eyes, 'tis an old man grey,
> With my outward, a thistle across my way.

In being so far conscious, he is only recognising the symbol, not admitting the reality.

In his earlier work, the symbol still interests him, he accepts it without dispute; with, indeed, a kind of transfiguring love. Thus he writes of the lamb and the tiger, of the joy and sorrow of infants, of the fly and the lily, as no poet of mere observation has

ever written of them, going deeper into their essence than Wordsworth ever went into the heart of daffodils, or Shelley into the
nerves of the sensitive plant. He takes only the simplest flowers
or weeds, and the most innocent or most destroying of animals,
and he uses them as illustrations of the divine attributes. From the
same flower and beast he can read contrary lessons without
change of meaning, by the mere transposition of qualities, as in
the poem which now reads:

> The modest rose puts forth a thorn,
> The humble sheep a threatening horn;
> While the lily white shall in love delight,
> Nor a thorn, nor a threat, stain her beauty bright.

Mr Sampson* tells us in his notes:
Beginning by writing:

> The rose puts envious . . .

he felt that 'envious' did not express his full meaning, and deleted
the last three words, writing above them 'lustful rose', and finishing the line with the words 'puts forth a thorn'. He then went on:

> The coward sheep a threatening horn;
> While the lily white shall in love delight,
> And the lion increase freedom and peace;

at which point he drew a line under the poem to show that it
was finished. On a subsequent reading he deleted the last line,
substituting for it:

> The priest loves war, and the soldier peace;

but here, perceiving that his rhyme had disappeared, he cancelled
this line also, and gave the poem an entirely different turn by
changing the word 'lustful' to 'modest', and 'coward' to 'humble',
and completing the quatrain (as in the engraved version) by a
fourth line simply explanatory of the first three.

* [*Editor's note:*] Editor of Blake's *Poetical Works*, a new text with
variorum readings, bibliographical notes and a preface, published by
the Oxford University Press, 1905.

This is not merely obeying the idle impulse of a rhyme, but rather a bringing of the mind's impulses into that land where 'contraries mutually exist'.

And when I say that he reads lessons, let it not be supposed that Blake was ever consciously didactic. Conduct does not concern him; not doing, but being. He held that education was the setting of a veil between light and the soul. 'There is no good in education,' he said. 'I hold it to be wrong. It is the great sin. It is eating of the tree of the knowledge of good and evil. This was the fault of Plato. He knew nothing but the virtues and vices, and good and evil. There is nothing in all that. Everything is good in God's eyes.' And, as he says with his excellent courage: 'When I tell the truth, it is not for the sake of convincing those who do not know it, but for the sake of defending those who do'; and, again, with still more excellent and harder courage: 'When I am endeavouring to think rightly, I must not regard my own any more than other people's weaknesses'; so, in his poetry, there is no moral tendency, nothing that might not be poison as well as antidote; nothing indeed but the absolute affirmation of that energy which is eternal delight. He worshipped energy as the wellhead or parent fire of life; and to him there was no evil, only a weakness, a negation of energy, the ignominy of wings that droop and are contented in the dust.

And so, like Nietzsche, but with a deeper innocence, he finds himself 'beyond good and evil', in a region where the soul is naked and its own master. Most of his art is the unclothing of the soul, and when at last it is naked and alone, in that 'thrilling' region where the souls of other men have at times penetrated, only to shudder back with terror from the brink of eternal loneliness, then only is this soul exultant with the supreme happiness.

(from *William Blake*, 1907)

PART FOUR

Recent Studies

T. S. Eliot

BLAKE (1920)

I

IF one follow Blake's mind through the several stages of his poetic development it is impossible to regard him as a naïf, a wild man, a wild pet for the supercultivated. The strangeness is evaporated, the peculiarity is seen to be the peculiarity of all great poetry: something which is found (not everywhere) in Homer and Aeschylus and Dante and Villon, and profound and concealed in the work of Shakespeare – and also in another form in Montaigne and in Spinoza. It is merely a peculiar honesty, which, in a world too frightened to be honest, is peculiarly terrifying. It is an honesty against which the whole world conspires, because it is unpleasant. Blake's poetry has the unpleasantness of great poetry. Nothing that can be called morbid or abnormal or perverse, none of the things which exemplify the sickness of an epoch or a fashion, have this quality; only those things which, by some extraordinary labour of simplification, exhibit the essential sickness or strength of the human soul. And this honesty never exists without great technical accomplishment. The question about Blake the man is the question of the circumstances that concurred to permit this honesty in his work, and what circumstances define its limitations. The favouring conditions probably include these two: that, being early apprenticed to a manual occupation, he was not compelled to acquire any other education in literature than he wanted, or to acquire it for any other reason than that he wanted it; and that, being a humble engraver, he had no journalistic-social career open to him.

There was, that is to say, nothing to distract him from his interests or to corrupt these interests: neither the ambitions of parents or wife, nor the standards of society, nor the temptations of success; nor was he exposed to imitation of himself or of anyone else. These circumstances – not his supposed inspired and untaught spontaneity – are what make him innocent. His early poems show what the poems of a boy genius ought to show, immense power of assimilation. Such early poems are not, as usually supposed, crude attempts to do something beyond the boy's capacity; they are, in the case of a boy of real promise, more likely to be quite mature and successful attempts to do something small. So with Blake, his early poems are technically admirable, and their originality is in an occasional rhythm. The verse of *Edward III* deserves study. But his affection for certain Elizabethans is not so surprising as his affinity with the very best work of his own century. He is very like Collins, he is very eighteenth century. The poem 'Whether on Ida's shady brow' is eighteenth-century work; the movement, the weight of it, the syntax, the choice of words –

> The *languid* strings do scarcely move!
> The sound is *forc'd*, the notes are few!

this is contemporary with Gray and Collins, it is the poetry of a language which has undergone the discipline of prose. Blake up to twenty is decidedly a traditional.

Blake's beginnings as a poet, then, are as normal as the beginnings of Shakespeare. His method of composition, in his mature work, is exactly like that of other poets. He has an idea (a feeling, an image), he develops it by accretion or expansion, alters his verse often, and hesitates often over the final choice.[1] The idea, of course, simply comes, but upon arrival it is subjected to prolonged manipulation. In the first phase Blake is concerned with verbal beauty; in the second he becomes the apparent naïf, really the mature intelligence. It is only when the ideas become more automatic, come more freely and are less manipulated, that we begin to suspect their origin, to suspect that they spring from a shallower source.

The Songs of Innocence and of Experience, and the poems from the Rossetti manuscript are the poems of a man with a profound interest in human emotions, and a profound knowledge of them. The emotions are presented in an extremely simplified, abstract form. This form is one illustration of the eternal struggle of art against education, of the literary artist against the continuous deterioration of language.

It is important that the artist should be highly educated in his own art; but his education is one that is hindered rather than helped by the ordinary processes of society which constitute education for the ordinary man. For these processes consist largely in the acquisition of impersonal ideas which obscure what we really are and feel, what we really want, and what really excites our interest. It is of course not the actual information acquired, but the conformity which the accumulation of knowledge is apt to impose, that is harmful. Tennyson is a very fair example of a poet almost wholly encrusted with parasitic opinion, almost wholly merged into his environment. Blake, on the other hand, knew what interested him, and he therefore presents only the essential, only, in fact, what can be presented, and need not be explained. And because he was not distracted, or frightened, or occupied in anything but exact statement, he understood. He was naked, and saw man naked, and from the centre of his own crystal. To him there was no more reason why Swedenborg should be absurd than Locke. He accepted Swedenborg, and eventually rejected him, for reasons of his own. He approached everything with a mind unclouded by current opinions. There was nothing of the superior person about him. This makes him terrifying.

II

But if there was nothing to distract him from sincerity there were, on the other hand, the dangers to which the naked man is exposed. His philosophy, like his visions, like his insight, like his technique, was his own. And accordingly he was inclined to attach more importance to it than an artist should; this is what makes him eccentric, and makes him inclined to formlessness.

> But most through midnight streets I hear
> How the youthful harlot's curse
> Blasts the new-born infant's tear,
> And blights with plagues the marriage hearse,

is the naked vision;

> Love seeketh only self to please,
> To bind another to its delight,
> Joys in another's loss of ease,
> And builds a Hell in Heaven's despite,

is the naked observation; and *The Marriage of Heaven and Hell* is naked philosophy, presented. But Blake's occasional marriages of poetry and philosophy are not so felicitous.

> He who would do good to another must do it in Minute
>   Particulars.
> General Good is the plea of the scoundrel, hypocrite, and
>   flatterer;
> For Art and Science cannot exist but in minutely organized
>   particulars. . . .

One feels that the form is not well chosen. The borrowed philosophy of Dante and Lucretius is perhaps not so interesting, but it injures their form less. Blake did not have that more Mediterranean gift of form which knows how to borrow as Dante borrowed his theory of the soul; he must needs create a philosophy as well as a poetry. A similar formlessness attacks his draughtsmanship. The fault is most evident, of course, in the longer poems – or rather, the poems in which structure is important. You cannot create a very large poem without introducing a more impersonal point of view, or splitting it up into various personalities. But the weakness of the long poems is certainly not that they are too visionary, too remote from the world. It is that Blake did not see enough, became too much occupied with ideas.

We have the same respect for Blake's philosophy (and perhaps for that of Samuel Butler) that we have for an ingenious piece of home-made furniture: we admire the man who has put it together out of the odds and ends about the house. England has produced a fair number of these resourceful Robinson Crusoes; but we are not really so remote from the Continent, or from our own past, as to be deprived of the advantages of culture if we wish them.

We may speculate, for amusement, whether it would not have been beneficial to the north of Europe generally, and to Britain in particular, to have had a more continuous religious history. The local divinities of Italy were not wholly exterminated by Christianity, and they were not reduced to the dwarfish fate which fell upon our trolls and pixies. The latter, with the major Saxon deities, were perhaps no great loss in themselves, but they left an empty place; and perhaps our mythology was further impoverished by the divorce from Rome. Milton's celestial and infernal regions are large but insufficiently furnished apartments filled by heavy conversation; and one remarks about the Puritan mythology an historical thinness. And about Blake's supernatural territories, as about the supposed ideas that dwell there, we cannot help commenting on a certain meanness of culture. They illustrate the crankiness, the eccentricity, which frequently affects writers outside of the Latin traditions, and which such a critic as Arnold should certainly have rebuked. And they are not essential to Blake's inspiration.

Blake was endowed with a capacity for considerable understanding of human nature, with a remarkable and original sense of language and the music of language, and a gift of hallucinated vision. Had these been controlled by a respect for impersonal reason, for common sense, for the objectivity of science, it would have been better for him. What his genius required, and what it sadly lacked, was a framework of accepted and traditional ideas which would have prevented him from indulging in a philosophy of his own, and concentrated his attention upon the problems of the poet. Confusion of thought, emotion, and vision is what we find in such a work as *Also Sprach Zarathustra*; it is eminently not a Latin virtue. The concentration resulting from a framework of mythology and theology and philosophy is one of the reasons why Dante is a classic, and Blake only a poet of genius. The fault is perhaps not with Blake himself, but with the environment which failed to provide what such a poet needed; perhaps the circumstances compelled him to fabricate, perhaps the poet required the philosopher and mythologist; although the conscious Blake may have been quite unconscious of the motives.

SOURCE: *The Sacred Wood* (1920).

NOTE

1. I do not know why M. Berger should say, without qualification, in his *William Blake: mysticisme et poésie*, that 'son respect pour l'esprit qui soufflait en lui et qui dictait ses paroles l'empêchait de les corriger jamais'. Dr Sampson, in his Oxford edition of Blake, gives us to understand that Blake believed much of his writing to be automatic, but observes that Blake's 'meticulous care in composition is everywhere apparent in the poems preserved in rough draft . . . alteration on alteration, rearrangement after rearrangement, deletions, additions, and inversions'.

Joseph Wicksteed

AN EXPOSITORY ESSAY
ADDRESSED TO MAX PLOWMAN
(1928)

My Dear Plowman,

Nothing is more certain than the fact that this book would never have been written but for you. Years ago I read a paper on 'The Tyger' to the Blake Society, but it had long lain untouched in my drawer, because 'The Tyger' is part of a book, and the book is part of a man. Without understanding the book one cannot understand the poem, and without understanding the man one cannot understand the book. For though these Songs were the first great expression of Blake's genius, the engraving of them comes in 'the middle of the journey' of his life, and if they are in a sense the beginning of his life-work it should never be forgotten that they are the culmination of more than twenty years of art, and more than thirty of passionate living. To treat them cursorily as early work is to miss much of what is most important and most exquisite in them.

Songs of Innocence and of Experience Shewing the Two Contrary States of the Human Soul is a title that ought to warn us that we are not dealing simply with a collection of songs about childhood and youth, but with a treatise and an exposition. And yet the word 'Songs' tells us truthfully that the form is poetry. Blake could write prose when he wished, and if the form is spoilt for us when the meaning is made clear, the book has failed of its purpose and we should be forced to make a choice between the meaning and the poetry. But Blake has not put us in this dilemma. He weaves his meaning over and under the surface of his song, and by tracking its course above and below, we need lose none of the music of the verse and may often discover rich harmonies of beauty resounding in the deeps. Many of the Songs, it is true, are simple enough. They are exactly what they seem; lyrics of birdlike beauty and Arcadian charm. Others have a double beauty, a beauty of simple meaning and an accompanying beauty of remoter thought. In a few the very poetry seems to recede into magic caves, whence it can only be unearthed by deep study of the charms of Blake's magicianry.

But both beauty and meaning are harnessed to an end. The word 'Shewing' betrays Blake's didactic purpose. He has set out to enlighten us about the Soul of Man, and to do this he must give us a living realisation of its 'Two Contrary States'.

Blake at this time saw all things twofold. If the soul had its contrary states, words and images had their secondary and deeper meaning, while vision itself, the organic faculty of speculation in the eye, was often vividly twofold. I believe that there were moments of exaltation when Blake quite literally saw double – not as the drunkard sees, one vision in two places, but two visions in one place, knowing there to be but one thing there. A tree by a stream in the sunshine appeared not only as a tree, but as a paradise of angels, and yet still as a tree, indeed only a tree seen in imaginative vision.

This ecstatic mystic experience is the foundation of Blake's power, but it is only towards the middle of his life that he begins attempting the supremely difficult task of expressing it in art; and these Songs, when we begin to understand them, appear as the record of the first, and in some ways most successful, of all his attempts.

Yet before I knew you I was very content (like most people) to understand some part of the *Songs of Experience*, and all (as I supposed) of the *Songs of Innocence*, and to leave the rest alone. Indeed I rather disliked the idea of attempting any complete understanding. This may have been partly due to the fact that some of Mr Ellis's interpretations in his facsimile edition of 1893 often seemed to me both unpoetic and unconvincing – partly, it certainly was, because (to be quite frank) I did not like what appeared to be the evident inner meaning of some of the Songs of Experience.

It was you who gradually persuaded me out of this attitude. Your keen and sympathetic interest in the fragmentary ideas I had gradually accumulated; your unfailing conviction that what was good enough for Blake was good enough for the rest of us; and your determination to do nothing yourself on the Songs till I had published my views, led me on, step by step, until one day, to my great surprise, I found myself able to read every one of the Songs with understanding. Since then I have been continually more and more surprised that I could ever have doubted the value of critical examination. Those rainbow mists, that hoar frost delicacy, which one is so afraid of desecrating and destroying, so far from melting in the sunlight, proves to be hard as tracery in chiselled marble, and the very ugliness of some of Blake's anger reveals the strength and beauty of the mind outraged and angered.

There is, I think, a reason almost in the nature of things why these Songs have remained so long undisturbed, or almost undisturbed, by interpretation. It is scarcely an exaggeration to say that Blake's modernity is so astonishing that a full century was needed since his death to prepare us for some of the things he had to say. I believe that there is a better chance than there ever was, at any other time, for some of his most lovely revelations of the 'human soul' to be understood.

Blake's system sometimes entangled him and helped to weave that vast complex of obscurity which envelops his later poetry. But his fundamental philosophy, as we find it here, is singularly simple and sane. Joy he conceives as the core of life, joy which we do not learn, or receive, or derive, from something else, but which is our being and essence. And yet no one better understood the part played by sorrow in the expansion of the soul. Grief and misunderstanding indeed may be so bad as to destroy souls, so far as anything can ever be destroyed. In 'A Little Boy Lost', and 'A Little Girl Lost', we have the stories of innocence thwarted and destroyed at the very moment when it was reaching out to experience. But every birth into a higher life may be through the portals of pain and distress; so that radiant as our essential Being is, there is no place too dark or dire for the mind to contemplate or for the soul to explore. If God is manifest as the Lamb 'by the stream and oer the mead', He can reveal Himself equally 'in the forests of the night' as the Tyger. And when the night yields to day it is a greater day.

Poetry itself can never be explained. We can never say why certain images and sequences of words produce an effect so magical on the ear and on the mind. But by understanding Blake's meaning we sometimes hear his poetry where we did not hear it before, and we are no longer obliged to conceive some of his most wonderful lines as 'a happiness that often madness hits on which reason and sanity could not so prosperously be delivered of'. For in truth this explanation, so long adopted by the world, is as untrue of Blake as it was originally of Hamlet. The happiness he hits on is neither accidental nor insane. It is, on the contrary, extraordinarily calculated and ordered. If the verses are baffling, it is often for the plain reason that we only understand the single meaning of words that have a double one, and until we have discovered the secondary content we sometimes lose the sense and sometimes even the song. For the magic of poetry is not for the ear alone, and without a clue to their meaning the words, however exquisitely assembled, fail to move, or move the surface and leave the depths unstirred.

And yet with all his maturity of meaning and mastery of craft Blake is in many ways singularly childlike. Indeed, he might almost be described as the boy who grew up to be a master, a genius, a prophet, without ever 'growing up'. Like other geniuses he shows a rare association of comparatively common powers which, finding themselves in company, are stimulated to an intense activity, and in moments of inspiration accomplish supreme achievements of the human mind. But taken separately very many of the strands which make up Blake's peculiar genius are characteristically childlike things. Children love to draw pictures and then paint them in bright colours; to make up little rhymes and sing them; they think it would be very nice if we all ran about naked and played with the animals; they like to imagine dreadful and lovely things happening; they are often very angry with the grown-up world, and if any god or gods dared to create such a place, then with them too. All these things Blake understood not as an outsider but because they were himself. The conviction that there is perfect well-being and enjoyment for us all, if only we were kind to one another; that the angels are good and (whatever the stupid world may think) that they are especially concerned with ourselves and our achievements; that the good and great of ages past are either very unimportant people, or our own particular friends with whom we hold easy discourse about things outsiders cannot understand – all these things, however true or untrue, are not things we first learn to think after we are grown up, and it takes a genius like Blake's to make them speak in Art and Poetry. It is true that in the Songs of Innocence Blake's childlikeness is to some extent deliberately assumed. But I consider that there is something of the child in his faith in the use of metaphor and symbol to explain and simplify the mysteries of being; and certainly the visionary faculty itself, though not confined to children, is almost universal in some form with children, and very seldom survives in full to later years.

There are certain other childlike features of the Songs. One of these is Blake's perfect indifference to being understood. He seems quite as happy talking to the angels as a child talking to its dolls, without a thought of being overheard. I do not believe he hid his meaning for fear of shocking his readers. On the contrary I think he rather enjoyed shocking them, as most clever children do. But he himself had a beautiful and childlike absence of reticence, and he was afraid of being hurt if he emerged too unprotected into a blighting publicity.

I think it is Blake's childlikeness that always subjects his genius to being put in its place by the grown-up world. They did it in his own day, and they will do it in days to come, but meanwhile there will always be new generations of youth discovering him afresh and who will put up with certain childish crudities, to find both rapture and wisdom in his attempt to express youth's most insistent visions.

A characteristic of Blake's which, though not in itself childlike, is closely connected with things that are, is his intense concentration of meaning. As you have often pointed out, he has so much to say (like a child he wants to say it all at once) that he can only express himself by using words that mean a great many things, and his symbols are often nothing else than bundles crammed with feelings and meanings, laboriously assembled, but, once completed, full of picturesque and dramatic possibilities, and indispensable to his intensely condensed expression. I cannot honestly say that I consider he uses them in the end with great success. *Jerusalem*, which is the noblest of his great prophecies and contains more precious nuggets than any, is not only burdened with a sevenfold obscurity, but is too prevailingly full of gloom and of unconvincing horror for really great poetry. Much of what he had to say was for his own relief of mind, and it becomes a burden upon ours. It was a thunderstorm following the exquisite sweetness of his morning song and the fierce heat of his midday, full of a certain splendour and power, but perhaps justified only vicariously as Art, through its effect in purging Blake's own heroic and beautiful mind. And yet I don't know. I think I will change my simile. Blake's greater prophecies are castles and estates he has left us, with too many dungeons in them, perhaps, and with many strange uncouth places, but where it happens that as one strays one sometimes meets the master unawares. Sometimes he flits away as though reluctant to be seen; but there are memorable hours when he holds forth in golden speech, and always when he does so he takes one to visit other chambers in his palaces and fairy lawns in the sweet gardens hanging on his hills.

But to return to these early lyrics. In them the concentration is often as great as in anything Blake ever uttered. There is comparatively little actual symbolism, but there is constant and abundant use of symbolical metaphor, which must be understood if we are to enjoy either the meaning or the beauty to the full.*

The music which he composed and to which he sang his songs is, we must fear, for ever lost. But much of his work suggests musical analogies, and I might almost describe my book in one aspect as the attempt to explain his *harmonies* of meaning in his

---

* When Blake uses the Serpent to represent the Priest, it has become a pure symbol, whatever its origin. But when he uses a tree, or green leaves, to represent the flesh, it is a metaphor expressive of the sweet earthiness of the unreflective life of man and animals.

verse and sometimes in his design. For except in some of the 'wren-like warblings' of *Innocence* almost all his greatest works are harmonies, a theme with a deeper and sometimes several deeper meanings reverberating below, or perhaps one should say within. 'The Blossom', for instance, is a pretty little song of the garden on the surface, but it is also (fairly obviously) a lullaby or cradle song. Closely examined, it turns out to be a unique and exquisite love-song, conveyed in symbol and closely associated with the exquisite inner theme of 'Infant Joy'. Deepest of all, it reveals itself in conjunction with the illustration as an essay on bodily Love, its beauty and its course in Human Life, not omitting also its expression in Art. All this is condensed into forty-four words, including the title (twenty-seven if we omit repetitions) and a few simple lines of decoration – the work certainly of a very great master and craftsman, but a master of childlike words, of unconventional but essentially childlike ideas, of a childlike absence of reticence, of childlike and joyous originality, and, as I have said, of a childlike indifference to being understood.

Closely connected with Blake's concentration of thought is his swiftness of expression. Many of these lyrics, as we find them in the manuscripts, appear to have been written rapidly without alteration. Others show a few minor changes. Others again, considerable and even repeated changes of great importance, and sometimes a poem is actually changed in the course of composition into something quite different in content and meaning. But the changes themselves are swift and striking. He often changes a great thing into something much greater, and seldom returns to an earlier form without an obvious reason. In fact, we seem to understand his dictum as we read his manuscripts, that it is in a 'Time, less than a pulsation of the artery', that 'the Poet's Work is Done'.

The work of exposition therefore is often nothing else than a slow motion picture produced from the manuscripts. With their help we can sometimes discover the process by which Blake arrives at his astonishing results, and watch the rapid notions of a mind that could combine, as in a flash, the most complex thoughts and feelings, till they seemed one swift and glorious sweep of the wing.

The work of analysing and criticising the Songs has become more and more fascinating as it has proceeded. And yet it was with no small hesitation, at first, that I contemplated offering the results of my labours to the public – not altogether from a fear of exposing the secret places of Blake's soul, but because human nature does not like being offered a key where it was conscious of no confinement. And the Songs of Innocence, at all events, have generally been considered to be as lucid as they were childlike. I must gratefully acknowledge that both the critics and the Blake public in general have been more than generous in their reception of my previous effort to unveil a work of Blake's that had not hitherto been regarded as veiled.[1] But I could hardly have ventured to 'profane with my unworthy hand This holy shrine' had I not been constantly assured that there was at least one other Blake enthusiast for whom the shrine grew holier as it was more closely explored. So, though I would not make you responsible for anything in the *form*, you cannot escape sharing my responsibility for the *fact* of this book which despite all its imperfections I wish, in the first place, to present to you.

The difference between interpreting the *Songs* and the *Job* that will first strike the uninitiated is that in the one case we have mainly to do with poems and in the other case with pictures. But this difference is not nearly as great as might appear; for Blake certainly turned almost indifferently from the one to the other as means of expressing exact ideas.[2]

A far more important difference lies in the fact that in studying the *Job* designs one had practically the whole of Blake's lifework for reference. Nearly everything he has left us had now been done, and any symbolism was almost certain to have been used somewhere before; any idea to have been somewhere else expressed. So that the merest hint in the symbolism of the designs often led with certainty to conclusions as to their intention.

But when Blake printed his *Songs of Innocence* he had produced very little of deep import, and even the interesting works dated between the Songs of Innocence and those of Experience[3] tell us less of his mind and mental history than the Songs themselves.

SOURCE: Preface to *Blake's Innocence and Experience* (1928).

NOTES

1. *Blake's Vision of the Book of Job* (1910 and 1924).

2. 'He [Milton] said he had committed an error in his *Paradise Lost*, which he wanted me to correct in a poem or picture' (Crabb Robinson, *Reminiscences* (1869)).

3. *The Marriage* is not dated, and though it is of incalculable importance for the interpretation of almost all Blake's works, it cannot itself be understood until the 'Two Contrary States' have been fully considered.

J. Harvey Darton

BLAKE AND VERSE FOR CHILDREN (1932)

I

BETWEEN Isaac Watts's day and the early years of the nineteenth century, very little verse was written specially for children. The Newbery scrap about 'Three children sliding on the ice', whatever its origin, and the dormouse poem in *Goody Two-Shoes*, whatever *its* origin ,were specks in a very small sea of adult condescensions. Nursery rhymes and rhymed alphabets, even if they were widely circulated in print, as to which the evidence is of a negative kind, were no more than traditional. Watts held a field which few people deemed worth tillage. It would be nearly true, but not quite, to say that between 1715 and 1804 no 'original poems for infant minds' were uttered.

Ann and Jane Taylor, who used that title with good warrant, were in fact both the successors of Watts and the creators of the Moral Tale in verse. But in the interval there were three writers who stand out as separate figures. They made verse, respectively, for, at, and about children.

The earliest was John Marchant, Gent., who, from the little that can be gathered from his works, must have been a strange fellow. He published some sturdy and even violent anti-papist books, and two very unusual volumes of verse for children – *Puerilia* (1751) and *Lusus Juveniles: or, Youth's Recreation* (1753). The sub-title to *Puerilia*, which is a well-printed book with a folding copperplate frontispiece and an engraved title-page, runs 'Songs for Little Misses, Songs for Little Masters, Songs on Divine, Moral, and other Subjects', which sounds like a mixture of Watts and Newbery, but is no more than common form. The interesting feature of both works is what he calls 'other Subjects'. There was apparently no limit to what he deemed suitable, except that 'Fables convey no other idea to the mind than that of a mere fiction', and 'tales, novels, and romances produce the same or the like effect'. He ranges freely, otherwise. He describes in joyful, even luscious rhyme the pleasures of a harvest feast – the dancing, the good food, the lashings of drink, and that capacious song 'Here's a health to the Barley Mow'. Another poem (in the *Lusus*) is called 'Decoy-Ducks: or, the Pleasures of a Brothel'. He liked music (the frontispiece to *Puerilia* shows a dancing lesson); he knew that children played with toys, tops and kites – rather foolishly, he thought, but still they could get a lesson from them; and above all, he had a quick eye for country sights and vivid little peepshows. He saw a great deal – more than many children's authors before or since; and what he saw was usually – not always, as 'Decoy-Ducks' shows – 'occurrences that happen within [children's] own little Sphere of Action'. But he had no true imagination. He was simply very much alive, very inquisitive, abruptly serious; as if he were immensely delighted with the bright surface of things and then suddenly remembered that he was a Puritan: an odd mixture, a little like Partridge in *Tom Jones*. So far as I can see, his books attracted little attention and were not reprinted.

Nathaniel Cotton, the second of these lonely figures, lived from 1705 to 1788, which, even had he not achieved it, would have been his proper span and sphere. He wrote *Visions in Verse, for the Entertainment and Instruction of Younger Minds* (1751). It went into many editions; Dodsley did a pretty one with a frontispiece of cherub heads. It will be remembered that Dr Cotton was a capable and humane alienist who had Cowper among his patients. His verse has deserved less long recollection. It is bland and equable, and the *Visions* instruct 'Younger' minds excellently, within their professed range; thus:

> See, the lark [preens] his active wings,
> Rises to heaven, and soars, and sings.
> His morning hymns, his mid-day lays,
> Are one continued song of praise. . . .
> Shall birds instructive lessons teach,
> And we be deaf to what they preach?

There was nothing in such fancies to excite any particular emo-

tion, good or evil. It is creditable to the author and his epoch that
they were highly esteemed at the time. It would have been strange
if they were not. That is their historical value today.

11

The third author is solitary and unique, in essence neither of his
own period nor of any other, for genius is lonely. In that period,
so far as children were concerned, he was little known. He transcended then and always all other poets whom children could
read; but it is only in the last fifty years or so that his spirit has
become a living spark in poetry meant for children. One can call
his a new voice in 1789. It is still a new voice in 1932. Then and
now its music is for those who are themselves the poets, the
dreamers,

> World-losers and world-forsakers,
> On whom the pale moon gleams.

It has never become a detail of history, a mere emblem or wit-
ness from ordinary English life.

It is simplest to quote outright the first poem in William
Blake's *Songs of Innocence*, for it can serve as a text for all that can
be said of him in a record of real children's books. It is often
quoted as 'The Piper', but that is not its title nor its strict connotation. The Songs of Innocence are usually treated as if they
were songs for Innocents, whereas they are nothing of the kind.
This is their 'introduction':

> Piping down the valleys wild
> Piping songs of pleasant glee
> On a cloud I saw a child.
> And he laughing said to me,
>
> Pipe a song about a Lamb:
> So I piped with merry chear,
> Piper pipe that song again –
> So I piped, he wept to hear.
>
> Drop thy pipe thy happy pipe
> Sing thy songs of happy chear.

> So I sung the same again
> While he wept with joy to hear
>
> Piper sit thee down and write
> In a book that all may read –
> So he vanish'd from my sight.
> And I pluck'd a hollow reed
>
> And I made a rural pen,
> And I stain'd the water clear,
> And I wrote my happy songs,
> Every child may joy to hear

(The punctuation is that of the engraved first edition. It is important. Line 8, for instance, is equivocal; a semi-colon or full-stop after 'piped' makes only one sense possible.) Blake, when he produced – literally produced: wrote, drew, engraved and put forth – his *Songs of Innocence* (1789, dated) and *Songs of Experience* (1794), was himself, in a spiritual sense, a child happy on a cloud, singing and desiring such songs as few but he could write. But he was also setting down what a child had thought, setting it down as an expression of human nature as he saw and had observed it – as innocent experience recorded, not as an offering to innocence; and the Introduction, to that extent, explains the very root of that experience, the immediate ecstasy of joy without shadow or reflection.

A great imaginative writer had, in fact, broken into this narrow library that others were toiling so laboriously to fill for children. Those others, the Edgeworths, the Wattses, the Taylors, the Lambs, the Trimmers (for they are all in the same gallery in this task), had their ideals, high, practical, long, severe, whatever you like to call them. But they never dreamt of knocking at the gate of heaven or playing among the tangled stars. At best they could only laugh a little and break a few weak chains of solemnity. They never saw the strange distance that is sometimes lifted up almost into sight beyond the clear clean horizon of sunset. They were never taken out of themselves. They always were themselves in a world of selves mutually communicable. Blake did not fit into their library, excellent though its accommodation was beginning to be. But today it is his spirit that its poets would like to recapture.

It is germane to the present purpose, however, to say only that at the stated time he brought these two books into the world, that he was received thus and thus, and that certain things were in his mind in the performance. As to his reception, whatever splendour we attribute to his genius now, under George III he was simply an obscure writer, painter and engraver: not the prophetic flame we see now standing out against a negligible background. Mrs Trimmer was better known and more widely read, as numbers go, than Blake or Lamb. Lamb had heard of her: there is no evidence that she had ever heard of Lamb. It should perhaps be unnecessary to say that kind of thing. But it is important to get the right local or temporary perspective. The plain fact is that when *Songs of Innocence* appeared, there was a large generation of young persons who had to have their faces washed, their bellies filled, and their minds garnished by a rough and ready habitual process rather than by a series of inspirations. The process ignored Blake for years to come. He was only a grubby old eccentric communing with God in a back garden, in a world where he, like everyone else, had to earn a living. A few intellectuals caught the flash of his curious eyes. But they too were eccentric, not of the general orbit.

Blake himself had to be aware of that fact, perforce. He did practical work which is curiously interwoven with the main thread of this record. Mary Wollstonecraft in 1788 wrote a children's book called *Original Stories from Real Life*. It was published in that year by J. Johnson, and in 1791 he issued an edition with plates designed and engraved by William Blake. About the same time, Blake was doing hack-work of another kind for him – adapting some designs of Chodowiecki, the German illustrator, and engraving them for English use. These designs – with others probably not adapted by Blake – adorned the *Elements of Morality*, by Christian Gotthilf Salzmann, the German semi-Rousseauist, which Mary Wollstonecraft had just translated. In adapting the drawings, Blake naturally read the book, or rather the translation, which included Salzmann's own preface. Salzmann had dwelt, in a very modern manner, on the question of teaching children purity. We should, he said, 'speak to children of the organs of generation as freely as we speak of the other parts of the body, and explain to them the noble use which they were designed for, and how they may be injured'. Blake, as Mr Joseph Wicksteed points out, did what Salzmann could hardly hope to do with safety if even his less (as they then were) advanced views on other matters were to be printed at all. He wove the theme, the facts, of purity and human physical nature into the fabric of the Songs of Innocence. But he did the almost mechanical task of engraving another man's drawings in order to earn a living – to be able to do his own designs for the Songs.[1] It is a strange conjunction of the worldly and the spiritual: not less strange, and even ironical, when one remembers that a year after Blake did these engravings, Mary Wollstonecraft herself was, in the eyes of the world, going to the devil with Imlay in Paris, for the sake of the flesh; but, in her own sight, for the sake of freedom and the spirit.

These high thoughts had then no real place in the furniture of the nursery library. In the eighties and nineties of that century, and earlier, it was doubtful whether the verse form itself ought to be on the shelves. Isaac Watts and Mrs Barbauld were far from sure of its value to the young intelligence. Their eyes were holden by the period's strong sense of hard clear pattern, a pattern not of colour but of well-proportioned shapes fitting one another. By poetry they meant metre and scansion, which were the antithesis of prose: and poetry, by involving these artifices, was unnatural and difficult to children. They were underrating their own public, really. They spoke as grown-up patrons, aloof though affectionate, kindly but alien.

SOURCE: *Children's Books in England* (1932).

NOTES

1. Mr Wicksteed pointed out Blake's familiarity with the Salzmann preface in the *Times Literary Supplement*, 18 Feb. 1932. He mentions there some of the dates of Blake's 'hack' work.

S. F. Bolt

THE SONGS OF INNOCENCE (1947)

THE substitution of exegesis for criticism which characterises the bulk of critical writing about the work of William Blake is only one manifestation of a misdirection of attention which has also resulted in concentration on a single fraction of his work – the Prophetic Books. In spite of their conventionally high rating, the Songs of Innocence in particular have suffered from the consequent neglect of that important part of his work which the interpretive analyst regards as 'obvious', and subsequent critics have advanced no further in their approach to them than Swinburne. 'It is indeed some relief to a neophyte serving in the outer courts of such an intricate and cloudy temple, to come upon this little side-chapel set about with the simplest wreaths and smelling of the fields rather than incense, where all the singing is done by clear children's voices to the briefest and least complex tunes.' The dismissal implied in the phrase 'side-chapel' defeats its own object. It is only in these Songs that Blake has communicated, in an unsophisticated form, the 'Divine Vision' which is central to all his work, but the only understanding which they admit is that wider understanding which poetry affords when images are realised in their peculiar context, not interpreted as universal symbols.

The problem of these Songs lies in their peculiar naïvety. This is not the simplicity of childhood, the simplicity of incomplete experience, but has its origin in no *experience* at all. Blake's condemnation of the 'perishing Vegetable Memory' as a substitute for 'inspiration', and his preference of 'the Eternal Image' to the actual object, are both relevant here. The images of the Songs of Innocence are seen in a vision, 'within a Moment, a Pulsation of the Artery'.

Such a statement can only be justified by detailed textual analysis. The 'Nurse's Song' is distinguished from the other Songs only by illustrating with greater clarity the method which is common to them all, and is therefore chosen for this purpose.

> When the voices of children are heard on the green
> And laughing is heard on the hill,
> My heart is at rest within my breast
>   And everything else is still.
>
> 'Then come home, my children, the sun is gone down
> 'And the dews of night arise;
> 'Come, come, leave off play, and let us away
> 'Till the morning appears in the skies.'
>
> 'No, no, let us play, for it is yet day
> 'And we cannot go to sleep;
> 'Besides, in the sky the little birds fly
> 'And the hills are all cover'd with sheep.'
>
> 'Well, well, go & play till the light fades away
> 'And then go home to bed.'
> The little ones leaped & shouted & laugh'd
>   And all the hills ecchoed.

The immediate apparent peculiarity of this poem is the total absence of metaphor. This is a clue to its unique structure. Metaphor is not needed, because there is no web of correspondences to be established and secured within the poem itself. Such correspondence as it does insist upon, as that the birds and the children are both small, is in no way peculiar to the poem, and far from presenting any startling breadth of imagery it verges on the banal, as in the line:

> 'Besides, in the sky the little birds fly'.

Simplicity of this kind means the absence of elements of individual experience, such as it is normally the function of poetry to control, but which are present in the simplest lyrics. In Wordsworth's 'Daffodils', for example, the source of the imagery in individual experience is explicit and plain, and the correspondences produced by means of the Pathetic Fallacy are peculiar

to an individual scene and an individual observer, who co-
operate in expanding and at the same time contracting the
implications of the actual situation which the poem presents. In
contrast with this the 'Nurse's Song' never leaves the bed-time
situation with which it opens, and the reason for this is that the
personality of the observer has been removed.

The laughter of the children does not 'rejoice' the hill, as it
might have done for a Wordsworthian observer. It is merely
'heard on' it. The hill does not 'feed' the sheep: it is merely
'covered with' them. The birds merely 'fly'. The use of adjectives
almost inevitably introduces the personality of the observer, but
here the only adjective used is 'little', and it is applied to objects
characteristically small. Even the setting sun is not invested
with private significance. This refusal to endow objects with
qualities which are not typical of them is characteristic of the
Songs of Innocence as a whole. The grass is simply 'green'; the
cock simply 'doth crow'; the fleece of the lamb is simply 'woolly'.
This is simplicity of a rare order, and has been carefully achieved.
The eleventh line of the 'Nurse's Song', for example, has been
altered to its present form from

> 'The flocks *are at play* and we can't go away'

thus eliminating a personally created correspondence between the
children and the sheep.

It is the difference between seeing 'a world in a grain of sand'
and 'sermons in stones'. If the observer limits the grain of sand
by seeing in it some different, specific thing, he makes it his own,
and has material for poetry of the usual order, but he will not see
a world in it.

> He who bends to himself a joy
> Does the winged life destroy.

In refusing to particularise, Blake is refusing to exclude the
'Immense World of Delight, closed to your Senses Five'. 'You
shall not bring me down to believe such fitting and fitted. I know
better and please your Lordship,' he retorts to Wordsworth's
passage in the 'Excursion' on the 'exquisite fitting' of the individual mind to the external world.

The associative use of words is dynamic, forming a poem out of their progressive inter-relation, but Blake's unambiguous, typifying use of words cuts them loose from one another, halting the usual process. Consequently, the movement of the Songs is not progressive but repetitive, a pendulum movement. Monotony is avoided in the 'Nurse's Song' by the variation in syllabic length which the use of 'sprung rhythm' allows to lines of equal metrical length: the long, four-stress lines vary between nine and twelve syllables in length, and the shorter, three-stress lines between six syllables and nine. Rhythmically, however, the lines merely repeat each other. No line runs over into its successor, giving impetus to the poem. Rhythmically and syntactically, each line is self-contained, each pair of long and short lines is self-contained, and each verse is self-contained.

> 'Then come home, my children, the sun is gone down
> 'And the dews of night arise;
> 'Come, come, leave off play, and let us away
> 'Till the morning appears in the skies.'

With the exception of the last verse, every verse is, as this, a single sentence broken into two halves, each of which halves is also halved again into the individual lines. In the long first and third lines this process is taken into the line itself, which similarly falls into two rhythmically and syntactically distinct halves, the break in sense coinciding with the caesura.

There is also the repetition of the rhyme scheme. This poem of sixteen lines contains fourteen formal rhymes, to which are added the frequent repetition of vowel sounds, as in the line:

> 'Besides, in the sky the little birds fly',

the partial repetition of whole syllables – 'the sun is gone down'– and the minute repetition of rhythm and vowel in the lines:

> 'Come, come, leave off play, and let us away',
> 'No, no, let us play, for it is yet day',
> 'Well, well, go & play till the light fades away'.

The most insistent repetition in the poem is that of the word *And*, with which every alternate line opens, with the exception of the last line of the second verse. This provides the tick-tock of the pendulum movement, as one moment succeeds another. It marks the separation of the lines, not their conjunction, a point which becomes obvious if comparison is made with the use of the same word in Shakespeare's 66th Sonnet, 'Tired with all these, for restful Death I cry...' In the Sonnet the opening of each line with *And* adds to its cumulative effect as part of a whole, but in the Song it has the opposite result, and makes a fresh start within the poem, constantly renewed.

Repetition of this kind is typical of the Songs in their entirety. The rhyme is always exhibited, never concealed.

> Little Lamb,
> Here I am;
> Come and lick
> My white neck.

Words and phrases are constantly repeated.

> Little Lamb, who made thee?
> Dost thou know who made thee?

Emphasis is gained by this repetition, but never significance. Its effect is static. This is the result of the careful selection of images in each poem, a selection which permits no heterogeneity. The reader has only to consider the effect of a substitution such as the following:

> When the voices of children are heard on the green,
> And *howling* is heard on the hill.

Here the emphasis which 'is heard on' gains by repetition is significant, because it unites two dissimilar images. Because the Songs lack such heterogeneity of imagery they have no need of dynamic movement to be organised into wholes. The images are immediately related, moment by moment, as they occur, because the poem, instead of seeking to develop and unify a personal complex of impressions, presents a vision of things which relates them without reference to past and future, and is therefore impersonal. The repetitive structure is therefore functional, constantly holding the attention at a single point.

It is this kind of impersonality which Blake terms innocence, and the note of innocent love which sounds throughout the Songs is similarly impersonal. The Lamb is loved for being a Lamb: it is not a particular lamb, but any lamb which is loved, and the typifying use of words already noted corresponds with this feeling. The problem of poetic method is how to endow typical objects with qualities which will make them loveable, without depriving them of their typicality by intruding the personality of the poet. In nearly all the Songs, natural objects are made to sympathise with human feelings.

> When the green woods laugh with the voice of joy,
> And the dimpling stream runs laughing by;
> When the air does laugh with our merry wit,
> And the green hill laughs with the noise of it.

But the qualities with which objects are endowed by this use of the Pathetic Fallacy are not strange to them, and have not been imposed by an individual sensibility. It is not an example of Wordsworth's 'fitting and fitted', because it is not the product of a specific situation, and thus there is no loss of typicality.

In the first place, the attribution of human feeling is linked with the attribution of the most obvious physical characteristics, such as the greenness of the woods in the passage quoted from the 'Laughing Song'. By association, the feelings attributed gain the same typicality as these characteristics, as in the opening verse of 'The Blossom':

> Merry, Merry Sparrow
> Under leaves so green,
> A happy Blossom
> Sees you swift as arrow
> Seek your cradle narrow
> Near my Bosom.

The merriment of the sparrow and the happiness of the blossom have the same inevitability as the speed of the arrow and the greenness of the leaves.

More intrinsic to the method is the propriety of the feelings attributed, a propriety made typical by an almost universal tradition, which Blake has utilised for his own ends. Wordsworth's cloud was lonely only because he had made it so, but it was not Blake who made the birds merry, and none of the values possessed by the images in the Songs of Innocence is peculiar to them. The recurring and almost interchangeable images are the child and the lamb:

> There's little Tom Dacre, who cried when his head,
> That curl'd like a lamb's back, was shav'd. . . .

Both the child and the lamb are types of innocent love, the all-embracing charity which does not pick and choose, but loves first and makes the particular discovery later. The Songs of Innocence deal only with the first of these stages – the second is reserved for the Songs of Experience – and it is for this reason that the particularised image is absent.

But to justify the use of these images, and preserve their traditional value intact, a highly organised context is necessary. It must be such that the one value of innocence, and no other, is permitted to them. The homogeneity of imagery already noted has a structural function additional to the immediacy of relation which it allows. Confront the lamb with a wolf, and it becomes an image of more than love and less than innocence. Any insistence to the contrary would destroy the poem's unity, for it would be an attempt to deny a relationship which the poem itself had established by bringing these two words together. For the most part the Songs succeed in preserving unity by the strict exclusion of all images of fear and doubt. In the world which Blake has created by a restriction of the Christian and pastoral traditions, there are no beasts of prey or lust, disease is unknown, and old age only means an access of dignity, not the approach of death. There is no need to exclude sorrow, for sorrow in another's distress, like joy in another's happiness, is an expression of innocence so long as it does not lead to fearful questioning.

> Can I see another's woe,
> And not be in sorrow too?

is as true to the note of innocent love as:

> Thou dost smile,
> I sing the while.

Fear, on the other hand, comes only from experience, and only by experience can it be reconciled with love. Words cannot, of course, be cut away from experience, but by the strict control of context all reference to individual experience can be excluded, so that only the typical experience remains. Here, as has been shown, the context is devised to cut away all conditional meanings. The word 'leaf', for example, stands only for something green and bright. Within the Garden of Eden enclosure of the Songs of Innocence, names have the same freshness which they had when Adam first gave them to the creatures.

Occasionally, however, as in 'Night', 'Holy Thursday', and 'The Little Boy Lost', the Songs adventure outside the charmed circle, and have to provide themselves with protection in the omnipotent image of a guardian power, or in a sudden protest, external to the world of the poem.

> The little boy lost in the lonely fen,
> Led by the wand'ring light,
> Began to cry; but God, ever nigh,
> Appear'd like his father in white.

Similarly in 'Night', although the lion can lie down with the lamb (for this is in accordance with its traditional nature), the wolf and tiger still 'howl for prey', and guardian angels are needed to keep them from the sheep. The break-down of the archetypal image results from this reference to experience outside the region of innocence. The range of association given to the words in a passage such as the following verse from 'Holy Thursday' makes necessary a reference to private experience.

> O what a multitude they seem'd, these flowers of London town!
> Seated in companies they sit with radiance all their own.
> The hum of multitudes was there, but multitudes of lambs,
> Thousands of little boys & girls raising their innocent hands.

In the phrase 'these flowers of London town' the words 'town' and 'flowers' are made by their juxtaposition to stand for complex experiences, from which the reader selects and matches particular elements. Similarly, in the third line, two widely different meanings of the word 'multitudes' – the multitudes of the 'charter'd streets' and the multitudinous flocks – are deliberately indicated and contrasted, a form of ambiguity which does not belong to the archetypal word which is alone consonant with the expression of innocence. The use of the word 'innocent' itself in the last line serves to complete this process, for innocence is now seen from the outside; just as the offer of 'aged men, wise guardians of the poor', which the next verse makes, involves a limiting criticism of innocence rather than the expression of it. The question: 'Did he who made the Lamb make thee?' is reserved for the Songs of Experience, and once it has been raised, however inadvertently, the introduction of guardian angels can only be a warning to read with reserve or an invitation to sentimentality.

Such failures, however, only serve to emphasise the unique achievement represented by the remaining Songs, and to illustrate the conditions of their success.

> I a child, & thou a lamb.

This line sums up the burden of the Songs of Innocence, and also their poetic method, which compels the reader to reduce complex verbal associations to essential images, and consider them moment by moment, the method of the vision itself.

S o u r c e: *Politics and Letters* (1947).

Author's Postscript 1967. An observation on 'Holy Thursday' in the foregoing article suggests that certain words enforce a reference to empirical truth which breaks the seal that should insulate the poem from mundane reality. This is an error. In fact this element of diction is an intrinsic part of the irony which informs the poem throughout – from the first line, with its suggestion that only special days are holy and that faces are only occasionally clean (and innocent), to the last, with its implication that the exercise of pity is a prudent precaution against the wrath of a God of thunder.

Wolf Mankowitz

THE SONGS OF EXPERIENCE (1947)

THE confusion which still obscures consideration of Blake as a serious poet is due partly to his historical coincidence with the Romantics. The teachers of literature in schools have usually found it convenient to bracket the Blake of the Innocent Experiences with the Shelley of inspired visionary poetry. The political and cultural isolation which forced Blake into the obliqueness of the *Prophetic Books* has been misconstrued in a way which typifies the emotional idiosyncrasy of a dominant class of untrained readers. Amongst readers of this class, it is not uncommon to find confusion existing over the distinction in consciousness between prophecy and poetry. Without prejudice to the intentions of the prophets, it can be pointed out that, whilst the *vatic* message is often emotionally right, it is frequently intellectually unacceptable; whilst the relevance of poetry follows from its interlocking emotional and intellectual appropriateness to verifiable, uninspired, human experiences. The difference, then, between the more successful and discussable poems of Blake, and his other prophetic writings, is a difference in consciousness. An examination of the Songs of Experience must be concerned with their *conscious* craft, with their *conscious* intention towards the reader, and with their *consciousness* of human experience, and with the level and extent of that *consciousness*.

I

The first two poems of the *Songs* state a number of problems rather than a formal or original theme with which the poet will concern himself, In 'Introduction', the Bard, calling 'the lapsed Soul', is aware that the Soul itself

> might controll
> The starry pole,

and though it has, by popular acceptance, 'fallen', may still act creatively and satisfactorily,

> And fallen, fallen light renew!

With the repeated *fallen* one is already aware that the perception lying behind so careful a use of language – a moment's consideration of the two different sets of associations activated in this repetition shows just how deliberately the word is selected and placed – possesses qualities quite other than those revealed by the romantic use of repetition. The latter is a use in which melancholy is suggested by the sigh and catch of the breath which the repetition mechanically produces. When a writer says, 'Tears, idle tears' or 'Break, break, break', he conveys feelingly no more than a lot of tears, or a large break. But in Blake's 'Introduction', to take the repetition as a merely emphatic description of 'light' is to represent an only too common incapacity of reading.

In the two latter stanzas of the poem, the Bard is speaking to the 'lapsed Soul'. The important qualification introduced here is twofold. Firstly, the Soul is addressed as 'Earth'.

> 'O Earth, O Earth, return!'

Secondly, this *return* is defined negatively. It is a movement away from all that the following images suggest – *lapsed, fallen, dewy, night, worn, slumberous mass.*

> 'Arise from out the dewy grass;
> 'Night is worn,
> 'And the morn
> 'Rises from the slumberous mass.'

Already the Returned Earth is associated with the morn rising. The final stanza, with its Elizabethan opening, concludes the argument for Return. When the last three lines are read properly

> 'The starry floor,
> 'The wat'ry shore,
> 'Is giv'n thee till the break of day.'

it appears that Blake is not hedonistically invoking us to enjoy the starry floor and the wat'ry shore. The Return to the rising morn, 'the break of day', is the positive, while *starriness* and *wateryness* are obviously in the same sequence as *lapsed, fallen, dewy*, etc. It is, again, a very careful use of words, demanding a very careful reading. The sense of the stanza depends upon our reading of *giv'n*. Here it is used more with the force of *imposed* than with the idea of *gift* behind it. Again we may note that we already have a statement which could only by the most superficial reading be classed with characteristic romantic verse. Blake's poem rejects as finalities the sensations which a romantic poet would regard as poetic ends.

In the second poem of the *Songs* the 'lapsed Soul' Earth answers.

> Earth rais'd up her head
> From the darkness dread & drear.
> Her light fled,
> Stony dread!
> And her locks, cover'd with grey despair

Earth raises her head from darkness, grey and despairing with absence of *light* – the anti-night argument of the first poem is extended here. From the speech of the Earth we are able to deduce broadly what Night stands for. We learn that Jealousy is 'the father of the ancient men', that Jealousy is selfish and cruel, and that he is associated with fear.

> 'Prison'd on wat'ry shore,
> 'Starry Jealousy does keep my den:
> 'Cold and hoar,
> 'Weeping o'er,
> 'I hear the father of the ancient men.
> 'Selfish father of men!
> 'Cruel, jealous, selfish fear!'

More specifically, Jealousy–Night force is condemned for its effect upon *delight*:

> 'Can delight,
> 'Chain'd in night,
> 'The virgins of youth and morning bear?'

And the importance of delight is that it is capable of *bearing* 'the virgins of youth and morning'. The idea of life implicit in this phase of the poem is extended in the following stanza.

> 'Does spring hide its joy
> 'When buds and blossoms grow?
> 'Does the sower
> 'Sow by night,
> 'Or the plowman in darkness plow?'

The honesty of *bearing*, the justification of fertility, is asserted here, and the association of the fertile forces with light is stated. The concluding stanza is the demand which Earth makes of the Bard:

> 'Break this heavy chain
> 'That does freeze my bones around
> 'Selfish! vain!
> 'Eternal bane!
> 'That free Love with bondage bound.'

Blake makes clear, then, what he conceives the function of the poet, the Bard, to be. He must break the heavy chain of Night which threatens to strangle fertility. Blake's readers should by now know sufficient of the poet to realise that he does not use words like *free*, *Love* and *bondage* loosely. They will look to him to define these experiences and others in the course of the Songs. He has already stated several of the problems with which he is concerned. The scope of these problems entitles him to call his songs *Experience*.

II

Blake's 'Sick Rose' belongs to his 'Garden of Love'. There,

> A Chapel was built in the midst,
> Where I used to play on the green.

> And the gates of this Chapel were shut,
> And 'Thou shalt not' writ over the door;
> So I turn'd to the Garden of Love
> That so many sweet flowers bore;

And I saw it was filled with graves,
And tomb-stones where flowers should be;
And Priests in black gowns were walking their rounds,
And binding with briars my joys & desires.

The Priests of the Chapel who bind joy and desire with briars are like Night and its attributes in the first two poems. They are black against the light of joy and desire, and their darkness is not only their own, but their Chapel's, and the society in which the institutional 'Thou shalt nots' are given rein. The joy and desire which are thwarted here are attacked by a worm in the 'Sick Rose' poem.

O Rose, thou art sick!
The invisible worm
That flies in the night,
In the howling storm,

Has found out thy bed
Of crimson joy;
And his dark secret love
Does thy life destroy.

Here it is immediately apparent that the rose which sickens is a mortal rose. The human rose is attacked by a worm which possesses a *dark secret* called *love*, and it is an evil power which destroys the life of the rose. The flower is attacked in its *bed of crimson joy*, and this last imageric phrase can only stand for the sexuality of the mortal rose. The argument of the 'Sick Rose' differentiates between *love* and sexuality. Love here is destructive, it is a night-force, one of the links in the chain which binds delight in the 'Earth's Answer'. But sexuality, the experience in the *bed of crimson joy*, is the very centre of the life of the rose. When it is attacked the flower sickens and dies. What then is the *love* which destroys it? Blake uses the word deliberately, and if we think of it as a counter in a commonly played game of communication we shall more clearly see his intention. He uses a personal expression to convey the experience of sexuality because it is a something which he has discovered, as it were, for himself. But if he has discovered it, it is in spite of *love* as it is commonly called. Blake is concerned in this short poem with an incredible area of experience. In it sexuality is revealed as the basis of life, the social concept of love, as something destructive to life. Love in its social definition is a negative creed of secretive joyless forbidding; love in Blake's experience is a vital matter of joy, open and sensuous. This insistence upon the need to keep sex open and honest, and not 'a dirty sore', is, incidentally, just one of the points at which Blake reminds one of D. H. Lawrence. The experience of the sick rose is one which both men recognised, deducing from it similar conclusions.

The 'Sick Rose' poem is the concrete expression of Blake's experience of the corruptive effects of 'social' love upon creative sexuality. In the third poem of the *Songs* the paradox of love against 'Love' is dealt with in the allegory of the Clod and the Pebble. Here the Clod asserts:

> 'Love seeketh not Itself to please,
> 'Nor for itself hath any care,
> 'But for another gives its ease,
> 'And builds a Heaven in Hell's despair.'

Now this is a clear account of the current idea of 'Love'. It is self-surrender, self-denial, acceptable to the Kingdom of Heaven – in the sense in which that phrase is loosely used in Christian society. But what is the fate of the Christian Clod?

> So sang a little Clod of Clay
> Trodden with the cattle's feet.

It is little, soft, passive, and though it could be argued that as clay it is the primal stuff out of which Man was made, we still would find it difficult to believe that its fate – to be trodden by the feet of cattle – is anything but undignified and uncreative. The resilient Pebble, on the other hand, is far less Christian in its statement on the nature of love:

> But a Pebble of the brook
> Warbled out these metres meet:

(let us note that Blake considers the Pebble's argument *meet*, appropriate to the situation),

> 'Love seeketh only Self to please,
> 'To bind another to Its delight,
> 'Joys in another's loss of ease,
> 'And builds a Hell in Heaven's despite.'

This argument is not as immediately acceptable as that of the Clod. Reacting from the same ideological position as the Clod occupies we find the attitude of the Pebble aggressive and lacking in consideration and tenderness. But an examination of Blake's words reveals that his experience is something quite other than our reaction to its statement. The Pebble's love is concerned with preserving and extending itself. It binds another to Its *delight*, *joys* in another's loss of ease. The delight and the joy which are the condition of love – the words are the same both here and in the 'Sick Rose' – follow the binding and the loss of ease. Submission of *another* to the condition of love is the surrendering of self-interest and self-concern to the demands of relationship. The relationship is a complex experience, and for those who accept the Clod's definition it is Hell. But, one feels, it is a Hell in which Pride is scarcely culpable, for in Blake's context Pride is what preserves the Pebble whole and wholly itself; though in the brook the waters are always passing over it, it remains untouched.

A great deal has been said, both to some point and for other reasons, about Blake's inverted use of the terms Heaven and Hell. For our purpose – that of adequately reading the Songs of Experience – it is perhaps sufficient to remember the poet's technique in 'The Clod and the Pebble' and in the 'Sick Rose'. Inversion there requires no philosophical formulae to aid its interpretation. It is a literary device and it yields to literary analysis; it does not necessarily indicate a completely private mythology on Blake's part, a private country from which no reader can return without the assistance of Professor Wellek or Dr Bronowski. It is more fruitful to analyse Blake's poetry locally, rather than attempt to take in his entire geography and organise it in a way in which he himself must have been too intelligent to have considered. The manner in which this technique of inversion operates is exemplified in the poem 'The Angel'. There a girl says,

> I Dreamt a Dream! what can it mean?
> And that I was a maiden Queen,
> Guarded by an Angel mild.

She is a Queen, but a *maiden* Queen, and the Angel is, of course, *mild* as an angel should be. But immediately the maiden begins to resent the presence of the angel:

> I wept both day and night,
> And hid from him my heart's delight

The hidden *heart's delight* is both the pleasure which the girl feels but feels constrained to hide, and the *delight* which she is capable of experiencing with the angel – we have already noted Blake's use of the word in the context of sexual experience. The maiden is prey to the worm that flies in the night, and to the briars in the Garden of Love. She is constrained by the Night which enchains the Earth. Her Angel 'took his wings and fled', and she 'arm'd [her] fears With ten thousand shields and spears'. Entrenched behind her fear of the experience which the angel represented, she successfully repulses any further advances he may make until 'the time of youth was fled, And grey hairs were on my head'. Obviously the angel in this very familiar case history is no angel so far as the Clod is concerned. The Clod might even consider him diabolical, for he does not mention marriage. But to Blake he is an Angel, an instrument of creative purpose.

The virtue which the maiden Queen exhibits would be socially classified as modesty. She is very like the modest rose in the poem 'The Lilly'.

> The modest Rose puts forth a thorn,
> The humble Sheep a threat'ning horn.

This modesty produces a defence, a thorn, shields and spears, which prevent the approach of the Angel. Humility, the Clod softness, produces aggression, a threat'ning horn. But –

> the Lilly white shall in Love delight,
> Nor a thorn, nor a threat, stain her beauty bright.

The lily does not attempt to protect itself. It leaves itself open to love's delight, and her beauty is like that of light, the familiar image of creation. It is interesting that Blake selects the lily here as the passionate recipient of love. The selection suggests that his observation was both original and serious. The tradition of poetry which offers the lily as purity and the rose as sensuality does not operate upon an active intelligence. Blake establishes his own terms of reference in order to communicate his own perception of experience.

The force of Blake's light imagery is perhaps most clearly illustrated in the poem 'Ah! Sun-Flower'. Here the sun-flower becomes the sun. It is *weary of time*, it seeks *that sweet golden clime* where there is neither time nor travelling and searching. There, in the sun, the Youth who *pined away with desire* whilst on the night-bound earth, and *the pale Virgin shrouded in snow*, his frustrated tormentor and co-sufferer, feel they will find fulfilment. The sun becomes in the poem, not a 'fine kissing carrion' but the creative life-source, which, without argument, it is.

III

The world in which the frustration of life the sequence of poems considered in Section II analyses, is expressed allegorically in the first two poems of the *Songs of Experience*. But Blake is too concerned with concrete examples to leave the allegorical analysis on its own to fulfil the poet's duty – 'Break this heavy chain'. In the poems 'The Little Girl Lost' and 'The Little Girl Found', the little girl is unable to sleep whilst her father and mother weep.* So long as weeping and the conditions which make weeping inevitable are dominant, the little girl will find the company of wild animals more gentle than that of human beings. There, in a non-human community where cruelty is natural, as it were, she and her parents are more likely to be happy than in society where 'Cruelty has a Human Heart'. There, 'in a lonely dell' they

* [*Editor's note:*] These poems are in *Songs of Innocence*.

cease to 'fear the wolfish howl, Nor the lions' growl'. The beasts of prey, in a sense, are not the wolves and lions, but the humans who perpetuate weeping.

This social state of weeping is considered in 'Holy Thursday'. There Blake observes that 'a rich and fruitful land' is not really fruitful if 'Babes [are] reduc'd to misery, Fed with cold and usurous hand'. On the contrary, no matter how rich such a land may be, with 'so many children poor', it is in every real sense 'a land of poverty.. . . It is eternal winter there.' It is in this country that

> A little black thing among the snow,
> Crying ' 'weep! 'weep!' in notes of woe!

is an affront to the pious parents 'who have gone to praise God'. For this same 'Little Vagabond' the warmth of the ale-house appears immediately to be preferable to the cold promises of the Church. In this country Blake's 'London' is certainly the principal city. There each street is *charter'd*, clearly defined, and like the *charter'd* Thames limited and confined by its definition. Every face in this London is charter'd, marked by the same lack of scope and the same misery and woe because of it. But this charter'd quality is not only due to 'social conditions' but, as Blake says,

> In every cry of every Man,
> In every Infant's cry of fear,
> In every voice, in every ban,
> The mind-forg'd manacles I hear.

Mind-forg'd is the important phrase here. The Earth is chained as much by its own psychological predisposition as by social injustice. The interdependent misery of the inhabitants of this London is most forcefully expressed in the poem's concluding stanza:

> But most thro' midnight streets I hear
> How the youthful Harlot's curse
> Blasts the new born Infant's tear,
> And blights with plagues the Marriage hearse.

It is important that the Harlot is youthful for it suggests that the new-born infant is itself not so far from the condition of the whore. Her curse is not only what she shouts against society, but the disease she is certain to succumb to. And this disease is not referred to to show how dreadful the fate of the harlot is, but because it is effective and destructively so towards the new-born infant's generation – it is blasted – and the marriages too are infected. Not only symbolically is the marriage car a hearse. The misery of these Londoners is not simply displeasure or discomfort. It is death following disease, disease which cannot be cured because it is neither acknowledged socially nor understood to be fundamental to society's disabilities. The mind-forg'd manacles are the more effective for not being recognized.

This incapacity to approach psychological truths is one which Blake most effectively attacks in the poem 'Infant Sorrow'. There the child speaks in a voice unsoftened by the usual sentiments:

> My mother groan'd! my father wept.
> Into the dangerous world I leapt:
> Helpless, naked, piping loud:
> Like a fiend hid in a cloud,
>
> Struggling in my father's hands,
> Striving against my swaddling bands,
> Bound and weary I thought best
> To sulk upon my mother's breast.

The child is born out of its mother's pain. The pain is accentuated by the misery which the father's tears suggest, a misery which is not only occasioned by the mother's pain. The inhabitants of Blake's world are used to pain in others, and can, we deduce, accept it more easily than pain in themselves. The father's tears are perhaps for the extra burden which the child constitutes. At all events it is an unwanted child, a child produced in joylessness, who is speaking. For it the world is immediately *dangerous*. It is energetic enough to leap into the world, and though helpless and naked, still has primal vitality enough to be a sort of fiend *hid in a cloud*, which suggests the swaddling bands the child struggles against (as well as the unconsciousness of both child and parent). Feeling itself in a dangerous world, perhaps feeling unwanted, at all events feeling joyless, it strives against its parents, and against the bonds which are immediately applied to it. In a short time it

learns that struggle is useless. It relinquishes its fiend-like qualities, its energy, really its life-force, and 'bound and weary' finds
it politic to resentfully 'sulk upon my mother's breast'. This is
the birth of a representative citizen of Blake's London. It is already in the process of forging its own mental manacles. It can
look forward to a life in which 'Love! sweet Love! [will be]
thought a crime'.

IV

The Songs of Experience are concerned, an analysis leads one to
conclude, with experience. It is not strictly necessary to attach
an adjective to the word, or would not be were the claims of
spiritual, religious, metaphysical, prophetic not at all urged upon
the reader. As it is it seems prudent to assert that the only adjective which *experience* requires is *human*. Blake is only concerned
incidentally with extra-human experience. It has already been
suggested above that he is not pre-eminently concerned with
home-made philosophy, or with the promotion of a new religion
of inversions, or with a personal mythology. All the problems
commented upon above are human and general; they need to be
negotiated by every intelligent human being sooner or later.
Blake's awareness of this fact is his intention to break Earth's
chain, and it forms the basis of his moral intention towards the
reader; for a concern with human experience is also a concern for
the behaviour of human beings.

To what extent Blake was concerned with the nature of God
may be debated elsewhere. The present analysis suggests that he
was more concerned with man. In fact the famous poem 'The
Tyger', so often taken to be an expression of naïve wonder at the
greatness of a god who could create both tiger and lamb, seems to
me to be more a comment on the limited capacity of man to
conceive God at all. The poem consists of a number of questions
posed in anthropomorphic terms – what shoulder, what art, what
dread hand, what dread feet, what the hammer, what the chain,
what the anvil, etc. – the cumulative effect of which is to suggest
that the poet is not only unable to conceive of a god in terms

other than human, but that he is unable to grasp the concept at all. The incredulity of 'Did he who made the Lamb make thee?' may be an incredulity at the whole notion of an all-creating god. Blake gives a capital letter to the lamb, a reality he can vouch for. God is *he*, conceived only as a series of questions. Similarly the little boy who asks too many questions and is burned in a holy place, says:

> 'Nought loves another as itself,
> 'Nor venerates another so,
> 'Nor is it possible to Thought
> 'A greater than itself to know:
>
> 'And Father, how can I love you
> 'Or any of my brothers more?'

Man is limited to being man. Blake's most considered conclusion appears to be that Man's most creative occupation is to develop to his fullest within that structural limitation.

SOURCE: *Politics and Letters* (1947).

C. M. Bowra

SONGS OF INNOCENCE AND EXPERIENCE (1950)

IN 1789, the year of the French Revolution, William Blake issued his *Songs of Innocence* as the first volume to be produced in his new manner of illuminated printing. In 1794 he reissued it in the same manner, but with the addition of *Songs of Experience* to form a single book. This book is noteworthy among Blake's works because it is the only volume of poems which he himself published. The *Poetical Sketches* of 1783 was published by the Reverend Henry Mathew, no doubt with Blake's approval or acquiescence but not with his own loving care. Blake's other publications were either prophetic books or prose works, not poetry in the strict sense. The fact that Blake published the Songs as he did shows what importance he attached to them. There can be no doubt that he intended them to be as good as he could make them both in contents and in appearance. The Rossetti manuscript shows not only what pains he took in revising his texts but what self-denial he exerted in omitting from the book poems which are among the best that he wrote but which for some reason he did not think suitable for publication in it. A book formed with such care deserves special attention. Blake was thirty-seven when he issued it in its complete form, and it represents his mature, considered choice of his own poems. It is perhaps not surprising that in recent years scholars have tended to neglect the Songs for the prophetic books; for the Songs look limpid and translucent, while the prophetic books are rich in unravelled mysteries and alluring secrets. But the Songs deserve special attention if only because they constitute one of the most remarkable collections of lyrical poems written in English.

Blake made in practice a distinction between poetry and prophecy. In the first place, he recognized and maintained a difference of form. In the Songs he uses the traditional metres of English songs and hymns without even repeating the experiment, made in *Poetical Sketches*, of lyrical blank verse; in the prophecies, modelling himself on the Bible and Ossian, he uses what is in fact free verse, and his reasons for this are given in the foreword to *Jerusalem*:

When this Verse was first dictated to me, I consider'd a Monotonous Cadence, like that used by Milton and Shakespeare and all writers of English Blank Verse, derived from the modern bondage of Rhyming, to be a necessary and indispensible part of Verse. But I soon found that in the mouth of a true Orator such monotony was not only awkward, but as much a bondage as rhyme itself.[1]

In the prophecies Blake speaks as an orator and needs an orator's freedom: in the Songs he sings and needs the regular measures of song. In the second place, Blake's purpose differs in the Songs and in the prophecies. In the prophecies he had a great message for his generation, an urgent call to awake from its slothful sleep, a summons to activity and to that fuller life which comes from exerting the imagination. At the beginning of *Milton* he displays his purpose:

Rouze up, O Young Men of the New Age! set your foreheads against the ignorant Hirelings! For we have Hirelings in the Camp, the Court and the University, who would, if they could, for ever depress Mental and prolong Corporeal War.

This is not the spirit in which Blake begins the Songs of Innocence with a poem significantly called 'Introduction':

> Piping down the valleys wild,
> Piping songs of pleasant glee,
> On a cloud I saw a child,
> And he laughing said to me:
>
> 'Pipe a song about a Lamb!'
> So I piped with merry chear.
> 'Piper, pipe that song again;'
> So I piped: he wept to hear.

These are the words of a poet who sings because he must, not of a prophet whose first wish is to summon his generation to a new life.

The differences of form and intention between the Songs and the prophetic books are paralleled by comparable differences in the presentation of material. When he completed the Songs, Blake had already written some of his prophetic books and begun that remarkable system of myths and symbols which gives them so special a character. In the Songs there is almost no trace of Blake's mythical figures. Though he wrote *Tiriel* and *The Book of Thel* at the same time as the Songs of Innocence, their characters do not appear in the Songs. And this is all the more remarkable since the experience in these prophetic books is ultimately not very dissimilar from that in the Songs and belongs to the same important years of Blake's life. In the Songs Blake pursued a more traditional and more lyrical art, because some deep need in him called for this kind of expression. It is therefore dangerous to try to explain the Songs too exactly by the prophetic books. There are undeniable connections between the two, but the Songs go their own way in their own spirit. In them Blake speaks of himself from a purely personal point of view. It is true that he uses his own remarkable symbols, but not quite in the same way as in the prophetic books, and certainly not with the same desire for a new mythology to supplement or correct that of the Bible.

It is possible to read the Songs and to be so enchanted by them that we do not stop to ask what in fact they mean. Such a procedure has the formidable approval of A. E. Housman, who says of them that 'the meaning is a poor foolish disappointing thing in comparison with the verses themselves'.[2] This is of course true. The mere meaning, extracted from the poems and paraphrased in lifeless prose, is indeed a poor thing in comparison with what Blake wrote. The poems succeed through the magnificence of their poetry, and no analysis can take its place. At the same time, it is almost impossible to read and enjoy poetry without knowing what it means, for the good reason that the meaning is an essential part of the whole and makes an essential contribution to the delight which the poems give. To acquiesce in ignorance of the meaning is more than can reasonably be asked of us. Human curiosity and the desire to gain as much as possible from a work of art reject this limited approach and force us to ask what the subjects of the poems are. Nor does this destroy our pleasure in them. When we know what Blake means, we appreciate more fully his capacity for transforming complex states of mind into pure song and for giving to his most unusual thoughts an appeal which is somehow both intimate and rapturously exciting.

That Blake intended his readers to understand what he said and to pay an intelligent attention to it is clear from his title-page, which describes the songs as 'showing the two contrary states of the human soul'. Blake groups his verses under two main headings, and there is plainly a great difference of character between the two parts. In so arranging his work, Blake followed his own maxim that 'without Contraries is no progression'. The contrast meant much to him, and we neglect it at the risk of misunderstanding his intention. So emphatic a division is not to be found in the prophetic books and shows that, when he chose, Blake could impose a fine architectural order on his work. Perhaps he was able to do this because the material and manner of the songs fall more easily into a definite shape than does the various stuff of the prophetic books. In the Songs Blake limits himself to a special section of material which is relatively clear in its outlines and limits. He has distilled his thoughts into the shape of song, and his appeal is more direct and more immediate than it can be in the more complicated technique of prophecy.

The two sections of Blake's book, the songs of innocence and the songs of experience, are contrasted elements in a single design. The first part sets out an imaginative vision of the state of innocence: the second shows how life challenges and corrupts and destroys it. What Blake intended by this scheme can be seen from the motto which he wrote for the book but did not include in it:

> The Good are attracted by Men's perceptions,
> And think not for themselves;
> Till Experience teaches them to catch
> And to cage the Fairies and Elves.

> And then the Knave begins to snarl
> And the Hypocrite to howl;
> And all his good Friends shew their private ends,
> And the Eagle is known from the Owl.

This little poem shows how the Songs are related to some of the most persistent elements in Blake's thought. Since for him the primary reality and the only thing that matters is the active life of the creative imagination, he has nothing but contempt for empiricist philosophers who build their systems on sense-perceptions instead of on vision. Blake believes that the naturally good are deceived by such theories and so corrupted by them that they cease to think for themselves, and restrict those creative forces which he calls 'Fairies and Elves'. When this happens, knavery, hypocrisy, and self-seeking enter into the soul, and the state of innocence is lost; but for those who have eyes to see, the free, soaring spirit of the eagle is visible in all its difference from the sleepy, night-ridden owl. This is the main theme of the Songs. In the first part Blake shows what innocence means, in the second how it is corrupted and destroyed.

Blake's state of innocence, set forth in symbols of pastoral life akin to those of the Twenty-third Psalm, seems at first sight to have something in common with what Vaughan, Traherne, and Wordsworth say in their different ways about the vision of childhood which is lost in later life, and it is tempting to think that this is what concerns Blake. But he is concerned with the loss not so much of actual childhood as of something wider and less definite. For him childhood is both itself and a symbol of a state of soul which may exist in maturity. His subject is the child-like vision of existence. For him all human beings are in some sense and at some times the children of a divine father, but experience destroys their innocence and makes them follow spectres and illusions. Blake does not write at a distance of time from memories of what childhood once was, but from an insistent, present anguish at the ugly contrasts between the childlike and the experienced conceptions of reality.

With a book which deals with so poignant a subject, it is tempting to look in Blake's own life for some event or circumstances which forced this issue so powerfully on him. That he was deeply troubled by it is clear not merely from the agonized poems of *Songs of Experience* but from the prophetic books, *Tiriel* and *The Book of Thel*, which seem to have been written in 1788 and 1789. In Thel Blake presents a symbolical figure who lives in an Arcadian state of innocence but finds herself appalled and helpless before the first appearances of reality; in *Tiriel* he makes his chief figure die when he realizes that he has erred in substituting the deadening rule of law for the free life of the imagination. Both books are, in a sense, concerned with the tragedy of innocence. Just as Thel is unable to endure reality when she sees it and flies back into eternity, so Har and Heva, who represent an innocence which has outlived its real strength, are unable to help Tiriel in his great need. The problems suggested in these two books are not the same as in the Songs, but there seems to be a common basis of experience, something which, even when he was writing the Songs of Innocence, deeply troubled Blake and forced him to think about this issue in more than one way.

When he composed the Songs of Experience, Blake seems to have passed through a spiritual crisis. He, who was in many ways the healthiest of men, wrote in 1793: 'I say I shan't live for five years, and if I live one it will be a wonder.' Something had shaken his trust in himself and in life. What this was we can only guess, and such clues as are available point to a combination of different causes. The trouble was already there in 1788 when he wrote *Tiriel*, but it seems to have grown and to have preyed more insistently on his mind in the following years. It did not in the least interfere with his creative powers. Indeed, at this time he did an astonishing amount of work both as a poet and as an artist, and most of it is as good as anything that he ever did afterwards. But Blake's genius was not discouraged by trouble and anxiety, and that he had these in full measure is beyond reasonable dispute. In the first place, his rapturous hopes in the French Revolution, expressed in his prophetic book called after it and written in 1791, were soon replaced by the recognition that events were taking a course not to his liking. The English Government was hostile to the Revolution, and Blake's own friends, like Thomas Paine, whom he saved from arrest by a timely warning in 1792, were in danger. What such a disillusionment meant to a visionary like Blake can be seen from his *Visions of the Daughters of Albion*, with its passionate denunciations of oppression and slavery. He was brought down with a terrible shock from his visions of reformed humanity to a realization of what political events really were.

In the second place, Blake's domestic life seems at this time to have passed through a strange phase. His excellent wife did not sympathise with his idealistic views of free love and resolutely opposed them. To Blake at first this was an unforeseen denial of the spirit, and it shook him deeply. It seems even for a time to have broken his trust in himself. He found his solution soon enough, and the rest of his life was spent in unclouded happiness with his wife. But what he felt at the moment can be seen from his strange poem 'William Bond', and especially from three verses in it:

> He went to Church in a May morning
> Attended by Fairies, one, two and three;
> But the Angels of Providence drove them away,
> And he return'd home in misery.
>
> He went not out to the Field nor Fold,
> He went not out to the Village nor Town,
> But he came home in a black, black cloud,
> And took to his Bed, and there lay down.
>
> And an Angel of Providence at his Feet,
> And an Angel of Providence at his Head,
> And in the midst a Black, Black Cloud,
> And in the midst the Sick Man on his Bed.

Since by 'Fairies' Blake means the impulses of the creative imagination, it is clear that in this crisis his inner life has received a terrible blow from 'Angels of Providence'. In his language they are the forces of legality and moralism in which he saw the most sinister enemies of the free life of the imagination. He, who had put all his trust in this free life, found himself frustrated and depressed by the forces which he most condemned. Partly in politics, partly in domestic life, partly no doubt in other matters, Blake seems to have discovered that his central and most cherished beliefs were not shared by others but were the object of hatred and persecution. At some date in these years the common world was revealed to him, and he found it more frightening than he had ever suspected. From this discovery the Songs were born.

Blake's crisis takes place in a spiritual order of things and involves spiritual values, and for this reason he has to speak of it in symbols. What he describes are not actual events as ordinary men see and understand them, but spiritual events which have to be stated symbolically in order that they may be intelligible. In the Songs of Innocence Blake's symbols are largely drawn from the Bible, and since he makes use of such familiar figures as the Good Shepherd and the Lamb of God, there is not much difficulty in seeing what he means; but in the Songs of Experience he often uses symbols of his own making, and his meaning is more elusive. Indeed, some poems in this section are fully understandable only by reference to symbols which Blake uses in his prophetic books; and since the meaning of most symbols tends to be inconstant, there is always a danger that we may make his meaning more emphatic or more exact than it is, especially since, as Blake grew older, he developed his symbols and by placing them in precise contexts gave them a greater definiteness. But in both kinds of song it is clear that Blake anticipates those poets of a hundred years later who forged their own symbols in order to convey what would otherwise be almost inexpressible, since no adequate words exist for the unnamed powers of a supernatural world. Blake's own view of his method can be seen from a letter to Thomas Butts:

Allegory addressed to the Intellectual powers, while it is altogether hidden from the Corporeal Understanding, is My Definition of the Most Sublime Poetry.

Since by 'Corporeal Understanding' Blake means the perception of sense-data, and by 'Intellectual powers' the imaginative spirit which is the only reality, it is clear that in his view poetry is

concerned with something else than the phenomenal world, and
that the only means to speak of it is what he calls 'allegory'. It is
true that elsewhere he sometimes speaks disparagingly of allegory,
but that is because he distinguishes between true and false allegory (*Vision of the Last Judgement*). For him allegory in the good
sense is not the kind of 'one-one correspondence' which we find
in *Pilgrim's Progress*, but a system of symbols which presents
events in a spiritual world.

In the Songs of Innocence the symbols convey a special kind
of existence or state of soul. In this state human beings have the
same kind of security and assurance as belongs to lambs under a
wise shepherd or to children with loving parents. Nor is it untrue
to say that both the shepherd and the father of Blake's poems is
God. It is He who is Himself a lamb and becomes a little child,
who watches over sleeping children and gives his love to chimney sweepers and little black boys. In the fatherhood of God,
Blake's characters have equal rights and privileges. But by it he
means not quite what orthodox Christians do. Blake, despite his
deeply religious nature, did not believe that God exists apart from
man, but says expressly:

Man is All Imagination. God is Man and exists in us and we in
him. . . . Imagination or the Human Eternal Body in Every Man.
. . . Imagination is the Divine Body in Every Man.
(Annotations to Berkeley's *Siris*)

For Blake, God and the imagination are one; that is, God is the
creative and spiritual power in man, and apart from man the idea
of God has no meaning. When Blake speaks of the divine, it is
with reference to this power and not to any external or independent godhead. So when his songs tell of God's love and care, we
must think of them as qualities which men themselves display
and in so doing realize their full, divine nature. For instance, in
'On Another's Sorrow', Blake says:

> Think not thou canst sigh a sigh,
> And thy Maker is not by;
> Think not thou canst weep a tear,
> And thy Maker is not near.

> O! He gives to us His joy
> That our grief he may destroy;
> Till our grief is fled and gone
> He doth sit by us and moan.

Blake means that every sigh and every tear evoke a response from our divine nature and through this are cured and turned to joy. Compassion is part of man's imaginative being, and through it he is able to transform existence. For Blake, God is the divine essence which exists potentially in every man and woman.

The power and appeal of this belief appear in 'The Divine Image'. The divine image, of course, is man, but man in part of his complex being and seen from a special point of view. Blake speaks quite literally and means to be taken at his word when he says:

> To Mercy, Pity, Peace, and Love
> All pray in their distress;
> And to these virtues of delight
> Return their thankfulness.
>
> For Mercy, Pity, Peace, and Love
> Is God, our father dear,
> And Mercy, Pity, Peace, and Love
> Is Man, his child and care.
>
> For Mercy has a human heart,
> Pity a human face,
> And Love, the human form divine,
> And Peace, the human dress.
>
> Then every man, of every clime,
> That prays in his distress,
> Prays to the human form divine,
> Love, Mercy, Pity, Peace.
>
> And all must love the human form,
> In heathen, turk, or jew;
> Where Mercy, Love, and Pity dwell
> There God is dwelling too.

The divine qualities which Blake enumerates exist in man and reveal their divine character through him. Though Blake says of man's imagination that 'it manifests itself in his Works of Art', he spread his idea of art to include all that he thought most important and most living in conduct. In mercy, pity, peace, and love, he found the creed of brotherhood which is the centre of his gospel. He knew that by itself love may become selfish and possessive and needs to be redeemed by other, generous qualities. It is in the combination of these that man is God. In the state of innocence, life is governed by these powers, and it is they which give to it its completeness and security. That is why Blake calls his Songs of Innocence 'happy songs' and says that every child will joy to hear them.

In his prophetic books Blake presents something like the state of innocence in what he calls Beulah, a kind of lower paradise, inferior indeed to the highest state of the active imagination which he calls Eden, but superior to the lower states in which reason inhibits and kills the imagination. His Beulah has its own peculiar charm, as of a world of dream:

> There is from Great Eternity a mild and pleasant rest
> Nam'd Beulah, a soft Moony Universe, feminine, lovely,
> Pure, mild and Gentle, given in mercy to those who sleep,
> Eternally Created by the Lamb of God around,
> On all sides, within and without the Universal Man.
> The daughters of Beulah follow sleepers in all their dreams,
> Creating spaces, lest they fall into Eternal Death.
>
> (*Vala, or The Four Zoas*, First Night)

When he wrote that, Blake had already decided that Beulah was not the highest state. It is not perfect because there is no effort or struggle in it as there is in Eden, and a full personality can be realized only if men leave Beulah for a state less confined and less secure. There can be little doubt that even when he wrote the Songs of Innocence, Blake had formed some of these ideas. He saw that though this state of childlike happiness, which he seems to have enjoyed in his first manhood, is wonderfully charming, it is not everything, and it cannot last. To reach a higher state man must be tested by experience and suffering. This is the link between the two sections of Blake's book. Experience is not only a fact; it is a necessary stage in the cycle of being. It may in many ways be a much lower state than innocence, and this Blake stresses with great power, but it is none the less necessary. The difference between the two states is reflected in the quality of Blake's poetry. Sweet and pure though the Songs of Innocence are, they do not possess or need the compelling passion of the Songs of Experience. In dealing with innocence Blake seems deliberately to have set his tone in a quiet key to show what innocence really means in his full scheme of spiritual development. He was careful to exclude from the first part of his book anything which might sound a disturbing note or suggest that innocence is anything but happy. That is why he omitted a striking verse which he wrote in the first version of 'A Cradle Song':

> O, the cunning wiles that creep
> In thy little heart asleep.
> When thy little heart does wake,
> Then the dreadful lightnings break.

The illusion of childhood and of the human state which resembles it must be kept free from such intruding suggestions, and there must be no hint that innocence is not complete and secure.

From innocence man passes to experience, and what Blake means by this can be seen from some lines in *The Four Zoas*:

> What is the price of Experience? do men buy it for a song?
> Or wisdom for a dance in the street? No, it is bought with the
>   price
> Of all that a man hath, his house, his wife, his children.
> Wisdom is sold in the desolate market where none come to
>   buy,
> And in the wither'd field where the farmer plows for bread
>   in vain.

(Second Night)

Blake knew that experience is bought at a bitter price, not merely in such unimportant things as comfort and peace of mind, but in the highest spiritual values. His Songs of Experience are the poetry of this process. They tell how what we accept in childlike innocence is tested and proved feeble by actual events, how much that we have taken for granted is not true of the living world, how every noble desire may be debased and perverted. When he sings of this process, he is no longer the piper of pleasant glee but an angry, passionate rebel. In 'Infant Sorrow' he provides a counterpart to his 'Introduction' and shows that even in the very beginnings of childhood there is a spirit of unrest and revolt:

> My mother groan'd! my father wept.
> Into the dangerous world I leapt:
> Helpless, naked, piping loud:
> Like a fiend hid in a cloud.
>
> Struggling in my father's hands,
> Striving against my swadling bands,
> Bound and weary, I thought best
> To sulk upon my mother's breast.

At the start of its existence the human creature feels itself a prisoner and, after its first efforts to resist, angrily gives up the struggle.

When experience destroys the state of childlike innocence, it puts many destructive forces in its place. To show the extent of this destruction Blake places in the Songs of Experience certain poems which give poignant contrasts to other poems which appear in the Songs of Innocence. For instance, in the first 'Nurse's Song' he tells how children play and are allowed to go on playing until the light fades and it is time to go to bed. In this Blake symbolizes the care-free play of the imagination when it is not spoiled by senseless restrictions. But in the second 'Nurse's Song' we hear the other side of the matter, when experience has set to work:

> When the voices of children are heard on the green
> And whisp'rings are heard in the dale,
> When days of my youth rise fresh in my mind,
> My face turns green and pale.
>
> Then come home, my children, the sun is gone down,
> And the dews of night arise;
> Your spring and your day are wasted in play,
> And your winter and night in disguise.

The voice that now speaks is not that of loving care but of sour age, envious of a happiness which it can no longer share and eager to point out the menaces and the dangers of the dark. It sees play as a waste of time and cruelly tells the children that their life is a sham passed in darkness and cold, like one of Blake's terrible prophetic scenes of desolation, as in *The Four Zoas*:

But from the caves of deepest night, ascending in clouds of mist,
The winter spread his wide black wings across from pole to pole:
Grim frost beneath & terrible snow, link'd in a marriage chain,
Began a dismal dance. The winds around on pointed rocks
Settled like bats innumerable, ready to fly abroad.

(Fifth Night)

The first and most fearful thing about experience is that it breaks the free life of the imagination and substitutes a dark, cold, imprisoning fear, and the result is a deadly blow to the blithe human spirit.

The fear and denial of life which come with experience breed hypocrisy, and this earns some of Blake's hardest and harshest words. For him hypocrisy is as grave a sin as cruelty because it rises from the same causes, from the refusal to obey the creative spirit of the imagination and from submission to fear and envy. He marks its character by providing an antithesis to 'The Divine Image' in 'The Human Abstract'. In bitter irony he shows how love, pity, and mercy can be distorted and used as a cover for base or cowardly motives. Speaking through the hypocrite's lips, he goes straight to the heart of the matter by showing how glibly hypocrisy claims to observe these cardinal virtues:

Pity would be no more
If we did not make somebody Poor;
And Mercy no more could be
If all were as happy as we.

In this corrupt frame of mind, selfishness and cruelty flourish and are dignified under false names. This process wrecks the world. Harsh rules are imposed on life through what Blake calls 'Mystery', with its ceremonies and hierarchies and its promise of 'an allegorical abode where existence hath never come' (*Europe*). It

supports those outward forms of religion which Blake regards as
the death of the soul:

> Soon spreads the dismal shade
> Of Mystery over his head;
> And the Catterpiller and Fly
> Feed on the Mystery.
>
> And it bears the fruit of Deceit,
> Ruddy and sweet to eat;
> And the Raven his nest has made
> In its thickest shade.
>
> The Gods of the earth and sea
> Sought thro' Nature to find this Tree;
> But their search was all in vain:
> There grows one in the Human Brain.

So Blake re-creates the myth of the Tree of Knowledge or of Life.
This tree, which is fashioned by man's reason, gives falsehood
instead of truth and death instead of life.

Perhaps the worst thing in experience, as Blake sees it, is that
it destroys love and affection. On no point does he speak with
more passionate conviction. He who believes that the full life
demands not merely tolerance but forgiveness and brotherhood
finds that in various ways love is corrupted or condemned. In
'The Clod and the Pebble' he shows how love naturally seeks not
to please itself or have any care for itself, but in the world of
experience the heart becomes like 'a pebble of the brook' and
turns love into a selfish desire for possession:

> Love seeketh only Self to please,
> To bind another to Its delight,
> Joys in another's loss of ease,
> And builds a Hell in Heaven's despite.

The withering of the affections begins early, when their elders
repress and frighten children. In 'Holy Thursday' Blake shows
what this means, how in a rich and fruitful land children live in
misery:

> And their sun does never shine,
> And their fields are bleak and bare,
> And their ways are fill'd with thorns:
> It is eternal winter there.

The horror of experience is all the greater because of the contrast, explicit or implicit, which Blake suggests between it and innocence. In 'The Ecchoing Green' he tells how the children are happy and contented at play, but in 'The Garden of Love', to the same rhythm and with the same setting, he presents an ugly antithesis. The green is still there, but on it is a chapel with 'Thou shalt not' written over the door, and the garden itself has changed:

> And I saw it was filled with graves,
> And tomb-stones where flowers should be;
> And Priests in black gowns were walking their rounds,
> And binding with briars my joys and desires.

In the state of experience, jealousy, cruelty, and hypocrisy forbid the natural play of the affections and turn joy into misery.

Blake's tragic appreciation of the restrictions which imprison and kill the living spirit was no purely personal thing. It was his criticism of society, of the whole trend of contemporary civilization. His compassionate heart was outraged and wounded by the sufferings which society inflicts on its humbler members and by the waste of human material which seems indispensable to the efficient operation of rules and laws. In 'London' he gives his own view of that 'chartered liberty' on which his countrymen prided themselves, and exposes the indisputable, ugly facts:

> I wander thro' each charter'd street,
> Near where the charter'd Thames does flow,
> And mark in every face I meet
> Marks of weakness, marks of woe.
>
> In every cry of every Man,
> In every Infant's cry of fear,
> In every voice, in every ban,
> The mind-forg'd manacles I hear.

How the Chimney-sweeper's cry
Every black'ning Church appalls;
And the hapless Soldier's sigh
Runs in blood down Palace walls.

But most thro' midnight streets I hear
How the youthful Harlot's curse
Blasts the new born Infant's tear,
And blights with plagues the Marriage hearse.

The child chimney-sweeper, the soldier, and the harlot are Blake's types of the oppressed – characteristic victims of a system based not on brotherhood but on fear. Each in his own way shows up the shams on which society thrives. The chimney-sweeper's condemned life is supported by the churches; the soldier's death is demanded by the court; and the harlot's calling is forced on her by the marriage-laws. The contrasts between truth and pretence, between natural happiness and unnatural repression, are stressed by Blake in these three examples, and through them we see the anguish in which he faced the social questions of his time.

The astonishing thing about the Songs of Experience is that, though they were inspired by violent emotions and have a merciless satirical temper, they are in the highest degree lyrical. Indeed, no English poet, except Shakespeare, has written songs of such lightness and melody. Yet Blake's subjects are not in the least like Shakespeare's. He writes not about fundamental matters like spring and love and death, but about his own original and complex views on existence; and the miracle is that in presenting themes which might seem to need comment and explanation, he succeeds in creating pure song. His words have an Elizabethan lilt, a music which emphasizes their meaning and conforms exactly to it. Despite his strong emotions and his unfamiliar ideas, Blake keeps his form miraculously limpid and melodious. This success is partly the result of a highly discriminating art. Blake made many changes in his texts before he was satisfied with a final version, and these show how well he knew what he was doing, how clear an idea he had of the result which he wished to reach. But this art was shaped by a creative impulse so powerful that it can only be called inspiration. Blake indeed believed that his words were often dictated to him by some supernatural power. As he wrote to Thomas Butts about a prophetic book, 'I may praise it, since I dare not pretend to be any other than the Secretary; the Authors are in Eternity.' In the strange workings of the creative mind there is a point at which words come with such force and intensity that they have a more than human appeal. Though the poet may not receive them all at once but gradually find, as Blake did, the exact words which he needs, yet these songs are miracles because their creation cannot be explained and because with them we feel ourselves in the presence of something beyond the control of man.

Two examples must suffice to illustrate Blake's art of song, and each is equally wonderful. The first is 'The Sick Rose':

> O Rose, thou art sick!
> The invisible worm
> That flies in the night,
> In the howling storm,
>
> Has found out thy bed
> Of crimson joy,
> And his dark secret love
> Does thy life destroy.

This illustrates in an astonishing way Blake's gift for distilling a complex imaginative idea into a few marvellously telling words. If we ask what the poem means, we can answer that it means what it says, and that this is perfectly clear. It conjures up the vision of a rose attacked in a stormy night by a destructive worm, and so Blake depicts it in his accompanying illustration. But, as in all symbolical poems, we can read other meanings into it and make its images carry a weight of secondary associations. We may say that it refers to the destruction of love by selfishness, of innocence by experience, of spiritual life by spiritual death. All these meanings it can bear, and it is legitimate to make it do so. But the actual poem presents something which is common and funda-mental to all these themes, something which Blake has distilled so finely from many particular cases that it has their common, quintessential character. And this Blake sees with so piercing and so concentrated a vision that the poem has its own independent life and needs nothing to supplement it. If we wish to know more about Blake's views on the issues at which the poem hints, we may find them in his prose works and prophetic books. But here he is a poet, and his thoughts are purified and transfigured in song.

My second example is 'Ah! Sun-flower':

> Ah, Sun-flower! weary of time,
> Who countest the steps of the Sun,
> Seeking after that sweet golden clime
> Where the traveller's journey is done:
>
> Where the Youth pined away with desire,
> And the pale Virgin shrouded in snow
> Arise from their graves, and aspire
> Where my Sun-flower wishes to go.

This raises questions similar to those raised by 'The Sick Rose'. Again a complex thought is distilled into two verses, and again what matters is the imaginative presentation which transports us in intense, excited delight. Here Blake's theme is not quite so single as 'The Sick Rose'. He has transposed into this song his central ideas and feelings about all young men and young women who are robbed of their full humanity because they are starved of love. Because of this, the youth pines away with desire and the pale virgin is shrouded in snow. It is the pathos of their earth-bound state that the song catches and makes significant through Blake's deep compassion. The central spring of the poem is the image of the sun-flower. The flower which turns its head to follow the sun's course and is yet rooted in the earth is Blake's symbol for all men and women whose lives are dominated and spoiled by a longing which they can never hope to satisfy, and who are held down to the earth despite their desire for release into some brighter, freer sphere. In this poem Blake expresses an idea which means a great deal to him, but he does not explain or elaborate it. He assumes that his poem will do its work by itself, and his

reward is that 'Ah! Sun-Flower' belongs to that very rare and
small class of poems in which inspiration carries words to a final
enchantment.

The Songs of Experience are more powerful and more magical
than the Songs of Innocence because they are born of a deep
anguish, from a storm in the poet's soul. Blake knows that one
kind of existence is bright with joy and harmony, but he sees its
place taken by another which is dark and sinister and dead. But
Blake was not content simply to complain or to criticize. He
sought some ultimate synthesis in which innocence might be
wedded to experience, and goodness to knowledge. That such a
state is possible he reveals in the first poem of *Songs of Experience*,
where he speaks with the voice of the bard and summons the
fallen soul of earth to some vast apocalypse:

> O Earth, O Earth, return!
> Arise from out the dewy grass;
> Night is worn,
> And the morn
> Rises from the slumberous mass.
>
> Turn away no more;
> Why wilt thou turn away?
> The starry floor,
> The wat'ry shore,
> Is giv'n thee till the break of day.

The world is still wrapped in darkness, but the stars which pierce
the night are a sign of other things to come, and the sea of eternity
beats on the narrow shore where mankind lives. The 'break of
day' is Blake's symbol for the new life in which both innocence
and experience are transformed, and the soul passes in its cycle
to a fuller, more active life in the creative imagination. As Blake
says in a note written on a page of *The Four Zoas*:

> *Unorgani\ʒ'd Innocence: An Impossibility.*
> Innocence dwells with Wisdom, but never with Ignorance.

The true innocence is not after all that of the Songs of Innocence,
but something which has gained knowledge from the ugly lessons

of experience and found an expanding strength in the unfettered life of the creative soul. Beyond experience Blake foresees this consummation and hints that it will come, even though he is concerned with the dark hither side of it.

Blake knows well that such a consummation will not come simply from good will or pious aspirations and that the life of the imagination is possible only through passion and power and energy. That is why he sometimes stresses the great forces which are hidden in man and may be terrifying but are none the less necessary if anything worth while is to happen. He sees that the creative activity of the imagination and the transformation of experience through it are possible only through the release and exercise of awful powers. He chooses his symbols for these powers in violent and destructive things, as when in his 'Proverbs of Hell' he says, 'The wrath of the lion is the wisdom of God', or 'The roaring of lions, the howling of wolves, the raging of the stormy sea, and the destructive sword, are portions of eternity, too great for the eye of man' (*Marriage of Heaven and Hell*). It was in such elemental forces that Blake put his trust for the redemption of mankind, and he contrasted them favourably with the poor efforts of the human intelligence: 'The tigers of wrath are wiser than the horses of instruction.' The wrath which Blake found in Christ, his symbol of the divine spirit which will not tolerate restrictions but asserts itself against established rules, was the means by which he hoped to unite innocence and experience in some tremendous synthesis.

The poetry of this desire and of what it meant to Blake can be seen in 'The Tyger'. Here, too, enraptured song conveys in essential vision some themes which Blake presents elsewhere in more detail. This is the pure poetry of his trust in cosmic forces. The images of 'The Tyger' recur in the prophetic books, but in the poem, detached from any very specific context, they have a special strength and freedom. The tiger is Blake's symbol for the fierce forces in the soul which are needed to break the bonds of experience. The 'forests of the night', in which the tiger lurks, are ignorance, repression, and superstition. It has been fashioned by unknown, supernatural spirits, like Blake's mythical heroes,

Orc and Los, prodigious smiths who beat out living worlds with their hammers; and this happened when 'the stars threw down their spears', that is, in some enormous cosmic crisis when the universe turned round in its course and began to move from light to darkness – as Urizen says in *The Four Zoas*, when he finds that passion and natural joy have withered under his rule and the power of the spirit has been weakened:

> I went not forth: I hid myself in black clouds of my wrath;
> I called the stars around my feet in the night of councils dark;
> The stars threw down their spears and fled naked away.
>
> (Fifth Night)

If we wish to illustrate 'The Tyger' from Blake's other works, it is easy to do so, and it adds much to our understanding of its background and its place in Blake's development. But it is first and last a poem. The images are so compelling that for most purposes they explain themselves, and we have an immediate, overwhelming impression of an awful power lurking in the darkness of being and forcing on us questions which pierce to the heart of life:

> Tyger! Tyger! burning bright
> In the forests of the night,
> What immortal hand or eye
> Could frame thy fearful symmetry?
>
> In what distant deeps or skies
> Burnt the fire of thine eyes?
> On what wings dare he aspire?
> What the hand dare sieze the fire?
>
> And what shoulder, and what art,
> Could twist the sinews of thy heart?
> And when thy heart began to beat,
> What dread hand? and what dread feet?
>
> What the hammer? what the chain?
> In what furnace was thy brain?
> What the anvil? what dread grasp
> Dare its deadly terrors clasp?

> When the stars threw down their spears,
> And water'd heaven with their tears,
> Did he smile his work to see?
> Did he who made the Lamb make thee?
>
> Tyger! Tyger! burning bright
> In the forests of the night,
> What immortal hand or eye,
> Dare frame thy fearful symmetry?

Just as early in the Songs of Innocence Blake sets his poem about the lamb, with its artless question,

> Little Lamb, who made thee?
> Dost thou know who made thee?

so early in the Songs of Experience Blake sets his poem about the tiger with its more frightening and more frightened questions. The lamb and the tiger are symbols for two different states of the human soul. When the lamb is destroyed by experience, the tiger is needed to restore the world.

In the *Songs of Innocence and Experience* there are only hints of the final consummation which shall restore men to the fullness of joy. The poems are concerned with an earlier stage in the struggle and treat of it from a purely poetical standpoint. What Blake gives is the essence of his imaginative thought about this crisis in himself and in all men. When he completed the whole book in its two parts, he knew that the state of innocence is not enough, but he had not found his full answer to his doubts and questions. From this uncertainty he wrote his miraculous poetry. Against the negative powers, which he found so menacingly in the ascendant, he set, both in theory and in practice, his gospel of the imagination. Strange as some of his ideas may be to us, the poetry comes with an unparalleled force because of the prodigious release of creative energy which has gone to its making. The prophet of gigantic catastrophes and celestial reconciliations was also a poet who knew that poetry alone could make others share his central experiences. In the passion and the tenderness of these songs there is something beyond analysis, that living power of the imagination which was the beginning and the end of Blake's activity. In *A Vision of the Last Judgement* he says:

'What,' it will be Question'd, 'When the Sun rises, do you not see a round disk of fire somewhat like a Guinea?' O no, no, I see an Innumerable company of the Heavenly host crying, 'Holy, Holy, Holy, is the Lord God Almighty.'

Because Blake pierced beyond the visible world to these eternal powers and made them his daily company, he was able to give to his poetry the clarity and the brightness of vision.

SOURCE: *The Romantic Imagination* (1950).

NOTES

1. All quotations are taken from *Prose and Poetry of William Blake*, ed. Geoffrey Keynes (Nonesuch Press, 4th ed., 1939).
2. A. E. Housman, *The Name and Nature of Poetry* (1933) p. 43.

Northrop Frye

BLAKE AFTER TWO CENTURIES

THE value of centenaries and similar observances is that they call attention, not simply to great men, but to what we do with our great men. The anniversary punctuates, so to speak, the scholarly and critical absorption of its subject into society. From this point of view, a centenary date might well be more impressive for those interested in William Blake than his birth on 28 November 1757. The year 1857 would bring us to a transitional point in the life of Alexander Gilchrist, who had recently got a life of Etty off his hands, married, moved to Chelsea to be near his idol Carlyle, was busy winding up some family business, and was preparing to start in earnest on *The Life of William Blake, Pictor Ignotus*. This last was no empty phrase. Scattered notices of Blake had appeared in collections of artists' biographies, but nothing like a full volume had been devoted to Blake in the thirty years since his death. Blake was fortunate in his first posthumous group of admirers. Gilchrist was a remarkable person, his wife Anne equally so, and Rossetti and Swinburne, if not exactly emancipated spirits, were at least sufficiently free of the more lethal Victorian virtues to admire Blake without undue inhibitions. They make an instructive contrast to the Ruskin who cut up one of the two coloured copies of *Jerusalem*, the anonymous worthy who apparently destroyed the great 'Vision of the Last Judgement', and the member of the Linnell family who erased the genitalia from the drawings on the *Four Zoas* manuscript.

Gilchrist died in 1861 with his masterpiece unfinished: Anne Gilchrist brought it out in 1863 in two volumes. The first volume was Gilchrist's biography: no better biography has been written since, for all our advance in understanding. The main part of the second volume was Rossetti's edition of the lyrics, where

Blake, however expurgated and improved in his metres, still did achieve something like a representative showing as a poet. Swinburne's critical essay appeared in 1868, and soon afterwards there began, a slow trickle at first, then a flood still in full spate, of critical studies, biographies, editions, illustrated editions, collections of paintings and engravings, handbooks, catalogues, appreciations, research articles, chapters in other books, and specialized studies pouring out of the presses of at least twenty countries. Max Beerbohm's Enoch Soames sold his soul to the devil in exchange for a glance at the future British Museum catalogue of critical work on him, only to discover that posterity took the same view of him that his contemporaries had done. Such irony is not for Blake, who in his lifetime was something of an Enoch Soames too, but an Enoch Soames who was right.

Much more than a Cinderella success story is involved here. In her little British Council bibliography, Miss Kathleen Raine remarks on the spontaneous personal affection shown in the public response to the recent discovery of a large and rather confused allegorical picture by Blake in a house in Devon. A new Michelangelo would have been more important, but it would not have aroused that specific reaction of affectionate pride. Blake's deep love of England is clearly not an unrequited love, nor is the sense that he is one of us confined to Englishmen. People get attracted to him through feeling that he is for them a personal discovery and something of a private possession. I constantly hear of doctors, housewives, clergymen, teachers, manual workers, shopkeepers, who are, in the most frequent phrase used, 'frightfully keen on Blake', who have bought every book on him they could afford, and kept him around like an amiable household god. I have taught Blake to Jesuits and I have taught him to Communist organizers; I have taught him to deans of women and I have taught him to ferocious young poets of unpredictable rhythms and unprintable (or at least privately printed) diction. His admirers have nothing in common except the feeling that Blake says something to them that no one else can say: that whatever their standards and values may be, Blake has the charity to include them, not as part of a general principle of benevolence, which Blake himself would have despised, but uniquely as individuals.

Undergraduates, too, have fewer barriers against Blake than against most poets: besides the absence of unfamiliar conventions of a special poetic language, he lacks the two qualities that undergraduates are most afraid of, sentimentality and irony. Again, some poets travel better than others, and just as Byron and Poe in the nineteenth century proved to be more readily exportable than Wordsworth or Hawthorne, so in the twentieth century Blake seems the easiest of all our poets to export to India or Japan. He can hardly ever lack admirers among the fellow countrymen of Rouault and of Gérard de Nerval, or of Hölderlin and of Novalis. Within ninety years after the first critical study of him was published, Blake appears to be headed for what at one time seemed his least likely fate: a genuine, permanent, and international popularity.

This popularity has been achieved in spite of Blake's reputation for being difficult and esoteric, someone not to be understood without preliminary study of a dozen occult systems of thought and several thousand pages of commentary. I have written one of the thickest of the commentaries myself, and I certainly meant all I said, but I quite realize how often the popular estimate of Blake is sounder in perspective than the scholarly one. Scholars will assert that the famous 'Jerusalem' hymn is crypto-Anglo-Israelitism or what not; but when it was sung in front of Transport House at the Labour victory of 1945 the singers showed that they understood it far better than such scholars did. Scholars will assert that the question in 'The Tyger', 'Did he who made the lamb make thee?' is to be answered with a confident yes or no: yes if Blake is believed to be a pantheist, no if he is believed to be a Gnostic. Most of those who love the poem are content to leave it a question, and they are right. 'You say', wrote Blake to the Rev. Dr Trusler, author of *The Way to be Rich and Respectable*, 'that I want somebody to Elucidate my Ideas. But you ought to know that What is Grand is necessarily obscure to Weak men. That which can be made Explicit to the Idiot is not worth my care.' Having thus brought his correspondent into focus, he goes on: 'But I am happy to find a Great Majority of Fellow Mortals who can Elucidate My Visions, & Particularly they have been Elucidated by Children, who have taken a greater delight in contemplating my Pictures than I even hoped.' Children have always found Blake easier than the Truslers have done.

II

Clearly, if Blake can be popular we need a new definition of popularity. Several very different things are included under the term popular, and the simple conception 'What the public wants' will not do. Best-seller popularity depends more on news value than on any aesthetic qualities, whether good or bad. But there is another sense in which the term popular may be used, as referring to the art which affords a key to imaginative experience for the untrained. The centre of gravity of popular fiction in this sense is the folk tale, and in American culture, for instance, it would be represented by *Huckleberry Finn*, *Rip van Winkle*, some tales of Poe, of Uncle Remus, and the various cycles of native humour like the Western tall tale. Much that is popular even in this context is still rubbish, and some of it may be quite unpopular in the best-seller meaning of the word. The popular in the second sense is the contemporary primitive, and it tends to become primitive with the passing of time. Such primitive and popular elements recur in great art, even very difficult and complex art. One thinks of Shakespeare's late romances, with their archaic nature myths and their improbable coincidences turning up 'like an old tale'. One thinks more particularly of the Bible, which is one long folk tale from beginning to end, and the most primitive and popular book in the world.

The two senses of popular seem to be, up to a point, connected with the distinction of content and form. 'What the public wants', as the first word suggests, relates primarily to content: certain conventional choices of subject – domestic, sentimental, heroic, sexually provocative – come into vogue by turns. Certain story types, on the other hand, which remain fairly constant from ancient myth to contemporary comic strip, are isolated in the art which is popular in the second sense. Like the corresponding primitive and popular forms in the plastic arts, they are abstract and stylized, and have a curiously archaic look about them whenever they appear. The generic term for such story types is myth, because myths are stories about divine beings which are abstract and stylized stories in the sense that they are unaffected by canons of realism or probability.

Blake's only fictions are in his Prophetic Books, and although they are certainly mythical enough, there are other aspects of popular literature in its formal sense more obviously relevant to him. The conceptual element in poetry is also a part of its content, and conceptual thinking in poetry is more or less assimilated to another kind of thinking which organizes the poetic structure. The unit of this formally poetic thinking is the metaphor, and the metaphor is inherently illogical, an identification of two or more things which could never be identified except by a lunatic, a lover, or a poet – one may perhaps add an extremely primitive savage. We are educated in conceptual thinking, and so usually find poetry which comes to terms with it easier to read, like Wordsworth's. Poetry which is popular in the sense of having a vogue is popular by reason of having such a conceptual content: it talks about the Deity in the eighteenth century, or Duty in the nineteenth, or it speaks to the eternal bourgeois in the heart of man, like Kipling's 'If', Longfellow's 'Psalm of Life', or Burns's 'A Man's a Man for a' that'. Poetry which concentrates on metaphor to the point of appearing to exclude conceptual thought altogether, like surrealist poetry, impresses most readers as wilfully crazy, or, if they are compelled to take it seriously, as incredibly difficult and esoteric.

Yet greater experience with literature soon shows that it is metaphor which is direct and primitive, and conceptual thought which is sophisticated. Hence there is a body of verse that can be called popular in the sense of providing the direct, primitive, metaphorical key to poetic experience for educated and uneducated alike. Most good teaching anthologies are largely composed of such verse, and in such anthologies the lyrics of Blake leap

into the foreground with a vividness that almost exaggerates
Blake's relative importance as a poet:

> O Rose, thou art sick!
> The invisible worm
> That flies in the night,
> In the howling storm,
>
> Has found out thy bed
> Of crimson joy,
> And his dark secret love
> Does thy life destroy.

I say exaggerates, because there are many fine poets who do not
have this specific kind of directness. One may always meet a
poem with a set of questions designed to avoid its impact: what
does it mean; why is it considered a good poem; is it morally
beneficial; does it say profound things about life, and so forth.
But such a poem as 'The Sick Rose' has a peculiar power of
brushing them aside, of speaking with the unanswerable authority of poetry itself. Blake's lyrics, with many of those of Herrick,
Burns, and Donne, the sonnets of Shakespeare, Wordsworth's
Lucy poems, and a few of the great ballads, are popular poetry in
the sense that they are a practically foolproof introduction to
poetic experience.

Metaphor, then, is a formal principle of poetry, and myth of
fiction. We begin to see how Blake hangs together: his prophecies
are so intensely mythical because his lyrics are so intensely metaphorical. At present his prophecies seem to have little to do with
popular literature in any sense of the word, but opinion will have
changed on this point long before the tercentenary rolls around.
It will then be generally understood that just as Blake's lyrics are
among the best possible introductions to poetic experience, so his
prophecies are among the best possible introductions to the
grammar and structure of literary mythology. His practice again
is consistent with his theory, which lays an almost exclusive emphasis on the imagination or forming power. However, there
comes a point at which our distinction of form and content breaks

down, and we have to raise the question of what kind of content formal art has.

'The Nature of my Work is Visionary or Imaginative,' said Blake: 'it is an Endeavour to Restore what the Ancients call'd the Golden Age.' By vision he meant the view of the world, not as it might be, still less as it ordinarily appears, but as it really is when it is seen by human consciousness at its greatest height and intensity. It is the artist's business to attain this heightened or transfigured view of things, and show us what kind of world is actually in front of us, with all its glowing splendours and horrifying evils. It is only the direct, metaphorical, and mythical perceptions, which work without compromise with unimaginative notions of reality, that can clearly render the forms of such a world. Such psychological experiments as those recorded in Mr Aldous Huxley's *The Doors of Perception* (the title of which comes from Blake, although taking mescalin is not precisely what Blake meant by 'cleansing' the doors of perception) seem to show that the formal principles of this heightened vision are constantly latent in the mind, which perhaps explains the communicability of such visions. For Blake, however, the Bible provides the key to the relation between the two worlds. The ordinary world is 'fallen', the manifestation of man's own sin and ignorance; the true world is the apocalypse presented at the end of the Bible and the paradise presented at the beginning of it: the true city and garden that is man's home, and which all existing cities and gardens struggle to make manifest in the lower world.

The apocalypse of the Bible is a world in which all human forms are identified, as Blake says at the end of his *Jerusalem*. That is, all forms are identified as human. Cities and gardens, sun moon and stars, rivers and stones, trees and human bodies – all are equally alive, equally parts of the same infinite body which is at once the body of God and of risen man. In this world 'Each Identity is Eternal', for 'In Eternity one Thing never Changes into another Thing'. It is a world of forms like Plato's except that in Blake these forms are images of pure being seen by a spiritual body, not ideas of pure essence seen by a soul, a conception which would rule out the artist as a revealer of reality. To Blake this vision of apocalypse and resurrection was the grammar of poetry and painting alike, and it was also the source of the formal principles of art. He lived in a way that brought him into the most constant contact with this world, for we notice that isolation, solitude, and a certain amount of mental stress or disturbance have a tendency to light up this vision in the mind. When Christopher Smart is shut into a madhouse with no company except his cat Jeffrey, the cat leaps into the same apocalyptic limelight as Blake's tiger;

For he keeps the Lord's watch in the night against the adversary.
For he counteracts the powers of darkness by his electrical skin
    and glaring eyes . . .
For he is of the tribe of Tiger.
For the Cherub Cat is a term of the Angel Tiger . . .
For by stroaking of him I have found out electricity.
For I perceived God's light about him both wax and fire.
For the electrical fire is the spiritual substance, which God sends
    from heaven to sustain the bodies both of man and beast.

Similarly when John Clare is confined to an asylum and is in the depths of schizophrenia, the luminous fragility of Blake's *Book of Thel*, along with the glowing lights and gemmed trees of Mr Huxley's adventures in heaven and hell, appear in his vision:

The birds sing on the clouds in that eternal land,
Jewel and siller are they a', and gouden is the sand.
The sun is one vast world of fire that burneth a' to-day,
And nights wi' hells of darkness for ever keeps away.
And dearly I love the queen o' that bright land,
The lily flowers o' woman that meeteth no decay.

Blake's attitude to art makes no psychological distinctions among the arts, and the same imagination that the poet uses appears in Blake's theory of painting as 'outline', which again is an intense concentration on the formal principles of the art. The abstract school of painting today assumes that the formal principles of painting are quasi-geometrical, but Blake, with the faded white ghosts of eighteenth-century classicism in front of him, warned sharply against the preference of 'mathematic form' to 'living form'. Blake despised everything that was amorphous or vague in art: the imagination for him could express itself only as rigorous and exactly ordered form. But by living form he meant a vitalized classicism, where the outline is held in the tight grip of imaginative intensity, a classicism that would have more in common with Van Gogh than with Flaxman or David. Blake's painting, though strongly formalized, is not abstract in tendency, but what one might call hieroglyphic in tendency. It presents the same world that his poetry presents; yet (except in lapses) it is not literary painting. The tense stylized figures of the Byzantines with their staring eyes and weightless bodies; mediaeval primitives with their glittering gold haloes and childlike sense of primary colour; Eastern 'mandalas' that communicate the sense of powerful spiritual discipline in repose; the calligraphic distortions of Klee: these all belong in different ways to the hieroglyphic tradition in painting, and are allied to the vision that Blake evolved from his study of Renaissance prints.

III

The conception of formally popular art which underlies the present argument is still an unexplored subject in criticism, and many aspects of it can be only suggested here. It has been neglected partly because the original proponents of it, notably Herder, confused it by mixing it up with a pseudo-historical myth of the Golden Age family. Formally popular art was supposed to have been derived from a 'folk' whose art was rural and spontaneous and communal and unspecialized and a number of other things that no art can be. When we remove this notion of a 'folk', we are left with a third conception of popular art as the art which is central to a specific cultural tradition. There is no question here of looking for *the* centre or isolating an imaginary essence of a tradition, but only of seeing what some of its prevailing and recurrent rhythms have been. The sources of a cultural tradition are, of course, its religious and social context as well as its own earlier products. In English culture we notice at once a strong and constant affinity with art which is popular in the formal sense, in striking contrast to, say, French culture, which has much more the character of something deliberately imposed.

One characteristic of the English tradition has obviously been affected by Protestantism. This is the tendency to anchor the apocalyptic vision in a direct individual experience, as the product, not of sacramental discipline, but of imaginative experiment. The experience may be as forced as *Grace Abounding* or as relaxed as Keats's speculations about a vale of soul-making, but it tends to be autonomous, to make the experience its own authority. The 1611 Bible is not a 'monument of English prose', but the exact opposite of what a monument is: it is a translation with a unique power of making the Bible a personal possession of its reader, and to this its enormous popularity as well as its importance in English culture is due. It has also fostered, of course, the kind of Biblical culture that has made *The Pilgrim's Progress* one of the most popular books in the language, that has given *Paradise Lost* its central place in English literature, and that has instigated some very inadequate performances of Handel's *Messiah* (a work with a unique power of catching this quality of direct vision in music) in Midland towns. Such Biblical culture, absorbed as part of a poet's own imaginative experience, was inspiring visions of revelation and resurrection at least as early as the *Pearl* poet, and had lost nothing of its intensity when Dylan Thomas was shattering the sedate trumpet of the B.B.C. with the same tones:

> Though they be mad and dead as nails,
> Heads of the characters hammer through daisies;
> Break in the sun till the sun breaks down,
> And death shall have no dominion.

Blake, who was brought up on the Bible and on Milton, is unusually close to this simple and naïve Biblism even for an English poet. The occult and esoteric elements in his thought have been grossly exaggerated by critics who, as Johnson said of Hume, have not read the New Testament with attention. What is so obviously true of most of his paintings is true also of his poetry: it is the work of a man whose Bible was his textbook. The prophecies re-create the Bible in English symbolism, just as the 1611 translation re-creates it in the English language, and, no less than *Paradise Lost* or *The Pilgrim's Progress*, they record a direct search for the New Jerusalem which exists here and now in England's green and pleasant land.

A second characteristic of the English tradition is of social origin, and is derived from an apparently permanent English tendency to political resistance. This tendency has taken different forms in different ages – Roundhead, Whig, radical, liberal, socialist – but is so constant that it may be actually a kind of anarchism, or what in a play of Bernard Shaw's is called an obstinate refusal to be governed at all. From Milton's defence of the liberty of prophesying to Mill's defence of the right to be eccentric, it is pervaded by a sense that the final cause of society is the free individual. This sense distinguishes it sharply from such revolutionary traditions as those of America or Russia, where a fundamental social pattern is established *a priori* by the revolution, and other patterns are rejected as un-American or counter-revolutionary.

In Blake's political outlook one finds a radicalism of a common English type, which includes a strong individual protest against all institutional radicalism. Blake was brought up in the centre of English social resistance, the city of London, in the period of Wilkes and the Gordon riots. His sympathy first with the American and then with the French revolution placed him as far to the left as he could go and still continue to function as an artist. Yet his denunciation of what he called the 'Deism' of the French revolutionaries, and of the ideology of Voltaire and Rousseau, is nearly as strong as Burke's. At the same time his poems point directly towards the English society of his time: even his most complex prophecies have far more in common with Dickens than they have with Plotinus. And though he said 'Houses of Commons & Houses of Lords appear to me to be fools; they seem to me to be something Else besides Human Life', this expresses, not a withdrawal from society, but a sense of the inadequacy of everything that falls short of the apocalyptic vision itself. Blake's is the same impossible vision that caused Milton to break with four kinds of revolt in England, and which still earlier had inspired the dream of John Ball, a dream based, like *Areopagitica* and *The Marriage of Heaven and Hell*, on a sense of ironic contrast between the fallen and unfallen worlds:

> When Adam delved and Eve span,
> Who was then the gentleman?

In breaking with all forms of social organization, however, Blake is merely following the logic of art itself, whose myths and visions are at once the cause and the clarified form of social developments. Every society is the embodiment of a myth, and as the artist is the shaper of myth, there is a sense in which he holds in his hand the thunderbolts that destroy one society and create another. Another busy and versatile English radical, William Morris, not a mythopœic poet himself but a mere collector of myths, nevertheless portrayed those myths in *The Earthly Paradise* as a group of old men who had outgrown the desire to be made kings or gods. In this cycle they are ineffectual exiles, but in Morris's later work they return as revolutionary dreams, though of a kind that, again, rejects all existing types of revolutionary organization.

The possibility is raised in passing that formally popular art has a perennially subversive quality about it, whereas art that has a vogue popularity remains subservient to society. We note that Russian Communism denounced 'formalism' as the essence of the bourgeois in art, and turned to vogue popularity instead, a vogue artificially sustained by political control, as part of its general policy of perverting revolutionary values. This tendency follows the example set by Tolstoy, who, though a greater artist than Morris, was also more confused about the nature of popular art.

Blake formed his creative habits in the age immediately preceding Romanticism: still, his characteristics are romantic in the expanded sense of giving a primary place to imagination and individual feeling. Like the Romantics, Blake thought of the 'Augustan' period from 1660 to 1760 as an interruption of the normal native tradition. This sense of belonging to and restoring the native tradition helps to distinguish Romanticism in England from Romanticism on the Continent, especially in France. It also enabled the English Romantic writers – in their fertile periods any rate – to lean less heavily on religious and political conservatism in their search for a tradition.

The great achievement of English Romanticism was its grasp of the principle of creative autonomy, its declaration of artistic independence. The thing that is new in Wordsworth's *Prelude*, in Coleridge's criticism, in Keats's letters, is the sense, not that the poet is superior or inferior to others, but simply that he has an authority, as distinct from a social function, of his own. He does not need to claim any extraneous authority, and still less need he take refuge in any withdrawal from society. The creative process is an end in itself, not to be judged by its power to illustrate something else, however true or good. Some Romantics, especially Coleridge, wobble on this point, but Blake, like Keats and Shelley, is firm, and consistent when he says, 'I will not Reason & Compare: my business is to Create'. The difficulties revealed by such poems as Shelley's *Triumph of Life* or Keats's *Fall of Hyperion* are concerned with the content of the poetic vision, not with any doubts about the validity of that vision as a mean between subjective dream and objective action. 'The poet and the dreamer are distinct,' says Keats's Moneta, and Rousseau in Shelley's poem is typically the bastard poet whose work spilled over into action instead of remaining creative.

Hence the English Romantic tradition has close affinities with the individualism of the Protestant and the radical traditions. In all three the tendency is to take the individual as the primary field or area of operations instead of the interests of society, a tendency which is not necessarily egocentric, any more than its opposite is necessarily altruistic. English Romanticism is greatly aided in its feeling of being central to the tradition of English literature by the example of Shakespeare, who was in proportion to his abilities the most unpretentious poet who ever lived, a poet of whom one can predicate nothing except that he wrote plays, and stuck to his own business as a poet. He is the great poetic example of an inductive and practical approach to experience in English culture which is another aspect of its individualism.

I have no thought of trying to prefer one kind of English culture to another, and I regard all value-judgments that inhibit one's sympathies with anything outside a given tradition as dismally uncritical. I say only that this combination of Protestant, radical, and Romantic qualities is frequent enough in English culture to account for the popularity, in every sense, of the products of it described above. There have been no lack of Catholic, Tory, and Classical elements too, but the tradition dealt with here has been popular enough to give these later elements something of the quality of a consciously intellectual reaction. During the twenties of the present century, after the shock of the First World War, this intellectual reaction gathered strength. Its most articulate supporters were cultural evangelists who came from places like Missouri and Idaho, and who had a clear sense of the shape of the true English tradition, from its beginnings in Provence and mediaeval Italy to its later developments in France. Mr Eliot's version of this tradition was finally announced as Classical, royalist, and Anglo-Catholic, implying that whatever was Protestant, radical, and Romantic would have to go into the intellectual doghouse.

Many others who did not have the specific motivations of Mr Eliot or of Mr Pound joined in the chorus of denigration of Miltonic, Romantic, liberal, and allied values. Critics still know too little of the real principles of criticism to have any defence against such fashions, when well organized; hence although the fashion itself is on its way out, the prejudices set up by it still remain. Blake must of course be seen in the context of the tradition he belonged to, unless he is to be unnaturally isolated from it, and when the fashionable judgements on his tradition consist so largely of pseudo-critical hokum, one's understanding of Blake inevitably suffers. We come back again to the reason for anniversaries. There may be others in the English tradition as great as Blake, but there can hardly be many as urgently great, looming over the dither of our situation with a more inescapable clarity, full of answers to questions that we have hardly learned

how to formulate. Whatever other qualities Blake may have had
or lacked, he certainly had courage and simplicity. Whatever
other qualities our own age may have or lack, it is certainly an
age of fearfulness and complexity. And every age learns most
from those who most directly confront it.

SOURCE: *University of Toronto Quarterly*, XXVII (1957).

F. W. Bateson

NOTES ON BLAKE'S POEMS (1957)

Preliminary Caution

BLAKE is one of the most difficult of the English poets, but the Victorian idea, still a popular one, that it is only the bad poems that are obscure is a vulgar error. With the exception of the early imitations and a few of the Songs of Innocence some degree of obscurity runs through *all* his poems, good, bad, and indifferent. There are three reasons why Blake's poetry is especially difficult – and why, therefore, it needs constant annotation:

(1) He never went to school – Henry Pars's Drawing School was nothing but a drawing school – and so he missed the mental discipline, or perhaps distortion, involved in learning Latin, to which almost every other English poet has been subjected. And, because he never had to worry out the special problems that translation into and out of an inflected language raises for English speakers, his grammar is often weak or vague. Prepositions in particular are used so loosely that the specific sense intended has to be worked out from the surrounding context.

(2) Blake's poetic eye is rarely wholly on the perceptual objects that the titles of his poems might suggest he is writing about – roses, nurses, tigers, little boys and girls, Milton, Jerusalem. In the well-known marginal note on Wordsworth's 'Influence of Natural Objects in calling Forth and strengthening the Imagination in Boyhood and Early Youth' (one of the preliminary extracts from *The Prelude* that Wordsworth published in 1815) he wrote that, in contradistinction to Wordsworth, 'Natural objects always did & now do weaken, deaden & obliterate Imagination in me'. Instead of the 'single vision' of eye-on-the-object poetry Blake cultivated what he called 'double vision'. The expository doggerel sent to Thomas Butts on 22 November

1802 gives two simple examples of this 'double vision'. One is a
thistle encountered on a walk from Felpham to Lavant; outwardly
a thistle but

> With my inward Eye 'tis an old Man grey.

And the thistle–old man is followed by a similar conjunction of
the sun and Los, who represents the Spirit of Prophecy in
Blake's mythological system:

> 'Twas outward a Sun; inward Los in his might.

Unfortunately such expositions are rare in Blake and the 'inward'
meanings of the symbols have to be reconstructed by the reader.
This particular poem ends apocalyptically in threefold and fourfold vision ("'Tis fourfold in my supreme delight'), for which he
does *not* provide keys. By this date, however, Blake was deliberately cultivating a certain unintelligibility. 'Allegory,' he told
Butts in a letter dated 6 July 1803, 'address'd to the Intellectual
powers, while it is *altogether hidden* from the Corporeal Understanding, is My Definition of the Most Sublime Poetry' (my
italics).

As a general guide to Blake's double vision the following list
of the principal symbols should be useful to the beginner:

Innocence symbols (pre-sexual and amoral as well as Christian):
children, sheep, wild birds, wild flowers, green fields, dawn, dew,
spring – and associated images, e.g. shepherds, valleys, hills.

Energy symbols (creative, heroic, unrestrained – as well as
revolutionary, righteously destructive): lions, tigers, wolves,
eagles, noon, summer, sun, fire, forges, swords, spears, chariots.
These overlap into:

Sexual symbols (from uninhibited ecstasy to selfish power over
the beloved and jealousy): dreams, branches of trees, roses, gold,
silver, moonlight – and associated images, e.g. nets, cages, fairies,
bows and arrows. These overlap into:

Corruption symbols (hypocrisy, secrecy, as well as town-
influences, including abstract reasoning): looms, curtains, cities,
houses, snakes, evening, silence, disease. These overlap into:

Oppression symbols (personal, parental, religious, political):

priests, mills, forests, mountains, seas, caves, clouds, thunder, frost, night, stars, winter, stone, iron.

Although it would be unwise to assume that the images in this list *always* carry the symbolic meanings indicated in every one of Blake's poems, they generally do. And the list is not by any means complete.

(3) Blake used his symbols – which are to be found even in some of the juvenilia in *Poetical Sketches* – to express increasingly subtle and complex intellectual distinctions. As the system developed, however, he found it necessary or convenient to reinforce the symbolism with an elaborate and cacophonous mythology that does not explain itself as the symbols usually do. At the same time the symbols become increasingly esoteric and he introduces a technical vocabulary of his own. The north, for example, stands for reason, the south for desire, the east for wrath, and the west for pity. And the new key words such as *spectre, opaqueness, mundane shell, emanation* and the like are almost as unintelligible as Ulro, Golgonooza and Ololon. (They can be learnt by heart, but the non-professional reader resents having to do so.)

The total effect of these idiosyncrasies is to make Blake's English, especially after *c.* 1793-4, so personal that at times it almost becomes a private language. The modern reader's difficulty is that, if he is to enjoy and understand Blake's poetry *as poetry* (as distinct from psychology or philosophy), he cannot afford to allow the private language to intrude too far into it. The poems only exist as poems within the total context of English literature, i.e. as memorable statements written in the English language and controlled by the literary conventions that English poetry employs. No doubt there is always a certain tension between what a new poet wants to say and what the English language and literary tradition permit him to say, but this tension is more acute in Blake's case than in any other because of the extremity of his individualism. The stars, for example, cannot lose their normal connotation of brilliance, however much he tries to restrict their meaning to tyrannic power or abstract thought. The problem, then, for the reader of Blake (as it was for Blake himself) is to maintain a semantic balance between what Blake was trying to say and what the traditions of English speech and poetry were trying to make him say. It is perhaps in this no-man's-land of meaning, which is neither private nor public, that the *Songs of Experience* achieve their peculiar successes. But the balance was a difficult one to hold. In the lyrics of the Pickering manuscript and the later Prophetic Books there are undeniable failures of communication. With patience a meaning is recoverable, but it is not exactly an English meaning. The reader must 'translate' Blake into English. In the special circumstances an editor can only provide the facts (both about Blake's private language, so far as that has been decoded, and about those aspects of the public poetic tradition that may not be generally known), arm the reader with this general caveat, and wish him *bon voyage*.

Songs of Innocence and Experience

Songs of Innocence was the first of the poetical works to be published by the special process of relief-etching on copper followed by hand-tinting in water-colours that Blake called 'Illuminated Printing'. The illustrated title-page is dated 1789, but as it was his regular practice in his later works to begin the engraving with the title-page, 1789 is not necessarily the year in which the thirty-one plates of illustrated or decorated text that make up *Songs of Innocence* in its final form were completed. Until he had acquired fluency from practice the necessity, as in all engraving of the written word, to cut a *mirror-image* of the text of each poem must have made every plate a formidably laborious undertaking. (The first experiment in Illuminated Printing, the prose tractate *There is No Natural Religion*, which immediately preceded *Songs of Innocence*, went wrong because Blake engraved the imprint on the title-page 'The Author and Printer W. Blake' in *reversed* characters.) In any case no copies of *Songs of Innocence* have survived that we can be certain were issued in 1789. The fact is more than a bibliographical nicety, because it provides additional evidence of the continuity of Blake's lyrical development from *Poetical Sketches* to *Songs of Experience*. What it means is that, though no doubt most of the Songs of Innocence had been written by 1789, a few *may* be later – just as a few others are certainly much earlier. Four of the songs were undoubtedly in existence in 1784. One is the early version of 'Laughing Song' which was copied out by an unidentified admirer with two similar 'Songs by Mr Blake' on to the flyleaf of a copy of *Poetical Sketches* that bears the inscription 'from Mrs Flaxman May 15 1784'. And among the heterogeneous songs that are sung in *An Island in the Moon*, which was written towards the end of 1784, are earlier versions of 'Nurse's Song', 'Holy Thursday' and 'The Little Boy Lost'. The fact that at least five years, and possibly six or even seven years, divides the composition of these poems from their illustration in *Songs of Innocence* suggests another critical corollary. It is simply that too much confidence must not be placed in the illustrations as providing clues to the interpretation of the symbolism. The Blake who engraved the poems was an altogether different man, with a totally different outlook on life, from the young man who wrote them. And a similar *caveat* applies, or may apply, with various degrees of probability, to many of the other Songs of Innocence as well as to almost all the Songs of Experience. The illustration of 'The Blossom', for example, has been used to give that poem an elaborate phallic interpretation – which has been widely accepted – that would never occur to anyone who had only the words in front of him. And in the case of the first plate of 'The Little Girl Lost', with its mature pair of lovers instead of the solitary seven-year-old Lyca of the text, it almost looks as if Blake had forgotten which song he was illustrating. (If the lovers are Lyca's parents they have no business on that plate.) It is wiser generally to look for the meaning of obscure lines not in the engravings but in the songs' words.

The Songs of Innocence can be divided into three strata, corresponding to the three periods in Blake's life in which they seem to have been written. The 1784 songs are all addressed to adults and not to children. They are closely connected with the later songs in *Poetical Sketches*, and like them they can reasonably be seen as a reflection of the ecstatic happiness of the years following Blake's marriage. In terms of literary history they represent a culmination of the cult of poetic 'simplicity' that began with Addison and his associates – Ambrose Philips, Thomas Tickell,

Henry Carey, etc. – and that, running through Shenstone, Collins and Percy to the so-called 'Della Cruscans', prepared the way for *Lyrical Ballads*. The Innocence is essentially a pastoral innocence, more sentimental than Christian, and with overtones of the classical Golden Age rather than of the Garden of Eden.

A second stratum is made up of the poems, specifically addressed to children, such as 'The Lamb', 'The Shepherd', 'The Little Black Boy' and 'The Blossom'. These *are* Christian poems, and they are often consciously didactic ('So if all do their duty they need not fear harm'). They belong to another recognized eighteenth-century genre, that of Bunyan's *Book for Boys and Girls* (1686), Isaac Watts's *Divine Songs Attempted in Easy Language for the Use of Children* (1715), a book that Blake knew well under its later title *Divine and Moral Songs*, and their numerous imitations (principally by Nonconformists) down to the *Hymns in Prose for Children* (1781) of Mrs Barbauld, a nice Unitarian schoolmistress and poetess whom Blake must almost certainly have met at Joseph Johnson's. An important difference is that Blake wrote most of these Christian-didactic pieces, which make up some two-thirds of the original *Songs of Innocence*, with at least one eye on their future illustration by himself. The collection is first of all a children's picture-book. The engraved title page, with its illustration of an extremely straight-backed elderly female who is showing a large picture-book to a fascinated little boy and girl, puts it firmly in its contemporary context. Between the autumn of 1784 and the first half of 1787 Blake and James Parker kept a print-shop next door to the family hosiery in Broad Street, and a collection of moral songs for children with coloured pictures in it would obviously have made an attractive and appropriate addition to Blake and Parker's meagre stock. But if the songs were written at this time, as many of them probably were, Blake did not hit on the medium for their illustration until a year or two later. According to J. T. Smith, who had been a personal friend of Robert Blake's, the process of Illuminated Printing was only expounded to William by Robert's ghost in a vision *after* his death. The story rings true. At any rate Robert did die in February 1787, and according to the colophon of 'The Ghost of Abel'

(1822), the last of the engraved poems (it is an unhappy postscript to Byron's 'Cain'), 'Blake's Original Stereotype was 1788'.

The third stratum in *Songs of Innocence* includes four poems – 'The Little Girl Lost', 'The Little Girl Found', 'The Schoolboy', and 'The Voice of the Ancient Bard' – that were finally transferred to *Songs of Experience*. The characteristic tone of these poems, and of one or two others like them, is more sombre and more adult than either of the other groups. Their author has abandoned the rôle he claims in the 'Introduction' ('Piping down the valleys wild') of the happy carefree piper for that of a prophet ('In futurity/I prophetic see') and inspired 'bard'. Even the questions his reluctant schoolboy asks society represent a significant change in attitude as well as in rhetorical form. (The earlier Songs make statements instead of asking questions; when a question *is* asked, as in 'The Lamb' or 'Infant Joy', it is answered immediately.) 'A Dream' also appears as a Song of Experience in some early copies of the combined series, though Blake soon restored it to Innocence. No doubt it is less out of place there, but it resembles 'The Little Girl Lost' and 'The Little Girl Found' in having an unhappy beginning and middle and a happy mystical end. 'Night', the greatest of the Songs of Innocence, also has obvious parallels with 'The Little Girl Lost' and 'The Little Girl Found', although unlike them it was never transferred to Experience. 'The Voice of the Ancient Bard' has the words of its text engraved in italic lettering, whereas all the other Songs are in minuscule roman – a technical difference that suggests it may have been engraved some time after them. In most copies it comes at the very end of *Songs of Innocence*. A more interesting difference is that in its message it has left behind the worlds of the pastoral and the nursery for contemporary social and political realities. Its 'truth new-born' may be Swedenborgianism or the French Revolution, or perhaps a combination of both of them, but whatever the precise meaning may be something new is clearly being attempted, even if it does not quite come off. This stratum can perhaps be dated *c.* 1788–90. The new interests and tone parallel Blake's gradual transition to a tragic philosophy of life in *Tiriel* (*c.* 1788), *The Book of Thel* (engraved 1789), and the marginalia in his copies of Lavater (early 1789) and Sweden-borg (1789–90). In any case his uncertainty whether to ascribe these poems to Innocence or Experience differentiates them sharply from the songs that the piper promised 'Every child may joy to hear'. It is not 'joy' that characterizes 'Night' or 'The Little Girl Lost' and 'The Little Girl Found', but a mystical certainty beyond either happiness or unhappiness.

The certainty proved more precarious than Blake had antici-pated – as *Songs of Experience* is there to prove. In October 1793 he issued a characteristic 'Prospectus' or sale catalogue of his engravings with the prices at which they could be bought. It included 'Songs of Innocence, in Illuminated Printing' and 'Songs of Experience in Illuminated Printing', each being obtainable for five shillings. The announcement certainly suggests (i) that *Songs of Experience* had been engraved by 1793, and (ii) that copies of it could be purchased separately. All the surviving copies, how-ever, have the date 1794 on the title-page and show no sign what-ever of having been issued separately. The whole point of *Songs of Experience* being the detailed contrast and deflation it presents to *Songs of Innocence*, the two series *have* to be read together. By way of underlining this interrelationship, Blake added in or about 1794 a fine general title-page for both series which reads 'Songs of Innocence and Of Experience Shewing the Two Contrary States of the Human Soul'. The plate, an illustration of Experi-ence rather than Innocence, shows a young Adam and Eve, naked except for their fig-leaves (which look more like vine-leaves), cowering in agonized terror before the leaping flames of God's anger.

Some four or five years, then, separate the engraving of *Songs of Innocence*, or most of the plates at any rate, from *Songs of Experience*. There is no similar gap between the composition of the last Songs of Innocence and the first Songs of Experience. Indeed, as we have seen, Blake eventually discovered that four of the later Songs of Innocence were sufficiently close to being Songs of Experience to merit inclusion in that series. Some of these transitional songs may have been written as late as 1790, and as the earliest of the Songs of Experience proper seem to have been written in 1791, they are a more reliable guide to the latter's meaning than the much later engravings. The position is much the same as with *Songs of Innocence*. The illustrations and decorations are attractive and occasionally impressive – for example, the moving and beautiful 'Holy Thursday' (Experience) – *in themselves*, but as a commentary on points of detail in the meaning of the poems they are normally unhelpful if not actually misleading. In some of the engraved copies, for instance, the rose of 'The Sick Rose' is not red but white – whereas the whole point of the poem is the suggestion of naked flesh in the rose's colour.

Incomparably the best commentary on *Songs of Experience* is the notebook now generally known as the Rossetti manuscript.* The Rossetti manuscript is an extraordinary document. Almost every inch of its 116 pages is covered with poems and doggerel, in every state of completion and incompletion, all sorts and varieties of prose, and dozens of more or less elaborate sketches in various media. Its total effect on the reader of Blake is like that of Keats's letters on the reader of Keats. It adds a new dimension to one's understanding. Originally it had been a sketchbook. Five of the early pages have drawings and sketches in a curiously stiff and angular style, quite unlike Blake's fluent curves, that have been attributed to his brother Robert (who died of consumption in 1787). When Blake acquired the notebook he began by using it sideways for sketches. (They start at the other end of the note-book from Robert's, only every other page being used so that the drawing can overflow on to the page below, and they continue up to page 96.) As far as they are decipherable these sketches appear to be illustrations of scenes in or suggested by *Paradise*

---

* Dante Gabriel Rossetti 'discovered' it and owned it for years. Rossetti bought it in 1847, for ten shillings, from William Palmer – a brother of Samuel Palmer the painter, one of Blake's most ardent disciples – who had somehow acquired it from Blake's widow. The manuscript is now in the British Museum; an excellent facsimile edited by Geoffrey Keynes was published by the Nonesuch Press in 1935. Photographs of the pages on which first drafts of the Songs of Experience (and the associated poems) appear are also to be found in Joseph H. Wicksteed's *Blake's Innocence and Experience* (1928), where the reproduction is decidedly clearer than in the Nonesuch edition.

Lost, and they can no doubt be connected with Joseph Johnson's abortive scheme for a magnificent illustrated Milton by Henry Fuseli that Blake was to engrave and Cowper the poet to edit. The drawings, especially the nudes, have the new vigour of line that Blake was now learning from Fuseli, and they may perhaps be dated 1790–1. About this time, or a few months later, Blake began to use the same end of the notebook for the poems that are the nucleus of *Songs of Experience*. Instead of using the pages sideways he now turned the notebook upside down and, starting with its last page but one (page 115), worked his way steadily back to page 98. The pages opposite the *Paradise Lost* drawings had generally been left blank, and when the sketch only consisted of a few tentative lines Blake did not hesitate to overwrite it with poems. Normally, however, the even-numbered pages have a *Paradise Lost* drawing sideways on the page ('Satan exulting over Eve', 'Satan defying God the Father, the Son interceding', 'The Trinity', 'Adam and Eve', etc.), while the odd-numbered pages, generally divided into two columns, contain the poems. Sometimes the poem's text is left without corrections, but most of the poems show deletions, alterations or additions, the revisions of 'Earth's Answer' and 'The Tiger' actually spilling over on to the illustrations.

It has been necessary to describe the Rossetti manuscript with this degree of minuteness, because the physical conditions under which the Songs of Experience were written probably contributed to their meaning. These poems are not fair copies. In the Rossetti manuscript we see Blake in the actual process of composition, and the poems obviously follow one another, with one or two possible exceptions, in the order in which they were written. May not the cramped conditions under which Blake was writing have unconsciously encouraged a greater verbal concentration than he usually achieved? The question is at least worth asking. Moreover the notebook probably once belonged to Robert, and as such it would always possess a special sanctity for Blake. 'Thirteen years ago', he wrote to Hayley in May 1800, 'I lost a brother & with his spirit I converse daily & hourly in the Spirit & See him in my remembrance in the regions of my

Imagination. I hear his advice & even now write from his Dictate.' Under these circumstances Blake may well have derived a special psychological stimulus from the notebook as an aid in the act of composition, a stimulus that would more than counterbalance the physical inconveniences that it created. The fact that he in time filled almost every blank inch in it certainly suggests that it did finally acquire for Blake some special spiritual virtue of its own. Nothing less, for instance, will explain the haphazard and untidy way in which Blake's last important poem, *The Everlasting Gospel*, is scattered through empty corners of the notebook. When the Songs of Experience were being written there were still, of course, plenty of blank pages left, but the compulsion not to waste the precious paper may have already begun to operate. If it did, the tendency to concision, an almost epigrammatic brevity, that characterizes all the poems, early and late, in the Rossetti manuscript would follow naturally. (The contrast with the general diffuseness, not only of the Prophetic Books, but of many of the earlier poems, too, certainly invites some such an explanation.)

Blake cannot have been unaware, either, of the sketches for *Paradise Lost*. As he looked up from the first verse of 'Earth's Answer' the contorted figure of Satan shrieking his defiance of God the Father would have met his eyes. And even when there could be no specific influence the drawings would at least tend to confirm and reinforce the background of Genesis myth in the poems. The symbolism of Experience draws heavily on the Fall of Man, the Fall of the Angels, the forbidden fruit, the serpent-tempter, and similar themes. The fact that Blake had recently been illustrating Genesis episodes and that the illustrations were often before his eyes as he worked out what were often their poetic equivalents is one that needs to be remembered in reading them.

There are sixty-one poems or poetical fragments in the last twenty pages of the Rossetti manuscript. How long a period their composition occupied it is difficult to determine, but my impression – partly derived from the handwriting, which varies noticeably both in the size of letters and the degree of its slope after page 105, and partly from the poems themselves – is that the first twenty or thirty pieces were written close together and that the others were spread over a much longer interval. Unfortunately the only poem in the Experience group that can be dated at all precisely is the last of the series. This describes in ballad form Lafayette's final betrayal, as it seemed to Blake, of the cause of the Revolution and the ironical reward of immediate imprisonment meted out to him by the Austrians when he crossed their border in August 1792. The news of Lafayette's fate did not reach England until the end of October, and Blake's poem would still have been topical in November or December 1792, though hardly later. This is a solid *terminus ad quem*. The *terminus a quo*, or the date when the poems began, is perhaps suggested by the twelfth poem in the series ('Why should I care for the men of thames'), which contains two couplets that may be topical:

> (i)   the little blasts of fear
>   That the hireling blows into my ear . . .
> (ii) The Ohio shall wash his stains from me:
>   I was born a slave but I go to be free.

The two allusions cannot be said to *prove* anything, but they combine to suggest that the poem was written in 1791, or perhaps early 1792. The 'little blasts of fear' may well refer to the circumstances under which Blake's poem *The French Revolution* was suppressed. Joseph Johnson printed this curious poem, or rather the first of its seven books, in 1791, but for some reason it was never actually published. Now, as it happens, Johnson had also printed and then failed to publish the first volume of Tom Paine's *Rights of Man* in the February of the same year. No doubt he was afraid of a Government prosecution in both cases. It is true that Paine did find another publisher, but within the year booksellers were being gaoled for selling it. Paine's revolutionary enthusiasms may also be responsible for the new glamour the Ohio had now acquired for Blake. Paine and Joel Barlow, a minor American poet whom Blake had read, were Joseph Johnson's guests from time to time from the spring of 1791 to the autumn of 1792, and Blake undoubtedly saw something of both of them. The indications are a bit nebulous, but they suggest to me a date in or about the summer or autumn of 1791.

If the poems of Experience in the Rossetti manuscript can be dated 1791–2 only a few months will have separated the last of the Songs of Innocence from the earliest of the Songs of Experience. The probability is of great interest because it provides one more example of the continuity of Blake's poetry. It is clear that Mary Wollstonecraft's advances, if she was indeed the disturbing influence, and the repercussions set up in Blake by his wife's jealousy, were only the climax to a process of gradual disillusionment that can be traced back to *Tiriel* and the prose tractates on natural religion, both of which are generally dated 1788, which may have had its emotional origins for Blake in Robert's death in 1787. *The Marriage of Heaven and Hell*, which was certainly started in 1790, reflects a similar disillusionment with Swedenborgianism. And the mood persisted after the Experience group in the Rossetti manuscript came to an end in 'Fayette', as is shown by the four poems in *Songs of Experience* in its final form that are neither in the Rossetti manuscript nor in the early copies of *Songs of Innocence*. The four are the 'Introduction' ('Hear the voice of the Bard'), 'A little Girl Lost', 'Ah! Sunflower' and 'To Tirzah', and they were presumably all written after the pieces in the Rossetti manuscript. About 'To Tirzah', indeed, there can be no question. Tirzah, the materialistic antithesis to Jerusalem, is a figure that was only added at a late stage in the evolution of Blake's mythological system. The early copies of *Songs of Experience* do not contain the poem at all, and it was probably written about 1800. The three other poems, all of them incomparably superior to 'To Tirzah', were presumably composed in 1793.

The preceding analysis has been primarily concerned to establish the order in which the Songs of Innocence and Experience were written. A chronological framework is the indispensable preliminary to the understanding of Blake's poetry. Unlike the poetry of Pope, for example, or that of Mr T. S. Eliot, Blake's progress was not through a succession of distinct styles, with intervals in which little or nothing is written. On the contrary, the controlling principle is one of continuous growth, an almost organic development of the symbolism, the poetic structure and the underlying human situations demanding communication.

Source: Introduction to *Selection of Blake's Poems* (1957).

Robert F. Gleckner

POINT OF VIEW AND CONTEXT
IN BLAKE'S SONGS (1957)

> A flower was offer'd to me,
> Such a flower as May never bore;
> But I said 'I've a Pretty Rose-tree,'
> And I passed the sweet flower o'er.
>
> Then I went to my Pretty Rose-tree,
> To tend her by day and by night;
> But my Rose turn'd away with jealousy,
> And her thorns were my only delight.

JOSEPH WICKSTEED, the only critic to devote an entire book to Blake's songs, said this about Blake's poem, 'My Pretty Rose-Tree': it 'shows how virtue itself is rewarded only by suspicion and unkindness'. And Thomas Wright, Blake's early biographer, commented on the poem as follows: ' "My Pretty Rose-Tree", Blake's nearest approach to humour, may be paraphrased thus: "I was much taken with a charming flower (girl), but I said to my-self, No, it won't do. Besides, I have an equally pretty wife at home. Then, too, what would the world say? On the whole it would be policy to behave myself." But his wife takes umbrage all the same. The thorns of her jealousy, however, instead of wounding him give him pleasure, for they excuse his inclination for the flower. Moral: See what comes of being good!'

On the contrary, the moral is that such off-the-mark commentary is what comes of ignoring the context of Blake's songs (that is, whether the poem is a song of innocence or song of experience) and the point of view from which a given poem is written. 'My Pretty Rose-Tree' is not about virtue perversely rewarded, nor does it have to do with 'policy' or morality in the ordinary sense of those words. Virtue by itself meant nothing to Blake unless clarified by context: in the state of innocence it is 'The Divine Image'; in experience it is perverted to 'A Divine Image' and 'The Human Abstract'. Real virtue Blake defined in *The Marriage of Heaven and Hell*: 'No virtue can exist without break-ing these ten commandments. Jesus was all virtue, and acted from impulse, not from rules.' In 'My Pretty Rose-Tree' the speaker acts from rules when he refuses the offer of the sweet flower. For, as Blake wrote elsewhere,

> He who binds to himself a joy
> Does the winged life destroy;
> But he who kisses the joy as it flies
> Lives in eternity's sun rise.

The speaker in 'My Pretty Rose-Tree' not only has let the moment go, but also has bound to himself a joy. Furthermore, since this is a Song of Experience, about the state of experience, the flower offered the speaker is the opportunity for a joy, a love, an ascent to a higher innocence. We recall that it was not just *any* flower, but a superb one, 'such a flower as May never bore'. Still, the offer is refused – because the speaker already has a rose-tree. Now, conventionally, this is admirable fidelity; for Blake, how-ever, it is enslavement by what he called the marriage ring. The speaker thus passes up the chance of a spiritual joy (sweet flower) to return to the limited joy of an earthly relationship (pretty rose-tree). He is sorely tempted – but his desire has fallen subject to an extrasensual force symbolized by the existence of, and his rela-tionship to, the rose-tree.

The result, of course, is the speaker's retreat from desire to the only substitute for desire in Urizen's world of experience, duty:

> Then I went to my Pretty Rose-tree,
> To tend her by day and by night.

The last two lines of the poem are the crushing commentary on the whole affair. Virtuous in terms of conventional morality, the speaker is rewarded with disdain and jealousy, ironically the same reaction which would have been forthcoming had the speaker taken the offered flower. It is Blake's trenchant way of showing the 'rules' to be inane.

How easily, then, in reading Blake's *Songs of Innocence and of Experience* we can ignore Blake's own individual method. Basically that method is simple, its roots lying in his concept of states and their symbols. Like many other artists Blake employed a central group of related symbols to form a dominant symbolic pattern; his are the child, the father, and Christ, representing the states of innocence, experience, and a higher innocence. These *major* symbols provide the context for all the 'minor', contributory symbols in the songs; and my purpose here is to suggest a method of approach that is applicable to all of them – and thus to all the songs.

Each of Blake's two song series (or states or major symbols) comprises a number of smaller units (or states or symbols), so that the relationship of each unit to the series as a whole might be stated as a kind of progression; from the states of innocence and experience to the Songs of Innocence and Songs of Experience, to each individual song within the series, to the symbols within each song, to the words that give the symbols their existence. Conceivably ignorance of or indifference to one word prohibits the imaginative perception and understanding of the whole structure. As Blake wrote in the preface to *Jerusalem*, 'Every word and every letter is studied and put into its fit place; the terrific numbers are reserved for terrific parts, the mild & gentle for the mild & gentle parts, and the prosaic for inferior parts; all are necessary to each other.'

For the serious reader of Blake's songs, then, a constant awareness of the context or state in which a poem appears is indispensable; and since each state is made up of many poems, the other poems in that state must be consulted to grasp the full significance of any one poem. Each song out of its context means a great deal less than Blake expected of his total invention, and occasionally it may be taken to mean something quite different from what he intended. Blake created a system of which innocence and experience are vital parts; to deny to the Songs of Innocence, then, the very background and basic symbology which it helps to make up is as wrong as reading *The Rape of the Lock* without reference to the epic tradition. Without the system, Blake is the simplest of lyric poets and every child may joy to hear the songs. Yet with very little study the child of innocence can be seen to be radically different from the child of experience, and the mother of innocence scarcely recognizable in experience. The states are separate, the two contrary states of the human soul, and the songs were written not merely for our enjoyment, or even for our edification, but for our salvation.

Closely related to the necessity of reading each song in terms of its state is the vital importance of point of view. Often it is unobtrusive, but many times upon a correct determination of speaker and perspective depends a faithful interpretation of the poem. Blake himself suggests this by his organization of the songs into series, *Innocence* introduced and sung by the piper, *Experience* by the Bard. Superficially there seems to be little to distinguish one from the other since the piper clearly exhibits imaginative vision and the Bard 'Present, Past, & Future sees'. Yet for each, the past, present, and future are different: for the piper the past can only be the primal unity, for the present is innocence and the immediate future is experience; for the Bard the past is innocence, the present experience, the future a higher innocence. It is natural, then, that the piper's point of view is prevailingly happy; he is conscious of the child's essential divinity and assured of his present protection. But into that joyous context the elements of experience constantly insinuate themselves so that the note of sorrow is never completely absent from the piper's pipe. In experience, on the other hand, the Bard's voice is solemn and more deeply resonant, for the high-pitched joy of innocence is now only a memory. Within this gloom, though, lies the ember which can leap into flame at any moment to light the way to the higher innocence. Yet despite this difference in direction of their vision, both singers are imaginative, are what Blake called the poetic or prophetic character. And though one singer uses 'mild and gentle numbers' and the other more 'terrific' tones, both see the imaginative (and symbolic) significance of all the activity in the songs. The inexplicit, Blake said, 'rouzes the faculties to act'. The reader of Blake, then, must rouse his faculties to consider this imaginative point of view always no matter who is speaking or seeing or acting in a poem.

Both singers are of course William Blake. And since he, or

they, sing all the songs, whether they are identifiable or not with a character in a poem contributes most importantly to the total meaning of the poem. To take an extreme example, in 'The Little Vagabond' of *Songs of Experience* there are four points of view: that of the mother, who is now out of her element and can no longer protect her child as she did in *Songs of Innocence*; that of the parson, who is a part of the major symbol of experience, father-priest-king; that of the vagabond himself, a child of experience, not the carefree, irresponsible, thoughtless child of innocence; and that of the Bard, through whose vision each of the other points of view can be studied and evaluated. Without an awareness of this complexity in 'The Little Vagabond' the poem dissipates into sentimental drivel. Another good example is 'Holy Thursday' of *Songs of Innocence*:

'Twas on a Holy Thursday, their innocent faces clean,
The children walking two & two, in red & blue & green,
Grey-headed beadles walk'd before, with wands as white as
  snow,
Till into the high dome of Paul's they like Thames' waters flow.

O what a multitude they seem'd, these flowers of London
  town!
Seated in companies they sit with radiance all their own.
The hum of multitudes was there, but multitudes of lambs,
Thousands of little boys & girls raising their innocent hands.

Now like a mighty wind they raise to heaven the voice of song,
Or like harmonious thunderings the seats of heaven among.
Beneath them sit the aged men, wise guardians of the poor;
Then cherish pity, lest you drive an angel from your door.

From a conventional point of view it is thoughtful and kind of the 'wise guardians of the poor' to run charity schools and to take the children occasionally to St Paul's to give thanks for all their so-called blessings. But from the piper's point of view (and Blake's of course) the children clearly are disciplined, regimented, marched in formation to church in the uniforms of their respective schools — mainly to advertise the charitable souls of their supposed guardians. The point here (seen only through the piper's vision) is that in the state of innocence there is, or ought to be, no discipline, no regimentation, no marching, no uniforms, and no guardians – merely free, uninhibited, irresponsible, thoughtless play on the echoing green. Accordingly the children in 'Holy Thursday' assert and preserve their essential innocence, not by going to church, but by freely and spontaneously, 'like a mighty wind', raising to 'heaven the voice of song'. This simple act raises them to a level far above their supposed benefactors, who are without vision, without innocence, without love: 'Beneath them sit the aged men, wise guardians of the poor.' The irony is severe, but lost upon us unless we are aware of context and point of view.

As a final example consider the 'Introduction' of *Songs of Experience*:

> Hear the voice of the Bard!
> Who Present, Past, & Future, sees;
> Whose ears have heard
> The Holy Word
> That walk'd among the ancient trees,
>
> Calling the lapsed Soul,
> And weeping in the evening dew;
> That might controll
> The starry pole,
> And fallen, fallen light renew!
>
> 'O Earth, O Earth, return!
> 'Arise from out the dewy grass;
> 'Night is worn,
> 'And the morn
> 'Rises from the slumberous mass.
>
> 'Turn away no more;
> 'Why wilt thou turn away?
> 'The starry floor,
> 'The wat'ry shore,
> 'Is giv'n thee till the break of day.'

The main difficulty here seems to be Blake's chaotic punctuation and the ambiguity it causes. Stanzas 1, 3, and 4 seem to be an invitation to Earth to arise from the evil darkness and reassume the light of its prelapsarian state. Such an orthodox Christian reading, however, is possible only if we forget (1) that this is a Song of Experience, and (2) that the singer of these songs is Bard, not God or a priest. In similar fashion, while ignoring the context or the point of view, one might quickly point out the obvious reference in stanza 1 to Genesis III and forget that the speaker in that chapter is the old Testament God, Jehovah, the cruel law-giver and vengeful tyrant who became in Blake's cosmos the father–priest–king image. And finally, the Holy Word in Genesis walked in the garden not in the 'evening dew' but in the 'cool of day', not to weep and forgive but to cast out and curse his children, to bind them to the soil, and to place woman in a position of virtual servitude to man. In view of this, if the second stanza is read as a clause modifying 'Holy Word', it is either hopelessly contradictory or devastatingly ironic.

Blake himself hints at the correct reading immediately by means of the ambiguity of the first stanza. There are actually two voices in the poem, the Bard's ('Hear the voice of the Bard'), and the Holy Word's ('Calling the lapsed Soul'); and the second stanza, *because* of its apparently chaotic punctuation, must be read as modifying both voices. The last two stanzas are the words of *both* voices, perfectly in context when the dual purpose of the poem is recognized. Only in this way can the poem be seen for what it is, an introduction to the state and the songs of experience, in which the Holy Word of Jehovah is hypocritical, selfish, and jealous, thinking and acting in terms of the physical phenomena of day and night and the earthly morality of rewards and punishments. The Bard, mortal but prophetically imaginative, thinks and acts by eternal time and according to eternal values.

But how does one discover the all-important point of view in Blake's songs? One way is to observe the reactions of various characters to the same symbolic act, object, or character, for both the characters and the symbols ultimately resolve themselves into aspects of the major symbol governing that particular poem. Thus the mother of 'Songs of Innocence' is symbolic in that her protection of the child contributes to the over-all picture of the child as major symbol of the state of innocence. In addition, many of Blake's symbols are recurrent, so that once a symbol's basic significance is revealed in a kind of archetypal context, each successive context adds association to association within the song series. When the beadle's wand appears in the first stanza of 'Holy Thursday' of *Innocence*, for example, its immediate connotation is authority. But since a *beadle* wields the symbol, it is also religious authority, the organized church, institutionalized religion. It also represents an act of restraint which forces the children to act according to rule rather than impulse. The wand is 'white as snow' to suggest the frigidity of man-made moral purity as opposed to the warmth of young, energetic, exuberant innocence. And finally, it suggests the worldly, non-innocent concept of duty (and its corollary, harm), the duty of worship which clashes with all of Blake's ideas of freedom and spontaneity. But all of this, it will be said, strongly suggests the world of experience, and 'Holy Thursday' *is* a Song of Innocence; the over-all point of view is the piper's. The point to be made here is simply this. If we do not read the poem as a Song of Innocence, about the *state* of innocence and its major symbol, the joyous child, we *can* read it as a rather pleasant picture of nicely dressed charity children being led to church by a gentle beadle to sing hymns; or as a terrible view of unfortunate, exploited charity children under the thumbs of their elders. And we would *not* see that despite outward appearance the children *are* innocent, essentially free and happy, as they spontaneously sing their songs. Without an awareness of context the symbols do not work as Blake intended them to, and the song becomes a fairly inconsequential bit of sentimental social comment.

Considering, then, the care Blake took with point of view, recurring symbols, and symbolic action, we can see that gradually many of Blake's characters merge. The final products of these mergers are what I have called the major symbols. Kindred points of view tend to unite the holders of these points of view; characters who are associated continually with the same or similar symbols tend to melt into one another; and a similar pattern of action reveals a fundamental affinity among the actors. In these ways the significance and value of any one character in any one song are intensified and expanded beyond the immediate context. The physical identity may shift, but the symbolic value remains constant – or better, is constantly enriched. When the beadle's wand in 'Holy Thursday' is recognized as part of the basic sceptre motif, the beadle's identity, while being retained as representative of church law, merges with that of Tiriel, say, and the father – and ultimately with the 'selfish father of men' in 'Earth's Answer', the pebble in 'The Clod and the Pebble'; the 'cold and usurous hand' of 'Holy Thursday'; God in 'The Chimney Sweeper'; the mother, parson, and Dame Lurch in 'The Little Vagabond'; Cruelty, Humility, and the Human Brain in 'The Human Abstract'; and Tirzah in 'To Tirzah'. Within the identity are inherent all the other identities which combine to make up the major symbol of the context. The priests of 'The Garden of Love' may bind with briars love and desire, but they do so because they are selfish, fatherly, cold and usurous, worldly, cruel, humble, hypocritical, and so forth.

One serious question remains: how does one distinguish among all these characters, or are they all precisely alike and hence redundant? Professor Mark Schorer answers the question this way – I know of none better: 'The point is', he says, 'that the individuality of these creations lies not in their rich diversity but in the outline that separates them from their backgrounds.' That is, each individual identity in its specific context is at once a part of the whole context and the whole of which it is a part. Both the priest of 'The Garden of Love' and the flower in 'My Pretty Rose-Tree' are self-sufficient for some understanding of these two poems. Blake simply asked his reader to do more than merely understand: that, he said, is a 'corporeal' function. He wanted them to imagine as he imagined, to see as he saw, even to re-create as he created. Only then does his method make sense, only then can one see the minor symbols as parts of a major symbol, only then can the individual song take its rightful place as a Song of Innocence or Song of Experience.

SOURCE: *Bulletin of the New York Public Library*, LXI (Nov. 1957).

Martin K. Nurmi

BLAKE'S REVISIONS OF 'THE TYGER' (1956)

In Blake's Notebook drafts of 'The Tyger' we have a valuable record of the growth of a great poem, a record which not only brings the poem itself into clearer focus but gives us as well another glimpse of the poet during a crucial but scantily documented period of his life. Yet, curiously enough, critics have largely neglected them. The fact that Blake revised this poem more than any other has been noticed, to be sure, and some critics have shown how a line or a stanza in the final poem is an improvement over earlier versions. But only one extended study of the drafts has been made, Joseph Wicksteed's attempt to reconstruct Blake's composition by association of ideas.[1] And that is incomplete: of the three full drafts of the poem (counting the final version as the third), and the additional drafts of two stanzas, Wicksteed studies thoroughly only the first draft and an additional draft of one stanza.

The present article is an attempt in some measure to fill in this critical gap, by tracing Blake's revisions through all his drafts, in order to clarify the poem's general meaning. In it I shall also offer a conjecture as to the occasion of the poem, based on the pattern in which it evolves, and shall include an accurate typographic transcription of Blake's manuscript drafts of the poem.

Because Wicksteed does not treat the drafts as a whole, he is led to view the evolution of 'The Tyger' too simply, as an undeviating expansion of meaning and increase in poetic effectiveness. It would be more accurate to regard it as a kind of dialectical struggle in which Blake strives to bring his emblematic tiger's two 'contraries' – its 'deadly terrors' and the divinity in which it participates by having been created by an 'immortal hand or eye'

– into the 'fearful symmetry' symbolized by the animal's natural symmetry of ferocity and beauty, and even by its contrasting stripes. This symmetry was the kernel of Blake's original conception, but he was not able to build his poem directly to embody it. If we follow his progress through his drafts, we will notice that his work falls into three stages in which this symmetry is significantly modulated. In the first stage he emphasizes the tiger's dreadfulness, portraying the beast as a cruel and bloody horror and asking pointed questions concerning its origin; in the second stage he swings to the opposite pole, shifting his emphasis to the tiger's divine origin by adding a stanza which rhetorically suggests that the tiger and the lamb do have a common creator and by omitting most of the tiger's dreadful attributes; in the third stage he retains the positive elements of the second stage, using the suggestion of the tiger's divine origin for the climax, but he also restores some of the dreadfulness of the first stage, though none of its horror, to effect a positively weighted synthesis of the two earlier stages in the complex affirmation of the final poem. Approached through its drafts, the final poem thus emerges quite clearly as a complex but essentially positive statement affirming the dread tiger's divinity, and not a probing of good and evil, as it has sometimes been interpreted.

In the drafts Blake does probe the meaning of the tiger as a symbol of 'evil' – in his ironic sense of the word – as a symbol of that creative cosmic energy so feared by the orthodox 'angels' in all its manifestations. In the drafts, indeed, he seems to pass through some kind of spiritual crisis concerning it. For his difficulty in fixing the tiger's symmetry is not merely a compositional one. In one sense it is that, of course. But when the poet who had written the superbly controlled lyrics of *Poetical Sketches* and *Songs of Innocence* successively exaggerates the two aspects of his symbolic tiger's nature as much as Blake's earlier drafts show him to do, we may plausibly attribute his compositional difficulties to a difficulty in accepting the implications of the tiger's meaning for himself. In the first stage of composition, Blake's pointed questions concerning a cruel and horrible tiger are not the result of imprecise diction, for he actually revised one stanza to make his questions more pointed; rather they hint that he was troubled and even repelled by his tiger's dreadfulness, despite his intention to show it as being harmonious with God's will. His transformation of this monster into the greatly ameliorated tiger of his second stage, who is only nominally dreadful, indeed almost benign, when compared with the tiger of either the first or third stage, similarly suggests that he overcame his initial doubts, experiencing such elation at being able to do so that he became even too optimistic. Finally, his adjustment of these two attitudes in the final poem seems to indicate that he had come to view the tiger's dreadfulness more philosophically than he was able to do in the first stage, and more realistically than he was able to do in the second.

That Blake went through some kind of crisis can be demonstrated from the drafts, but specifically what kind of crisis it was we can only conjecture. Several signs, however, seem to point to his revolutionary sympathies. From their position in the Notebook, the drafts of 'The Tyger' appear to have been written some time during 1792, or at the latest 1793,[2] the period of violence in France when many who had supported the revolution were having second thoughts about it. Since Blake seems to have conceived of tigers as natural symbols for energy, and even hinted at their connection with the revolutionary manifestation of energy, in *The Marriage of Heaven and Hell* (1790–3), his bloody and repellent characterization of the tiger of the poem in the first stage of composition may show a temporary disillusionment with revolution, a disillusionment parallel to that expressed in the bitter quatrain sometimes added to the preludium of *America*, where the Bard shatters his harp in rage, 'asham'd of his own song'. This possibility is supported by the indication that his mood changes to one of optimism when he writes, in his pivotal second stage, the crucial lines containing the symbolic action of stars throwing down their spears and weeping, for this action closely echoes his symbolic descriptions of the surrender and repentance of kings in both *The French Revolution* (1791) and *America* (1793).

This is not to imply that 'The Tyger' is, after all, nothing more than a sublime piece of political allegory. Such an interpretation would both fail to square with our experience of the poem and mistake Blake's intention and method. 'The Tyger' has many meanings, not only because it is an emblematic masterpiece which by itself supports a variety of valid interpretations, but because its context in Blake's thought as a whole gives it many. The poem describes an apocalypse – by definition a vast and inclusive event – which occurs in a cosmos knit by interpenetrating 'correspondences' uniting any one event with all others. No single interpretation, therefore, whether political, religious, ethical, or sexual can be sufficient in itself. On the other hand, these considerations do not prevent us from talking about the poem concretely. Its very inclusiveness of meaning enables us to approach it through any relevant particular meanings, and to suggest that it may have been connected with a specific point in history, without implying any limitation of the poem as a whole.

I mentioned that Blake's introduction of stars and heavens into the poem marks a turning point in his composition. Since we shall have to be quite clear about this symbolism as we consider the drafts in detail, and since it has puzzled many readers, some explication of it here will be useful. The lines in question are those later forming the fifth stanza:

> When the stars threw down their spears,
> And water'd heaven with their tears,
> Did he smile his work to see?
> Did he who made the Lamb make thee? (p. 73)

We can approach these symbols most clearly and concretely through Blake's use of them in his contemporary historical prophecies. In his work in general, stars and heavens symbolize the rigidly categorical restrictions imposed upon man by laws derived from abstract reason, and the weeping of stars symbolizes at the cosmic level an apocalyptic melting or breaking down of these barriers separating man from his own humanity, a return of man from the 'forests of night'.[3] But in the works of 1791–3 an important particular meaning of these symbols, as Erdman has shown, is that of political repression, specifically the agents of repression, kings and nobles.[4] In *The French Revolution*, the King's bosom expands 'like starry heaven' (p. 169) when he assembles the nobles, the 'heavens of France' (p. 175); aristocratic privilege is a 'marble built heaven'; its destruction a 'starry harvest'; and the king's armies, who are to defend the heavens, are 'starry hosts' (p. 170). In *America* the thrones of kings are similarly 'heav'nly thrones', and Urizen, the god of kings, sits 'above all heavens' (pp. 207–8).

In these same works are to be found several echoes of the action in the fifth stanza of 'The Tyger'. Blake, when he describes the repentance or defeat of tyrants, consistently shows the starry forces throwing down their spears (and swords and muskets) and weeping. In *The French Revolution* the Abbé de Sieyès, as the voice of the people, hopes that the king's soldier will 'Throw down ... [his] sword and musket, / And run and embrace the meek peasant', and predicts that when this happens, the 'Nobles shall hear and shall weep, and put off / ... the crown of oppression' (p. 176). A similar throwing down of weapons and weeping occurs twice in *America*, not as a hope but as an accomplished fact, and it is, furthermore, produced by the appearance of the fiery Orc, just as the action in our poem is brought about through the creation of the burning tiger. When the spirit of Orc inspires the Americans, 'The British soldiers thro' the thirteen states sent up a howl / Of anguish, threw their swords & muskets to the earth, & ran' (p. 206). And a little later, when the red fires of Orc have driven the plagues sent upon the Americans back upon George III himself, the royal forces 'sent up a howl of anguish and threw off their hammer'd mail, / And cast their swords & spears to earth' (p. 207). When this happens, Urizen adds to their tears of anguish by weeping himself; indeed, he literally waters the heavens above which he sits, shedding tears in a grotesque 'deluge piteous' (pp. 207–8).

No one would argue that this symbolic action in the historical prophecies is exactly equivalent in meaning – or effect – to the action in the fifth stanza of 'The Tyger'. But the pattern of the starry kings' armies throwing down their weapons and weeping, whether in repentance or in the unrepentant anguish of defeat, is similar to the action in the first two lines of the stanza to indicate that these lines do at one level describe a victory for political liberty, if only as a symptom or a result of the apocalypse.[5] And the context of the rest of the poem shows that this victory is a result of the creation of the dread tiger. Knowing Blake's republican sympathy and the transcendent values he attached to political liberty, we can be certain at this level that the creator of a tiger which could thus advance the cause of freedom was none other than 'he who made the Lamb', and we can be just as certain that this creator smiled 'his work to see'. Moreover, because the unity of Blake's cosmos assures us of consistency in the general import of his symbolism through all of its levels of meaning, we can be confident that the fifth stanza shows the dread tiger to be not only a divine creation but also, despite its dreadfulness, an aspect of the divine will, at whatever level we read the poem.[6]

With this much preparation, let us then turn to examine the three stages of Blake's composition in some detail. The first two stages are to be found in the Notebook, and the third in the final poem itself.

I

The first stage consists of the first draft (p. 109, col. 2 of the Notebook) and the revisions of the second stanza of this draft, the interlineal revisions as well as the new draft of the stanza on the page opposite (Notebook, p. 108, col. 1; the pages run backwards because Blake was using his Notebook in reverse at this time).

That Blake's initial attitude toward the dreadfulness of the tiger and his creator is a troubled one is shown by his repellent portrayal of the tiger in the deleted stanza of the first draft (the fourth stanza in order of composition, but heavily deleted, and omitted as the stanzas were later numbered). 'And when thy heart began to beat / What dread hand & what dread feet', he asks,

> Could fetch it from the furnace deep
> And in thy horrid ribs dare steep
> In the well of sanguine woe
> In what clay & in what mould
> Were thy eyes of fury rolld

Even though Blake is evidently thinking on paper here, trying lines as they come, we can scarcely take expressions such as 'horrid ribs', 'sanguine woe', and 'eyes of fury' to be merely crudely exaggerated characterizations of a dread power that was viewed as a means to Eden. Blake had too much control to be guilty of this much exaggeration even in a rough draft. Nor does this kind of horror form a part of his conception of revolutionary energy. Though Orc in *America* is 'terrible', he never becomes 'horrid', and though his raging fires produce tears of anguish among the enemies of liberty, they never produce anything remotely approaching 'sanguine woe'. The tiger's dreadfulness is appalling here, we must conclude, because Blake was unable to accept it easily; an implied rejection of it crept into his verse even as he wrote to justify it as being symmetrical with God's purpose.

This attitude of uncertainty is maintained and given more explicit expression by the revision of the second stanza of this draft. In the stanza as originally written, dreadfulness is general and evocative:

> In what distant deeps or skies
> Burnt the fire of thine eyes
> On what wings dare he aspire
> What the hand dare sieze the fire

It was consistent with Blake's intention in the poem as a whole that dreadfulness should not be too horrible and that the questions asked about the tiger should be rhetorically general enough, as they are here, not to demand answers other than those supplied by the image of the tiger itself. Indeed, Blake used this original evocative form of the stanza in the final poem, where he realizes his intention.

But he does not, in the first stage of composition, allow this form of the stanza to stand. Evidently the rather generalized questions in these lines, however appropriate to his purpose in the poem, are not sharp enough to express his real attitude toward the tiger's dreadful aspect. For he makes interlineal revisions which change the question in the first two lines from one which asks evocatively *where* the tiger got the fire of his eyes to one which asks more pointedly *whether* he got it from 'distant deeps or skies'; furthermore, the fire now becomes cruel:

> Burnt in distant deeps or skies
> The cruel fire of thine eyes

Did the 'cruel' fire come from the Devil (deeps) or from God (skies)? Or did it have an eternal source at all? These questions demand an answer; the original question does not. The original question, to be sure, asks us formally to name the source of the fire, but it does not ask whether the fire has an eternal source, for it assumes that it has. It asks only from which of a number of distant deeps or skies it came, calling attention to the transcendent qualities of the tiger's eyes. A real answer is demanded by the revised question, whichever way it is read. Read one way it asks us to choose between deeps and skies as alternatives and may even urge deeps, since it tells us that the fire is cruel. Read the other way it flatly demands an answer of 'yes' or 'no'.

This sharp question was the one Blake wanted to ask in this stage, for though he struck out the revisions made between the lines, he transcribed this stanza as revised, on the following page (Notebook, p. 108, col. 1). The position of the transcribed stanza on the page indicates that it belongs with the first draft.[7]

II

Blake's second stage of composition is represented by a new stanza (Notebook, p. 108, col. 1), written below and presumably after the transcription of the revised second stanza, and by the second full draft of the poem (p. 108, col. 2). In this stage Blake swings to the other pole, displaying such enthusiasm over the tiger's positive side that he pushes its dreadfulness into the background.

The crucial lines of this stage are those of the new stanza (eventually to become the fifth stanza of the final poem), in which Blake shifts away from the tiger to introduce the results of its creation, in the symbolism of stars and heavens. (The number

5 evidently indicates the place of the stanza in the final draft; the deleted 3 was originally a stanza number and then left as a line number. Words crossed out by the poet are here italicized.)

```
5          dare he smile laugh
3     And did he laugh his work to see
          ankle
      What the shoulder what the knee
Dare
4     Did he who made the lamb make thee
1     When the stars threw down their spears
2     And waterd heaven with their tears
```

These lines show a marked change in mood. Blake apparently conceives the whole poem somewhat differently than before, since he proposes to substitute for his original third stanza, which had described the sinews of a dread tiger's heart, a stanza which he begins (taking the lines in order of composition) in such a positive and joyful mood that he cannot decide whether to ask if the creator laughed or only smiled. He is simply not in the mood for dread, and when he attempts to carry on more or less in his original vein in the second line, he is led away from the creator's forging and twisting shoulder to the bathos of knee and even ankle. In the third line ('Did [or Dare] he', etc.) he gets to the heart of the matter in the central question of the poem. But the answer is pretty clear in his mind, for, in context with the mood implied by his indecision over 'smile' and 'laugh' and the bathetic 'ankle', this question scarcely could be answered 'no'. The answer is, in any case, made clearer in the following two lines by the apocalyptic symbolism of the stars throwing down their spears and weeping.

Blake's rearrangement of the lines by numbering them 3, 4, 1, and 2, and his omission of the bathetic line, make the stanza firmer and much more clearly positive in mood. Placing the lines about stars and heavens first qualifies the question concerning the creator's response to his dread creation in such a way that the answer is obvious: 'Did he smile (or laugh) his work to see [?]' no longer asks simply whether the creator was in general pleased with his tiger, but asks more specifically whether he was pleased with it *when* it caused the stars to throw down their spears and weep. Put this way, the question becomes obviously rhetorical. And the line ending the stanza in the new arrangement, 'Did (or Dare) he who made the lamb make thee [?]' becomes a positive rhetorical climax which sums up the whole poem.

This mood of certainty is maintained in the second full draft of the poem (Notebook, p. 108, col. 2). In this draft, a fair copy written out without revisions and spaced on the page as if it were final, Blake omits most of the dreadfulness of the first stage. He omits altogether the second stanza; he omits the bloody deleted stanza, and thereby also reduces the questions of the third stanza, 'What dread hand & what dread feet [?]' to mere suggestions of dreadfulness, for he has removed the verb needed to complete these questions; and he omits the next to the last stanza, which had asked what 'dread grasp' could clasp the 'deadly terrors' of the tiger's brain. The result of these omissions is a poem of only four stanzas, in which all the dreadfulness is in the ambiguous suggestions of the strophic first and last stanzas – powerful suggestions in the final poem in context with the restored stanzas, but ambiguous by themselves – and in the truncated question without a verb. We must now accept the tiger's fearful aspect merely because we are told that there is a fearful symmetry in him and that his creator has a dread hand and a dread foot. Blake seems to rush over the tiger's unpleasant aspect to get to the rhetorical affirmation in the new stanza, which is included here. In this abbreviated poem the new stanza overbalances the tiger's symmetry so much that it no longer seems very fearful. It is not because of Blake's usually casual orthography that 'Immortal' is capitalized in the first stanza of this draft; he wishes to stress the tiger's divine aspect.

III

In his third stage, in the final poem itself, Blake retains the assurance he had gained in the second, using the stanza about stars and spears as the climax of the poem. But now he is more realistic about the tiger, for he restores some of its original dreadfulness. He restores the stanzas beginning 'In what distant deeps or skies' and 'What the hammer? what the chain?' (the second and fourth stanza of the final poem), to give the tiger's creator once more a 'dread grasp' and the tiger itself a brain of 'deadly terrors'. But if he is more realistic than in the second stage, he is also more philosophical than in the first. He no longer portrays the tiger's dreadfulness with the harsh immediacy of his original characterization, but brings it into perspective by ameliorating and generalizing it. He does not restore the bloody stanza of the first draft, and consequently allows the truncated questions, 'And what dread hand? and what dread feet?' (stanza three) to remain mere suggestions of dreadfulness, grammatically incomplete, as they had been in the second draft.[8] And though he does restore the second stanza of the first draft, he uses it in its evocative form, in which it asks vaguely *where* the tiger got the fire of his eyes, no longer cruel. Viewed against its drafts, the final poem shows Blake to have a tight control of his materials because he can perceive clearly and steadily the unity underlying the tiger's symmetry: The tiger *is* dreadful, but its dreadfulness is an 'accident' and not its 'substance', to use one of his favourite philosophical distinctions; its substance is power, the power of that energy which will return man to Eden.

This conceptual unity is embodied not only in the final image but in the very structure of the poem itself. The structure of the final poem almost perfectly illustrates Blake's hard dictum that a truly unified work of art must have its unity 'as much in the Part as in the Whole' (p. 582), and reminds one of the structure of a Gothic cathedral (to Blake 'living form', p. 583), in which each stone, often even each slate in the roof, may be said to support its own weight. For each of the questions of which the poem is composed, even those which show the tiger's dreadfulness, provides its own answer, not as simple rhetorical questions would, but by contributing to the complex but unified total image in which all questions are answered. The tiger thus comes to be its own justification.

From the vantage point of the final poem it is easy to see why

Blake's overbalanced moods in his first two stages prevented him from achieving a symmetrical tiger, for the final poem shows that both aspects of the symmetry must be advanced at the same time. The second stanza cannot be omitted, as it had been in the exultant second stage, nor can it ask the sharply limiting questions it had asked in the first. It must be there in its evocative form, not only to support the suggestion of immortality given in the first stanza, but to supply a spacious context for the dreadfulness in the following two stanzas, so that the image they build up can become awesome, and not merely dreadful. In this context the third stanza (used in the second stage almost as a hasty concession that the tiger had an unpleasant aspect) and the fourth stanza (omitted in the second stage) bring out the tiger's dreadfulness, by showing its 'deadly terrors' to be the work of a dread hand twisting and forging; but at the same time, paradoxically, they make the tiger seem actually less dreadful, because it becomes more and more awesome, as they build the total image. As a result, the rhetorical affirmation of the fifth stanza no longer shifts the reader arbitrarily to the tiger's positive side, as it had done in the second stage, but culminates the characterization of the preceding stanzas, forming a kind of climactic modulation to a major key which clearly and triumphantly provides a final resolution to the progression that had been moving toward resolution all along. The real climax, of course, which resolves everything, is the word 'Dare' that is substituted for 'Could' in the closing return to the strophic stanza. Coming after the image of the tiger is completed, the last two lines are not a question, not even a rhetorical one, but a cry of wonder.

Thus the final poem is essentially positive. The dread it expresses, though real – and deplorable, apart from its role in melting starry repression – has been assimilated to the larger imaginative vision of the poet-prophet, 'Who Present, Past, & Future, sees' (p. 65). As one of the *Songs of Innocence and of Experience*, 'The Tyger' belongs to that complex stratum of lyrics composed of poems like 'The Little Black Boy' and 'The Chimney Sweeper' (of *Innocence*), which shows both states at once. And it expresses the general idea that the ultimate Edenic

Innocence is to be attained only through the bitterness of Experience. But it also goes beyond this conception of the 'two contrary
states of the human soul', to show that Innocence, when it is in
danger of being destroyed by the repression of a fallen 'God &
his Priest & King' (p. 70), may even temporarily take on some of
the characteristics of its contrary state, becoming transformed
into a wrathful energy which may itself occasion bitterness. The
lamb, as Schorer observes, turns 'into something else, indeed into
the tiger' (p. 250). To attain the dawn, man may have to act in
'the forests of the night'. In its immediate context in Blake's
lyrics of this period, 'The Tyger' thus shows the apotheosis of
that armed Innocence portrayed in a manuscript lyric that comes
three pages later in the Notebook (p. 105), where the sun, a symbol of peaceful Innocence throughout the songs,[9] becomes wrathful, 'Clothd in robes of blood & gold ... Crownd with warlike
fires & raging desires'. But this wrathful state is a temporary one.
As Blake expresses it some years later in another poem (Notebook, p. 12), transforming the symbolism of the fifth stanza of
'The Tyger', the path leads through the 'Gates of Wrath' to the
'break of day', where the corporeal war of 'swords & spears /
Melted by dewy tears / Exhales on high. ...'

It seems to me that the change of mood which we have observed
Blake to pass through in his first two stages can be most easily
accounted for as reflecting his responses to events in France in the
late summer and early autumn of 1792. Several lines of evidence
converge to suggest this: the date of the drafts, the historical
echoes in the pivotal fifth stanza, and above all the fact that the
course of the revolution in this period was such that it could –
and did – arouse this kind of response among humanitarian
republicans.

Such cruel excesses of revolutionary energy as the Rising of
August and the September Massacres furnish a plausible occasion
for Blake's troubled mood in the first stage. There was always
something of the 'gentle visionary' about Blake, and he must have
deplored these early terrors, despite his ardent Jacobinism.
Though his apocalypses may sometimes stream with blood (e.g.,

the end of *Milton*), he preferred to think of revolutions as blood-less, hoping in *The French Revolution* that the struggle would end by the king's soldier simply embracing the 'meek peasant'. Even in *America*, where he must treat a military victory won by American armies, he would rather not show the Americans as actually fighting; they merely 'rush together', owing their vic-tory to the fact of their solidarity and to the spiritual manifesta-tion of revolution in the flaming Orc.

Then in late September came news that violence was appar-ently over, news which could have prompted the shift in mood seen in Blake's second stage. Viewed prophetically, such events as the defeat of the Austrians at Valmy on the twentieth (to which Erdman, p. 178, has called attention in connection with the fifth stanza), the formation of the National Convention on the twenty-first, and the announcement of the French Republic on the twenty-second must have made the attainment of Innocence seem close enough to cast the bloody actions of August and mid-September pretty well into the background. This view, according to Wordsworth and Coleridge, was even typical. The 'lamentable crimes' of the September Massacres, writes Wordsworth, re-membering the period after the announcement of the Republic,

> 　　　　　　　　　　　　　　　　　were past,
> Earth free from them for ever, as was thought, –
> Ephemeral monsters, to be seen but once!
> Things that could only show themselves and die.[10]

'The dissonance ceased,' recalls Coleridge, 'and all seemed calm and bright . . .'[11]

Blake is not, to be sure, writing merely a revolutionary lyric. His tiger is not another Orc, another portrayal of the spirit of revolt, but something much more inclusive, a symbol showing the creative power of energy, even of wrathful energy, wherever it appears. But because the revolution was for Blake a crucial contemporary manifestation of energy, events in the progress of the revolution would affect even his larger conception.[12]

For Blake to have been thus affected by contemporary events, his Notebook would have had to lie idle for a period of ten days or even several weeks, since the manuscript drafts are on successive pages. This is easily possible. He did not write in his Notebook exclusively or constantly, but used it at this time for lyrics, which, according to H. M. Margoliouth, were written in response to events of one kind or another.[13] Moreover, if his uncertainty concerning such an important concept as that of energy was unresolved during his first stage, it is unlikely that he could work very productively until it was resolved, in the second stage. That an interruption did occur is suggested, indeed, by the appearance of the pages of the manuscript – and even the appearance of a manuscript page could conceivably have had some significance for the inventor of 'illuminated printing'. Whereas the first draft ends a page crowded with lyrics, the other drafts occupy a page that is otherwise blank, except for a light sketch. The empty space at the top of the second page, coming after the profusion poems on the first, thus seems a visual parallel to the mournful and unproductive 'blank in Nature' declared by Los in *Milton* (p. 383).

Blake's last revision is another matter. The final poem cannot be accounted for as a response to specific events. Though the Terror of late 1792 and early 1793 could have shown him that his relatively mild tiger of the second stage was premature, his restoration of dreadfulness to the poem in its final version does not show the influence of events – and certainly not of events like the Terror – as do his exaggerations of the two earlier stages. On the contrary, Blake's being able to handle dreadfulness and assimilate it in the unified symmetry of the final poem shows him to gain precisely that control of his material which his concern with revolution seems to have prevented him from gaining in his earlier stages. He is now able to transcend the limitations of specific events and give his symbol the comprehensive scope of an 'eternal principle'. This is the result of hard thought, not of events. Blake can now give the tiger's dreadfulness symbolic distance because he can see it in a perspective in which it no longer has the immediacy of an issue. And he can portray its symmetry as containing a really fearful component because he can see clearly and fully, at this point, the place of the tiger in the divine plan.

Transcription of the Drafts of Blake's 'The Tyger'

First draft, Rossetti manuscript, p. 109 (*italics indicate deletions*)

The Tyger

	1	Tyger Tyger burning bright
		In the forests of the night
		What immortal hand or eye
Dare		*Could* frame thy fearful symmetry

Burnt in

2 In what* distant deeps or skies

The cruel   *Burnt the* fire of thine eyes
On what wings dare he aspire
What the hand dare sieze the fire

3 And what shoulder & what art
Could twist the sinews of thy heart
And when thy heart began to beat
What dread hand & what dread feet

Could fetch it from the furnace deep
And in thy horrid ribs dare steep
In the well of sanguine woe
In what clay & in what mould
Were thy eyes of fury rolld

Where   where

4 *What* the hammer *what* the chain
In what furnace was thy brain

            dread grasp

What the anvil what *the arm grasp clasp*

Dare   *Could* its deadly terrors *clasp grasp* clasp

6 Tyger Tyger burning bright
In the forests of the night
What immortal hand & eye
       frame
Dare *form* thy fearful symmetry

[The manuscript has a vertical deletion line reaching from the first line of the first stanza through the first line of the sixth.]

* 'In what' deleted, but deletion line erased.

Additional stanzas on opposite page (p. 108), column 1 of the Notebook

> Burnt in distant deeps or skies
> The cruel fire of thine eyes
> Could heart descend or wings aspire
> What the hand dare sieze the fire
> [Three vertical deletion lines.]

5 dare he *smile laugh*
3 And *did** he laugh* his work to see
    ankle
  What the shoulder what the knee
Dare
4 *Did* he who made the lamb make thee
1 When the stars threw down their spears
2 And waterd heaven with their tears

Second full draft on page 108, column 2

> Tyger Tyger burning bright
> In the forests of the night
> What Immortal hand & eye
> Dare frame thy fearful symmetry

> And what shoulder & what art
> Could twist the sinews of thy heart
> And when thy heart began to beat
> What dread hand & what dread feet

> When the stars threw down their spears
> And waterd heaven with their tears
> Did he smile his work to see
> Did he who made the lamb make thee

> Tyger Tyger burning bright
> In the forests of the night
> What immortal hand & eye
> Dare frame thy fearful symmetry

[Three vertical deletion lines, one crossing the other two.]

* Above 'did' is an illegible blotch, perhaps a deletion.

THE FINAL FORM OF BLAKE'S 'THE TYGER'

Tyger! Tyger! burning bright
In the forests of the night,
What immortal hand or eye
Could frame thy fearful symmetry?

In what distant deeps or skies
Burnt the fire of thine eyes?
On what wings dare he aspire?
What the hand dare sieze the fire?

And what shoulder, & what art,
Could twist the sinews of thy heart?
And when thy heart began to beat,
What dread hand? & what dread feet?

What the hammer? what the chain?
In what furnace was thy brain?
What the anvil? what dread grasp
Dare its deadly terrors clasp?

When the stars threw down their spears,
And water'd heaven with their tears,
Did he smile his work to see?
Did he who made the Lamb make thee?

Tyger! Tyger! burning bright
In the forests of the night,
What immortal hand or eye,
Dare frame thy fearful symmetry?

SOURCE: *Publications of the Modern Language Association of America*, LXXI (1956).

NOTES

1. *Blake's Innocence and Experience* (1928) pp. 246–51. Stanley Gardner, in *Infinity on the Anvil* (1954) pp. 123–30, uses the drafts to some extent to show the greater effectiveness of the final poem.

2. See 'Proverbs of Hell', no. 44: 'The tygers of wrath are wiser than the horses of instruction.' Also the fiery creature appearing 'to the east, distant about three degrees' (the distance of Paris from London), which the angel's metaphysics distorts into Leviathan, has a tiger's

forehead. (The beast who emerges from the sea in Revelation XIII 2, the most plausible model for this one, was 'like unto a leopard', but had the feet of a bear and the mouth of a lion.) *Blake's Poetry and Prose*, ed. Geoffrey Keynes (1948) pp. 184, 189–90. Unless otherwise indicated, page references to Blake's works will cite this edition.

3. *Europe*, p. 216. Famous exceptions to stars as symbols of repression are illustration XIV to *Job*, 'When the morning Stars sang together, and all the Sons of God shouted for joy', where Blake is, of course, illustrating another's work, and the early lyric 'To the Morning Star' in *Poetical Sketches* (1783). On the place of stars in Blake's symbolic cosmography, see S. Foster Damon, *William Blake, His Philosophy and Symbols* (1924) pp. 143–4.

4. David V. Erdman, *Blake: Prophet against Empire* (Princeton, 1954) pp. 15, 153, 178–80, 436–7.

5. That this stanza includes an historical meaning has been suggested by Mark Schorer, *William Blake: the Politics of Vision* (New York, 1946) pp. 250–1, and Erdman, *Blake*, pp. 178–80.

6. As has often been noted, the action of the stars throwing down their spears, both in 'The Tyger' and in *The Four Zoas*, Fifth Night, line 224 (p. 299) – where Urizen recounts his defeat – is related to Milton's account of the war in Heaven. The relation, however, is a complicated one, and in a way inverted. The tiger is not to be equated with Satan-Urizen; he is, if anything, closer to Orc. And the action in *The Four Zoas*, as the historical allegory in the Fifth Night makes clear, has also an apocalyptic aspect, in Blake's sense of that term (p. 647), for Urizen in recapitulating the collapse of the hosts of reaction in the American war and after, giving an account that matches the last page of *America* and the first of *Europe* (Erdman, *Blake*, pp. 343–9). If we wish a Miltonic-Scriptural equivalent for the tiger, it must be the militant Christ – as the Lamb is the forgiving Christ. Professor Erdman has called my attention to the fact that the plot of *Europe* hinges on the distinction between these two aspects of Christ. That the tiger is an active force fighting for 'divine humanity' is further shown by Blake's re-use of the action of the fifth stanza, with the actors and mood changed, in the Ninth Night of *The Four Zoas*, where he spells out, as it were, the apocalyptic implications of 'The Tyger'. This time it is the 'tygers from the forests' (as well as horses, bulls and lions) who put aside their weapons. Not, however, in defeat, and sorrow, or even in Urizen's mixed mood of repentance, but in the unalloyed joy of victors in the final apocalypse: They 'throw *away* [not down, italics mine] / The spear, the bow, the gun, the mortar'; and, instead of weeping, they 'sing' and 'seize the instruments of harmony' (p. 355).

7. Transcribing this stanza, the uppermost entry on the left-hand

column of p. 108, would very likely have been Blake's next work on the poem after writing the first draft.

8. These questions are grammatically complete in the versions of the poem given by Benjamin Malkin in *A Father's Memoirs of His Child* and Allan Cunningham in *Lives of the Most Eminent British Painters*, vol. II (1830). Malkin gives the line as 'What dread hand forged thy dread feet?' (in Arthur Symons, *William Blake* (New York, 1907) p. 326), and Cunningham as 'What dread hand formed thy dread feet?' (Symons, p. 394). With this and one other less important exception, Malkin's version agrees with extant printed versions, and his alteration of the line may have been approved by Blake, whom he knew personally; Mona Wilson seems certain that Blake did approve it (*The Life of William Blake* (1948) p. 192). But Cunningham's text of the poem as a whole departs so far from any other version ('spears' becomes 'spheres', for instance, and the last stanza is omitted altogether) as to indicate that it is simply inaccurate, perhaps written from memory. His version of the lines in question, however, does happen to agree with the only alteration which we know Blake to have authorized, found in one extant issue of *Innocence and Experience* (copy *P* in Geoffrey Keynes and Edwin Wolf II, *William Blake's Illuminated Books* (New York, 1954) p. 61), in which the last line of the stanza is changed in ink to read, 'What dread hand Formd thy dread feet?'

9. See especially 'The Little Black Boy', 'The Chimney Sweeper' (of *Innocence*), 'Introduction' to *Experience*, 'Earth's Answer', and 'The Voice of the Ancient Bard'.

10. *The Prelude* (1850), ed. Ernest de Selincourt (1926) x 41–7.

11. 'France: An Ode', in *Poems*, ed. Ernest Hartley Coleridge (1912) p. 245.

12. The Orc component of the tiger may be seen in the general similarities between the tiger and Orc in *America*, who, like the tiger, burns in the night as if he had been forged, glowing 'as the wedge / Of iron heated in the furnace' (p. 202), and whose origin is a little ambiguously either in the Satanic deeps or the divine Atlantic mountains (p. 202). Very bloody revolutionary tigers indeed are associated with Orc in *Europe*, where Enitharmon's premature belief that Eden had come – a situation parallel to Blake's second stage of composition – is shattered by the resumption of strife (p. 219). These tigers, however, are far removed from the tiger of the poem, representing a limit of this use of the symbol by Blake.

13. *William Blake* (1951) p. 54. Margoliouth remarks that the occasion of 'The Tyger' is unknown, but believes that this poem too is occasional (p. 58).

Kathleen Raine

BLAKE'S DEBT TO ANTIQUITY (1963)

BLAKE paid Socrates the compliment of calling him 'a kind of brother', and allowed Plato the honour of having anticipated his own ideas on poetry and the arts; but of only two masters did he write with unqualified admiration, and these were Alchemists. In *The Marriage of Heaven and Hell* he says, 'Any man of mechanical talents' might from the writings of Paracelsus or Jakob Boehme 'produce ten thousand volumes of equal value with Swedenborg's'; and in a verse letter to Flaxman he recalls his early masters: Isaiah and Ezra, Shakespeare and Milton, then

> Paracelsus & Behmen appear'd to me, terrors appear'd in
> the Heavens above
> And in Hell beneath....

From these passages we may gather that what fired Blake's imagination in the Alchemical philosophy was the teaching of the famous Smaragdine Table of Hermes Trismegistus (Blake names this work in *Jerusalem*): 'That which is above is like that which is beneath, and that which is beneath is like that which is above, to work the miracles of one thing.' *The Marriage of Heaven and Hell*, often said to contain Blake's most original thought, is in truth an impassioned re-statement of the philosophy of Alchemy.

From the enthusiasm of his praise we know that finally he was with the Alchemists and not with those neo-Platonists who see all that is 'beneath' as evil. Plotinus urges the soul to fly to 'our father's delightful land', as Thel does; but that was not Blake's answer, and in *The Book of Thel* we first find Blake presenting the philosophy of Alchemy as the solution of the problems of duality.

Thel herself may be named from the charming figure of Thalia ('the blossoming one'), who in Thomas Vaughan's *Lumen de Lumine* initiates the Alchemist Eugenius Philalethes into the mysteries of 'that which is beneath'. Philalethes meets Thalia in a living 'temple of nature', where the murmur of bees – the generating souls – may be heard; thence she leads him into the underworld, where she shows him an altar shaped as a cube (the traditional symbol of earth), where a young snake hatches from the roots of an old rotten tree. Still deeper is a cave, smelling of the grave; and this, Thalia tells her initiate, is the inmost sanctuary of Nature's mysteries, where death perpetually gives place to regeneration; as Thel was shown

> ... the secrets of the land unknown.
> She saw the couches of the dead, & where the fibrous roots
> Of every heart on earth infixes deep its restless twists. ...

The roots of life are in death.

Thel's motto summarizes the theme of the poem that bears her name, later expanded in the *Marriage*:

> Does the Eagle know what is in the pit?
> Or wilt thou go ask the Mole?

The answer (given in *Visions of the Daughters of Albion*) is that of the Alchemists:

> 'Does not the eagle scorn the earth & despise the treasures
> beneath?
> 'But the mole knoweth what is there, & the worm shall tell
> it thee.
> 'Does not the worm erect a pillar in the mouldering church
> yard
> 'And a palace of eternity in the jaws of the hungry grave?'

In *The Gates of Paradise* we see a figure of the grave, wearing the winding-sheet and encircled by the worm, and below her the words, 'I have said to the Worm: Thou art my mother & my sister.' In 1788 Blake wrote in the margin of an aphorism by Lavater, which expresses contempt for the natural creation, 'It is the God in *all* that is our companion & friend, for our God himself says: "you are my brother, my sister & my mother". . . . God is in the lowest effects as well as in the highest causes; for he is become a worm that he may nourish the weak.'

This is the philosophy taught to Thel by the matron Clay, who speaks as 'that which is beneath' – matter:

> 'Thou seest me the meanest thing, and so I am indeed.
> 'My bosom of itself is cold, and of itself is dark;
> 'But he, that loves the lowly, pours his oil upon my head,
> 'And kisses me, and binds his nuptial bands around my breast,
> 'And says: "Thou mother of my children, I have loved thee
> 'And I have given thee a crown that none can take away." '

– the marriage of heaven and earth, the highest with the lowest. Paracelsus writes of the relation of the star-souls above to the bodily creatures below; in the beginning, he says, the upper heaven or stars and the inferior terrestrial nature were but one thing; but 'God separated the subtle from the gross', the superior masculine from the inferior feminine watery nature; but there remains a concordance and 'the things beneath are so related to the things above as Man and Wife'. The title-page of the *Marriage* illustrates this Paracelsian theme; many pairs of spirits meet in loving embrace, and the female comes from the dark abyss to meet the male, who descends from 'above' on a bank of cloud.

But the divine principle 'beneath' is a prisoner, whose release is the 'great work' of the Alchemists. Vaughan, following Paracelsus, writes that 'Heaven here below differs not from that above but in her captivity, and that above differs not from that below but in her liberty. The one is imprisoned in the matter, the other freed from all the grossness and impurities of it, but they are both one and the same nature, so that they easily unite'; and he concludes with an image that reminds us of matron Clay, 'and hence it is that the Superior descends to the Inferior to visit and comfort her, in this sickly infectious habitation'. 'He, that loves the lowly', of whom the Clay speaks, and who pours 'oil' upon her head, as the bride is anointed in the Jewish marriage-ceremony, is the Heavenly Father considered as husband of the Earthly Mother;

and as matron Clay is given a 'crown', so Vaughan writes that the stars 'shed down their golden locks, like so many bracelets and tokens of their love'.

Earth's traditional attributes, according to the Alchemists, are cold, moisture, and darkness, as both Paracelsus and Vaughan write; and Blake's matron Clay speaks of herself as 'cold' and 'dark', like Vaughan's matter, 'a horrible confused qualm of stupefying spirit of moisture, cold, and darkness'. This is the feminine principle or 'Adamic earth'; and when Blake writes, in the *Marriage*, 'Red clay brought forth', he is summarizing the teaching of Paracelsus; for all colours, Paracelsus says, are latent in her darkness; and Vaughan, 'what rare pearls are there in this dunghill? . . . A pure eternal green overspreads her. . . . Roses red and white, golden lilies, azure violets, the bleeding Hyacinth, with their several celestial odours and spices.' This is the wilderness that in Blake's *Marriage* is about to blossom as the rose, and Lyca's 'desart wild' that is to 'become a garden mild'. Vaughan describes the Father 'filling his powerful hands' and saying, 'Receive from me, O Holy Earth! that art ordained to be the Mother of all, lest thou shouldest want anything; when presently opening such hands as it becomes a God to have, he pour'd down all that was necessary for the constitution of things.'

Paracelsus and, though less splendidly, Vaughan, studied and practised Alchemy as a means to practical ends; to Boehme it was a symbolic language purely and simply; his theme was the divine essence, good and evil, Heaven and Hell. In Boehme's writings the fire-principle is the Father, source of nature, and, as he repeats in countless passages, the abyss of Hell. From the fire proceeds the light, the Son, the principle of heaven; yet fire and light spring from a single root: 'For the God of the holy World, and the God of the dark World, are not two Gods; there is but one only God.' It is on the authority of Boehme that Blake wrote of the Jehovah of the Bible as 'no other than he who dwells in flaming fire'. This fire is Boehme's first principle of the Divine Essence. It is, in Blake's words, 'Energy, call'd Evil', and in its fires the devils dwell, as 'living Spirits in the Essences of the Eternal Original', as angels live in the principle of light; and each spirit is confined within its own principle. The devils can never enter Paradise; and yet, says Boehme, it has 'no Wall of Earth or Stones about it, but there is a Great Gulph (or Cliff) between Paradise and this World, so that they who will pass from thence, thither, cannot; and they who would come to us cannot neither'.

The Marriage of Heaven and Hell shows a 'mighty Devil' in his fires, his energies chained within his own principle as he vainly attempts to advance towards an angel who stands in the light. But the opposite of this is also true. Blake writes in the same 'Memorable Fancy', 'As I was walking among the fires of hell, delighted with the enjoyments of Genius, which to Angels look like torment and insanity . . .'; for energy – or, as Boehme also calls the fire-principle, desire – is 'Eternal Delight'; and in 'The Voice of the Devil' he says, 'It indeed appear'd to Reason as if Desire was cast out; but the Devil's account is, that the Messiah fell, & form'd a heaven of what he stole from the Abyss.'

The energies of the abyss are the 'Giants who formed this world into its sensual existence, and now seem to live in it in chains. . . .'

Orc, Blake's 'frowning Babe', the Messiah of the New Age, comes from the Abyss, as his name (akin to Orcus, or Hell) implies. Blake depicts him always in his flames, the fire-principle to which he belongs; 'the Eternal Hell revives'. From the same rich context of Alchemical paradox arises the great unanswered question of 'The Tyger', 'Did he who made the Lamb make thee?'

Tigers and other savage beasts were a fashionable subject of painting at the end of the eighteenth century, an aspect of the Romantic revolt of evil, or energy. The vogue was introduced in England by Stubbs, whose famous tiger, now in the Tate Gallery, was exhibited at the Society of Artists of Great Britain, in Somerset Street, in 1769. Blake was then a boy of twelve years old, in his second year at Pars's drawing-school, held in the same house. Is there, in 'The Tyger', an echo of a boy's enthusiasm for Stubbs's glorious beast?

One of Blake's 'Proverbs of Hell' seems to relate the Tyger to Boehme's 'wrath-fires' of the Father; 'The tygers of wrath are wiser than the horses of instruction.' But in his *Aurora* Boehme writes that evil beasts were never intended in the divine plan, and originated with the corruption of the world by Lucifer and his fallen angels. If there had been no Fall, there would have been no serpents, toads, or venomous insects; but when Lucifer exalted himself, and corrupted the fountains of creation, then the life-principle took on forms of evil, 'as a fiery serpent, or Dragon, and imaged and framed all manner of fiery and poisonous Forms and Images, like to wild, cruel and evil Beasts'; for Lucifer, says Boehme, 'half-killed, spoiled and destroyed' the source of life; so the beast 'which had most of the Fire, or the bitter, or the astringent quality became also a bitter, hot and fierce beast'.

From many passages in Blake's longer poems it seems that the Tyger is an embodiment of evil; and a corruption of humanity; tigers and lions are called 'dishumaniz'd men', and

> ... the Tyger fierce
> Laughs at the human form. ...

As Lyca in the Lion's den was met by animal forms, so in the world 'beneath' those who have lost the vision of eternity become mere human animals;

> Troop by troop the beastial droves rend one another ...
> ... those that remain
> Return in pangs & horrible convulsions to their beastial state;
> For the monsters of the Elements, Lions or Tygers or Wolves,
> Sound loud the howling music ... terrific men
> They seem to one another, laughing terrible among the
> banners.

These 'monsters of the Elements' do not belong to the world of the divine logos, nor to the primal fire-principle, but to error or creation; and 'Error, or Creation, will be Burned up, & then, & not till Then, Truth or Eternity will appear. It is Burnt up the Moment Men cease to behold it.' It is, Blake says, a 'most pernicious Idea' to believe that 'before the Creation All was Solitude and Chaos'; for, as Plato also taught, all things exist in 'their Eternal Forms' in the divine mind. But in this world of illusion, there are 'horrid shapes & sights of torment'; men are meta-morphosed into serpents – that is to say, fall into the power of the serpent, matter. In the caves and dens of this world, we meet 'the terrors of the Abyss', serpents and scorpions, and beasts of prey. Lamb and child live in the vision of eternity, the world of 'Jesus the Imagination'; but the Tyger roams 'the forests of the night', removed from the light of the spiritual sun.

Forests, in Blake's symbolic landscape, represent creation and are always evil. Vala, the Shadowy Female, roams 'In forests of eternal death, shrieking in hollow trees'; there blind Tiriel and his serpent-haired daughter wander 'to the covert of a wood ... where wild beasts resort ... but from her cries the tygers fled'. Everywhere we find the same image combined – darkness, forests, beasts of prey; and with forests we find associated images of smoke and fire.

In this association Blake is following Paracelsus, who likens nature, the 'great mystery', to a forest that burns as it grows, issuing from nothing and returning to nothing again, 'as a forest which the fire burneth into a little heap of ashes ... such is the beginning, such is the end of the creatures'. So Blake's lions and tigers 'roam in the redounding smoke, in forests of affliction', the ever-growing, ever-consuming mystery of nature. The forests and their creatures are themselves the smoke, for as Para-celsus writes: 'All bodies shall pass away and vanish into nothing but smoke, they shall all end in a fume.' Thus Vala, as Nature, is is called 'the demoness of smoke'; and in the Last Judgement, Mystery, who is both goddess and tree, is burned up:

> In the fierce flames the limbs of Mystery lay consuming. . . .
> . . . The tree of Mystery went up in folding flames.

In his painting of the Last Judgement Blake describes a group of figures representing 'the Eternal Consummation of Vegetable Life & Death with its Lusts. The wreathed Torches in their hands represents Eternal Fire which is the fire of Generation or Vegetation; it is an Eternal Consummation.' But the symbol is more ancient than Paracelsus; it is Heraclitus' image of the earth as a great fire, parts kindling, parts going out; Yeats too writes

> A tree there is that from its topmost bough
> Is half all glittering flame and half all green. . . .

As with all great symbols, the burning tree of Nature is, as Blake says, permanent in the human imagination.

So Blake's Tyger 'burning bright' is itself part of the ever-burning ever-consuming forest of nature. Blake's Nameless Shadowy Female (nameless surely because she is the Great Mystery itself) speaks of her children as a 'progeny of fires'; in 'The Tyger' Blake asks

> What the hand dare sieze the fire?

and in the poem *Europe* we are given a possible answer; for the Shadowy Female seizes the fire of the stars above in order to generate creatures in the nether abyss, according to the Alchemical teaching of the concordance of the stars with the natural creation:

> 'Unwilling I look up to heaven, unwilling count the stars:
> 'Sitting in fathomless abyss of my immortal shrine
> 'I sieze their burning power
> 'And bring forth howling terrors, all devouring fiery kings,
>
> 'Devouring & devoured, roaming on dark and desolate
>   mountains,
> 'In forests of eternal death, shrieking in hollow trees.
> 'Ah mother Enitharmon!
> 'Stamp not with solid form this vig'rous progeny of fires.
>
> 'I bring forth from my teeming bosom myriads of
>   flames. . . .'

Is not the Tyger 'burning bright' one of this 'progeny of fires', the 'all devouring fiery kings', 'Consumed and consuming' in the 'immortal shrine' in the abyss, immortal as darkness and matter, the eternal opposite of light and spirit?

Another Alchemical symbol has become partly obscured in the final draft of the poem, 'The Tyger', which reads

> In what distant deeps or skies
> Burnt the fire of thine eyes?
> On what wings dare he aspire?

But a cancelled draft in Blake's notebook brings out the contrast of above and beneath:

> Burnt in distant deeps or skies
> The cruel fire of thine eyes?
> Could heart descend or wings aspire?

– did the Creator draw his Tyger forth from Heaven or Hell? In the final draft Blake has implied an identity of the deeps and the skies; but unless we realize that his starting-point is their opposition, we shall miss the force of the paradox, which suggests that Heaven and Hell may be, after all, aspects of the One Thing. Thomas Vaughan paraphrases the Smaragdine Table.

> Heaven above, heaven beneath,
> Stars above, stars beneath,
> All that is above is also beneath.
> Understand this and be happy.

But the figure who seizes the fire to create the Tyger is male; and while we may conclude a resemblance and affinity with the Shadowy Female we must look farther.

> On what wings dare he aspire?
> What the hand dare sieze the fire?

The theft of fire suggests Prometheus; the daring aspiration, Satan, who in *The Marriage of Heaven and Hell* 'formed a heaven with what he stole from the Abyss' – the flaming fires of the Father. Whoever made the Tyger cannot have been the Son or Logos, for he is a thief and a rebel, who in order to create must possess himself of fires not his own. Crabb Robinson, Wordsworth's friend, the diarist, recalls Blake as saying – and he had Wordsworth in mind – that 'whoever believes in Nature disbelieves in God – for Nature is the work of the Devil. On my [Robinson] obtaining from him [Blake] the declaration that the Bible was the word of God, I referred to the commencement of *Genesis* – in the beginning God created the Heavens and the Earth. But I gained nothing by this, for I was triumphantly told that this God was not Jehovah, but the Elohim, and the doctrine of the Gnostics repeated with sufficient consistency to silence one so unlearned as myself.'

Blake he calls a Gnostic; and it is quite possible that Blake did know something of the Gnostics from the writings of Joseph Priestley and elsewhere. Common to all schools of Gnosticism is the belief that the creator of the temporal world was not the supreme God; and among Jewish Gnostics, the Creator of Genesis is identified with this second creator. Blake's Urizen is recognizably the God of the Old Testament; grey-bearded and venerable in his 'aged ignorance', he carries with him the Books of the Law. In Blake's *Job* we see him as the author of the Ten Commandments; but that he also is the Devil we know from his cloven foot. Yet Blake's creator is not wholly evil; for as the Ancient of Days we see the Creator with his golden compasses, like the demiurge of the Gnostics who, though in part fallen, 'derived his birth from the supreme god; this being fell, by degrees, from his native virtue, and his primitive dignity'. But whatever grandeur there may be in his work, Blake called the creator of the temporal world 'a very cruel being'.

Paracelsus too wrote of 'another creator of the mysteries, besides the chiefest and most high'; for the creatures, he says, 'are always egged on and provoked to do evill, compelled thereto by the fates, stars, and by the infernal one; which by no means could have bin, if they had proceeded out of the most high himself, that we should be forced into these properties of good and evil'.

Two poems in *Songs of Experience*, 'The Human Abstract' and 'A Poison Tree', identify the Tree of Good and Evil as mystery, or Nature: Mystery bears

> ... the fruit of Deceit
> Ruddy and sweet to eat;

and the Poison Tree 'an apple bright' that slays the man who eats it. The Poison Tree grows from 'wrath' and the 'apple bright' from anger; and we are led, again, to Boehme. For Boehme also this Tree is Nature: 'it grew out of the Earth and has wholly the Nature of the Earth in it' and 'as the earth is corruptible, and shall pass away in the End, when all goes into its Ether'. He might be paraphrasing Paracelsus. Of the two trees in the old legend – the Tree of Life and the Tree of Good and Evil – Boehme writes that they are the same tree, but manifested in two different principles: in the light of Heaven, the principle of the Son; and in the fires of Hell, the 'wrath of the anger of God', the Father. Adam, who might have lived upon the 'fruits of life' – Blake too uses the phrase – chose instead the earthly nature of the tree. The words 'wrath', 'poison', and 'anger' that recur in these two poems point unmistakably to Boehme, who writes that the Tree, corrupted by the Fall, brought forth Fruits, according to its comprehensible, palpable, hard, evil, wrathful, poisonous, venomous, half-dead kind'; and he asks that human question, '*Why* did God suffer this Tree to grow, seeing Man should eat it? Did he not bring it forth for the fall of Man? And must it not be the Cause of Man's Destruction?' In Blake's Poison Tree

> ... my wrath did grow. ...
> And it grew both day and night
> Till it bore an apple bright. ...

The figured man who lies outstretched in death beneath the tree is, by implication, the victim of God's anger. This myth is expanded in *The Four Zoas*; not only do poisonous fruits grow from the tree, but the serpent itself issues from 'writhing buds'. From this 'deadly root' of poison and wrath the Mystery branches and extends endlessly,

> In intricate labyrinths o'erspreading many a grizly deep

– those 'labyrinths' of nature, where Enion hid herself.

Man's 'Mortal part' is the cruel work of nature and vanishes with the Mystery; on the Laocoön Group he wrote, 'What can be Created can be Destroyed. Adam is only the Natural Man & not the Soul or Imagination'; he is created from the 'red clay'; and the Tyger also is moulded in clay:

> In what clay & in what mould
> Were thy eyes of fury roll'd?

Man as a clay vessel moulded by a potter is a Biblical metaphor;
but those grand images of the moulding of the Tyger,

> And what shoulder, & what art
> Could twist the sinews of thy heart?
> And when thy heart began to beat
> What dread hand? & what dread feet?

lead us also another source. The Fifth Book of the *Hermetica*,
that source-book of the Alchemical philosophy, is written in
praise of the demiurge; the Pymander here describes the cunning
of the Workman who frames man in the womb:

Who circumscribed and marked out his eyes? Who bored his
nostrils and ears? Who opened his mouth, who stretched out and
tied together his sinews? Who channelled the veins? Who hard-
ened and made strong the bones? Who clothed the flesh with
skin? Who divided the fingers and the joints? Who flatted and
made broad the soles of the feet? Who digged the pores? Who
stretched out the spleen, who made the heart like a Pyramis?

Even the rhetoric – those questions that in being asked are
answered – is that of Blake's poem; the twisting of the sinews, the
eyes 'circumscribed and marked out', the flattening of the broad
soles of the feet, the heart 'like a Pyramis', with its suggestion of
πυρ, Blake's 'furnace'. The association of 'Nostrils, Eyes & Ears'
recurs in later poems. In Urizen's 'dens' the 'dishumaniz'd men'
are called tigers, lions, serpents, and monsters; and this same
image describes the closing of their senses:

> . . . their Ears
> Were heavy & dull, & their eyes & nostrils closed up.

In the poem 'To Tirzah' it is again the female principle who is
held responsible for this binding:

> Thou, Mother of my Mortal part,
> With cruelty didst mould my Heart,
> And with false self-decieving tears
> Didst bind my Nostrils, Eyes & Ears:
>
> Didst close my Tongue in senseless clay,
> And me to Mortal Life betray.

The workman of the Tyger (so we may deduce from early drafts of the poem) is both potter and blacksmith; he moulds the eyes in clay, but he also works with hammer, anvil, and furnaces.

> What the hammer? what the chain?
> In what furnace was thy brain?
> What the anvil? what dread grasp
> Dare its deadly terrors clasp?

Blake's Los, the time-spirit, is also both potter and blacksmith; he beats out in heart-beats on his anvil the chains of time; and he is master also of '. . . the Potter's Furnace among the Funeral Urns of Beulah' – the male's 'Furnace of beryll' associated with the looms of the Naiades; for the funeral urns which he moulds are the mortal bodies – an image also found in the *Hermetica* that leads us back to the bowls or urns of Porphyry's cave. But Los's famous furnaces belonged first to Urizen the demiurge:

> Then Los with terrible hands siez'd on the Ruin'd Furnaces
> Of Urizen: Enormous work, he builded them anew,
> Labour of Ages. . . .

They were 'Ruin'd' by the demiurge, at the beginning of creation; and again we are pointed back to Boehme and the corrupting of the source. Los the time-spirit must labour to rebuild what was ruined in the beginning – enormous work indeed. The Hermetic workman was called 'god of the fire, and the Spirit'; for 'the Mind which is the Workman of all, useth the fire as his instrument'. It is the demiurge who seizes the fire; and now it is the time-spirit of evolution who must labour to restore what was lost in the beginning. Los's 'Labour of Ages' is the traditional work of Alchemy, to perfect the creation in the resurrection of the hidden god.

The Furnaces of Los are seven in number; so are Boehme's qualifying spirits, or fountains; and the identity of the furnaces with these fountains we know, because at the end of the time-process their original purity is restored:

> . . . the Furnaces became
> Fountains of Living Waters flowing from the Humanity Divine.

But there are also seven planetary spirits; Plato describes them turning round the Spindle of Necessity: seven *elohim*, or creators, in the Jewish mystical tradition, retained as the sevenfold gifts of the Holy Ghost in Christianity. Los's furnaces retain also a strange affinity with the planetary spheres; for they are 'Sevenfold each within other', like Plato's Spindle of Necessity. Paracelsus compares the whole created world to a furnace 'wherein the Seeds of the Sun and Moon, by their various astral influences are corrupted and concocted and digested, for the Generation of all things'. Los's furnace is the *Athanor* of the Alchemists, built, as Paracelsus says, 'in imitation of the Foundation of Heaven and Earth', where the Alchemist labours at the great work in which nature also, as St Paul says, 'groans and travails' towards redemption.

Whenever Blake writes of the stars he understands them as the planetary rulers of destiny. Urizen he calls 'the Starry King', or as Satan, 'Prince of the Starry Wheels', 'Starry Jealousy', and leader of the 'starry hosts'. The Zoas he calls 'immortal starry ones'. They are 'the Starry Eight', the seven planets, and the eighth sphere of the fixed stars, ruled by Urizen. (Boehme's God the Father is also described as ruler of the firmament; and if he can be likened to anything, Boehme says, it is 'to the round Globe of Heaven'.) Los, who is called 'the fourth immortal starry one', is given the traditional number of the sun, proper to his solar nature, throughout the Prophetic Books.

Souls who enter the created world from beyond the galaxy become subject to the demiurge. In the 'Introduction' to *Songs of Experience* Blake reminds the fallen soul that she herself comes from eternity, and

> ... might controll
> The starry pole
> And fallen, fallen light renew!

But in this world she is subject to 'Starry Jealousy', who, like the Hermetic demiurge, 'containing the Circles and Whirling them about, turned round on a Wheel his own Workmanships and suffered them to be turned from an indefinite Beginning to an undeterminable end'.

Thus prepared, we can turn to the stars as they appear in 'The Tyger'.

> When the stars threw down their spears,
> And water'd heaven with their tears,
> Did he smile his work to see?

In *The Four Zoas* Urizen himself recalls the same event:

> ... I hid myself in black clouds of my wrath;
> I call'd the stars around my feet in the night of councils dark;
> The stars threw down their spears & fled naked away.
> We fell. I siezed thee, dark Urthona. In my left hand falling
>
> I siez'd thee, beauteous Luvah; thou art faded like a flower
> And like a lilly is thy wife Vala wither'd by winds.

The stars who threw down their spears when the demiurge fell are the same as the stars in 'The Tyger'; they are the planets, Blake's Zoas, the energies of the human soul, some of whom are here named. As in all traditional accounts of the Fall, the demiurge draws down with him the planetary spirits whom he governs.

The throwing down of the spears echoes Milton's account of the same event, the fall of the rebel angels, driven out of heaven by Messiah's chariot:

> ... they astonisht all resistance lost,
> All courage; down thir idle weapons drop'd;
> O're Shields and Helmes, and helmed heads he rode. ...

They flee,

> ... witherd all thir strength,
> And of thir wonted vigour left them draind,
> Exhausted, spiritless, afflicted, fall'n

– as Luvah and Vala are *faded* and *wither'd*. It is these same stars whom in illustrating the Book of Job Blake has shown in their renewed brightness,

> When the morning stars sang together, and
> all the sons of God shouted for joy.

What, then, in the light of all this, is the answer we are to give to the final question of 'The Tyger?' 'Did he who made the Lamb make thee?' Are we to answer it in Boehme's words:

The God of the holy World, and the God of the dark World, are not two Gods; there is but one only God. He himself is all Being. He is Evil and Good; Heaven and Hell; Light and Darkness; Eternity and Time. Where His Love is hid in anything, there His Anger is manifest.

This is the god of the Alchemists, beyond the contraries. But the answer of the Platonists, and of the *Hermetica*, would be No: the Tyger belongs to the fallen time-world. Yet on the deepest level, all these traditions converge, for the time-world exists only by divine permission. Blake, I believe, left his great question unanswered not because he was in doubt, but because the only answer is a No and Yes of such depth and complexity.

Nor must we overlook, in analyzing the meaning of the text, all that is conveyed by the powerful exaltation of the metre, by the fiery grandeur of the images. If the discoverable meaning of the poem suggests that the Tyger is the work of a creator ambiguous or evil, the emotive force of metre and image is all affirmation, praising the fiery might, the energy, and the intelligence of the mortal God. 'The Tyger' is preparing the way for the *Marriage*, with its vindication of Hell or Energy:

The roaring of lions, the howling of wolves, the raging of the stormy sea, and the destructive sword, are portions of eternity, too great for the eye of man.

Instead of seeking to find a Yes or a No, we will be nearest to the truth if we see 'The Tyger' rather as an utterance of Blake's delight, not in the solution, but in the presentation of the problem of evil as he found it in the Hermetic and Alchemical tradition.

SOURCE: *Sewanee Review*, LXXI (Summer 1963) – an abridged version of the Mellon Lectures delivered in Washington 1962.

SELECT BIBLIOGRAPHY

BOOKS

Books referred to in the Introduction have not been included in this list, which is chronological in arrangement.

Mark Schorer, *William Blake: the Politics of Vision* (Henry Holt, 1946). This presents Blake as 'a visionary deeply immersed in radical religious and political movements of the eighteenth century'. The Songs do not come in for a great deal of comment; the *Marriage of Heaven and Hell* is taken as the central document.

Bernard Blackstone, *English Blake* (Cambridge U.P., 1949). Less a work of scholarship (though it examines Blake's relationship to Locke, Berkeley, etc.) than of enthusiastic evangelism. The Songs are treated rather rhapsodically, and Blake is presented as the best interpreter in the modern Western world of the Everlasting Gospel.

H. M. Margoliouth, *William Blake* (Oxford U.P., 1951). This little volume in the Home University Library is a very good introduction, balanced and scholarly, not over-simplified.

Stanley Gardner, *Infinity on the Anvil* (Blackwell, 1954). A study of Blake's symbolism in which the Songs, collectively and individually, receive plenty of attention. The later books are regarded as marred by 'explicatory comment'.

William Gaunt, *Arrows of Desire: a Study of William Blake* (Museum Press, 1956). A useful book, biographical rather than critical, that fills in the background of Blake's life, both personal and intellectual.

Harold Bloom, *Blake's Apocalypse* (Yale U.P., 1962; Gollancz, 1963). More than half the book is devoted to *The Four Zoas*, *Milton* and *Jerusalem*. Little exegesis of individual lyrics, but the general comments on the two series of Songs is valuable. Students can also look up comments on Blake in *The Visionary Company* (Faber, 1962).

John Beer, *Blake's Humanism* (Manchester U.P., 1968).

Vincent Buckley, *Poetry and the Sacred* (Chatto & Windus, 1968). This contains a chapter on Blake's originality which is useful to the student of the Songs.

Stanley Gardner, *Blake*, in the Literature in Perspective series (Evans, 1968). Gardner's edition of Blake's *Selected Poems* was published in 1962 by London U.P.

John Holloway, *Blake: the Lyric Poetry*, Studies in English Literature 34 (Arnold, 1968).

Raymond Lister, *William Blake* (Bell, 1968).

Kathleen Raine, *Blake and Tradition* (Routledge & Kegan Paul, 1969).

Deborah Dorfman, *Blake in the Nineteenth Century* (Yale University Press, 1969). Students will find this a very useful study of Blake's reputation from Gilchrist to Yeats.

John Beer, *Blake's Visionary Universe* (Manchester U.P., 1969).

Morton D. Paley, *Energy and the Imagination* (Oxford U.P., 1970).

Alvin H. Rosenfeld, *William Blake: Essays for S. Foster Damon* (Brown U.P., U.S.A.).

ESSAYS AND ARTICLES

D. W. Harding, 'William Blake', in *Pelican Guide to English Literature*, ed. Boris Ford, vol. v. *From Blake to Byron*, 1957. This chapter was reprinted in *Experience into Words* (Chatto & Windus, 1963) entitled 'Experience and Symbol in Blake'. Because it is easily available, it has not been included here, but it should certainly be read.

Northrop Frye, 'Poetry and Design in William Blake', in *Journal of Aesthetics and Art Criticism*, X (1951) i. This draws interesting parallels between the Songs and emblem-books.

V. de S. Pinto, 'William Blake, Isaac Watts and Mrs Barbauld', included in *The Divine Vision* (Gollancz, 1957). A collection of studies in the poetry and art of William Blake edited by Professor Pinto for the Bicentenary Committee. This essay deals, though not exhaustively, with the links between *Songs of Innocence* and earlier books for children.

A. M. Wilkinson, 'Blake's *Songs of Innocence and Experience*' in *Use of English*, XIII (1962) iv. A straightforward and quite helpful article. Wilkinson edited the Songs with introduction and notes for the University Tutorial Press in 1957.

Discussions of William Blake, ed. J. E. Grant (1961). Reprints of articles from learned periodicals, many of them close readings of difficult passages and poems, all written since 1950.

S. Foster Damon, *A Blake Dictionary* (Brown U.P., 1965). Described by Nurmi as 'a compendium of a lifetime of imaginative scholarship' and recommended by Keynes.

An exhaustive checklist of studies on every aspect of Blake is *A Blake Bibliography* by G. E. Bentley, Jr. and Martin K. Nurmi (University of Minnesota P., 1964).

A most valuable selective bibliography of Blake is to be found in *The English Romantic Poets and Essayists: A Review of Research and Criticism* ed. C. W. Houtchens and L. A. Houtchens, revised edition, published for the Modern Language Association of America by New York U.P. in 1966. The English publishers are London U.P. The review of Blake studies contributed in 1957 by Northrop Frye was brought up to date (1964) by Martin K. Nurmi.

BIBLIOGRAPHY

The fullest descriptive bibliography is still that of Geoffrey Keynes, published in 1921.

NOTES ON CONTRIBUTORS

F. W. BATESON was a Fellow of Corpus Christi College, Oxford, editor of the *Cambridge Bibliography of English Literature* and founder-editor of *Essays in Criticism*. He died in 1978.

S. F. BOLT is Senior Lecturer at the Cambridgeshire College of Arts and Technology. His publications include *The Right Response* (1966) and *Poetry of the 1920s* (1967). Poetry editor of *Delta*.

C. M. BOWRA (1898–1971) was Warden of Wadham College, Oxford, a classical scholar and critic of European and English literature. His publications include *The Heritage of Symbolism* (1943) and *The Romantic Imagination* (1950).

S. T. COLERIDGE (1772–1834). Poet, critic and philosopher. Crabb Robinson in a letter to Dorothy Wordsworth (1826) reported that Coleridge had visited Blake 'and I am told talks finely about him'.

H. CRABB ROBINSON (1775–1867) was acquainted with many notable persons, especially writers, of his day. His *Diary* and *Reminiscences* contain numerous personal impressions of Blake.

ALLAN CUNNINGHAM (1748–1842) was the author of the widely circulated *Lives of the most eminent British Painters, Sculptors and Architects* (1830), translated into German in the same year. The 'Life of Blake' occupies pp. 142–79 of the second volume.

H. NORTHROP FRYE is Professor of English Literature at Victoria College, Toronto. His study of Blake, *Fearful Symmetry*

(1947), has been a seminal work. He was responsible for the section on Blake in *The English Romantic Poets and Essayists*, published for the Modern Languages Association of America in 1957.

ALEXANDER GILCHRIST (1828–61), Blake's biographer, drew on the recollections of those who had known and befriended Blake in his latter years – John Linnell, Samuel Palmer, Edward Calvert, George Richmond, etc. His *Life of Blake* was published posthumously (1863). As revised by Ruthven Todd (Everyman Library, 1945) this remains the standard biography.

ROBERT F. GLECKNER is Professor of English at the University of California, Riverside. *The Piper and the Bard*, his study of Blake's *Songs of Innocence and Experience*, was published in 1959. He was co-editor of *Romanticism: points of view* (1962).

JOHN LINNELL (1792–1882), the painter, was introduced to Blake in 1818 and remained to the end an admirer, friend and patron. Mrs Blake kept house for him for a few months after her husband's death.

BENJAMIN HEATH MALKIN (1792–1842) published in 1806 *A Father's Memoirs of his Child*, the frontispiece to which was designed by Blake and engraved by Cromek. Several pages in the Dedicatory Epistle are devoted to Blake's works 'for the purpose of descanting on merit, which ought to be more conspicuous, and which must have become so long since, but for opinions and habits of an eccentric kind'.

WOLF MANKOWITZ is the author of many successful novels, plays, short stories, films and musicals, besides some critical essays.

MARTIN K. NURMI is Professor of English Literature at Kent State University, Ohio. He is a distinguished Blake scholar and is co-editor with G. E. Bentley of *William Blake: a Bibliography* (1964).

SAMUEL PALMER (1805–81), the painter, was one of the young artists who venerated Blake during the last phase of his life. For a while his own work had a visionary, magical quality.

EDWARD QUILLINAN (1791–1851), minor poet, translator of Camoëns, married Dora, daughter of William Wordsworth, and lived at Ambleside.

KATHLEEN RAINE, poet and critic, author of *William Blake and Traditional Mythology* (Andrew Mellon Lectures, 1962) and of numerous articles on Blake. Her *Collected Poems* appeared in 1956.

DANTE GABRIEL ROSSETTI (1828–82), painter and poet, founder member of the Pre-Raphaelite Brotherhood, worked on Gilchrist's *Life of Blake*, and printed poems from the Notebook that came into his possession and now usually bears his name.

W. M. ROSSETTI (1829–1919), critic and editor, was involved, like his brother, in extending Gilchrist's commemorative work.

JAMES SMETHAM (1821–89), painter and essayist, befriended by the Rossettis and Ruskin.

ARTHUR SYMONS (1865–1945), poet and critic, author of *The Symbolist Movement in Literature* (1899), was introduced to Blake's poetry by W. B. Yeats in 1893. His own book on Blake (1907) included reprints of all available accounts of the poet printed prior to Gilchrist's *Life* (1863) with the exception of the biographical sketch by Frederick Tatham (see below).

FREDERICK TATHAM (1805–78), a sculptor and miniature-painter, was introduced to Blake by Linnell about 1825 and saw him frequently till he died. He was one of the few friends to attend the funeral. After the death of Mrs Blake, who acted for a while as his housekeeper, Tatham came into possession of the whole stock of Blake's drawings, engravings, etc., besides some manuscripts which he is reputed to have destroyed on conscientious grounds.

JAMES THOMSON (1834–82), journalist and poet, author of 'The City of Dreadful Night'.

JOSEPH WICKSTEED (1870–1959), a noted schoolmaster and student of religion, produced three valuable commentaries on Blake's pictorial and poetic symbolism – *Blake's Vision of the Book of Job* (1910), *Blake's Innocence and Experience* (1928) and *Commentary on William Blake's Jerusalem* (1954).

J. J. GARTH WILKINSON (1812–99) was a noted Sweden-borgian, which may account for his interest in Blake, whose *Songs of Innocence and Experience* he reprinted, with an introduction, in 1839. He published a volume of verse, *Improvisations from the Spirit* (1857), which attracted the notice of James Thomson (see above) and led him to discover Blake's poetry.

INDEX